(Continued from front flap)

that is both cultural and personal. Several contributors and the editor, in a long epilogue, reflect on solutions to the identity crisis that can maintain a viable balance between continuity and growth and the degree to which such solutions have actually been achieved.

About the Editor

ROBERT N. BELLAH holds A.B. and Ph.D. degrees from Harvard, the latter in Sociology and Far Eastern Languages, and has worked as a Research Fellow at the Institute for Islamic Studies at McGill University. Currently he is Associate Professor of Sociology and Regional Studies at Harvard. He is the author of *Tokugawa Religion* (The Free Press, 1957) and is presently writing a book on the sociology of religion.

Religion and Progress
in
Modern Asia

EDITED BY ROBERT N. BELLAH

The Free Press, New York

Collier-Macmillan Limited, London

Asia - Religion
Relig. & sociology

Preface

THIS VOLUME is based on papers presented to a conference on Cultural Motivations to Progress in South and Southeast Asia held in Manila from the third to the eighth of June, 1963, and on excerpts and summaries of the discussions that took place during the conference. The conference was sponsored by the Congress for Cultural Freedom and the University of the Philippines. General Carlos P. Romulo, President of the University of the Philippines, and his staff extended gracious hospitality to the participants. The Ateneo de Manila University and a number of individual Filipinos were also most hospitable. Miss Marion Bieber of the Congress for Cultural Freedom handled the arrangements and contributed greatly to the comfort and welfare of the participants.

The Conference was very much the brain child of its director, Soedjatmoko of Indonesia. He provided the inspiration, many of the focal ideas, and a guiding spirit during our discussions. Much of whatever we achieved is due to his efforts.

The editor is responsible for the summary of the discussions that appears in the Introduction. Actual excerpts from the transcript of the discussions have been checked by the participants quoted and therefore should accurately represent their views.

The editor's Epilogue is an independent retrospective essay representing only an individual point of view and not the conclusions of the conference.

One participant has questioned the title the editor has chosen for the book. Does it not, he suggests, by its inclusion of the word "modern," beg the very question of the conference? To avoid this implication let me state that "modern" in the title means only "recent" and does not imply anything one way or the other about the success of modernization in contemporary Asia.

A bibliography and a list of participants in the conference can be found at the back of the book. The bibliography, compiled by the editor, makes no pretense at comprehensiveness but merely suggests the range of relevant material.

Finally, the editor gratefully acknowledges the assistance of the staff of the Center for Advanced Study in the Behavioral Sciences, Stanford, California, in the final preparation of the manuscript and in particular the index during the period of his residence there in the academic year 1964–65.

R.N.B.

Contents

ROBERT N. BELLAH

Introduction

IF IT WERE POSSIBLE to describe in a single phrase the problem of this book and of the conference that lies behind it, it might be "the modernization of the soul." The very incongruity of the phrase perhaps suggests some of the complexity, paradox, and doubt inherent in our subject. Religion, after all, deals with matters of eternity and ultimate truth. How can it be involved in change, modernization, and progress? Religion is the source of ultimate values and criteria of judgment. How can it be judged in terms of its "potential for modernization"? Yet it is generally agreed by most of the contributors to this book that religion, whatever its ultimate orientation, is very much bound up with the totality of the social process and the concreteness of individual existence, especially in Asia, where religion still largely shapes the traditional forms of culture. And being so deeply involved in social and personal life, inevitably, it is felt, religion often has profound implications for the course of historical development, encouraging or inhibiting economic, political, and social modernization. Recognizing the extraordinary difficulty of the conceptual problems involved and the extreme paucity of good empirical data in the area, the editor and contributors offer this volume as a set of tentative explorations of what we believe is an important aspect of the great social and cultural changes taking place in our contemporary world.

The Conference

The Conference on "Cultural Motivations to Progress in South and Southeast Asia" was held in Manila from the third to the eighth of June, 1963, under the joint sponsorship of the Congress for Cultural Freedom and the University of the Philippines and with the generous support of the Ford Foundation. The idea for the conference had developed at a Congress for Cultural Freedom conference in India some eighteen months earlier. Present at the earlier conference were several participants in the Manila seminar. Mr. Soedjatmoko, perhaps more than anyone else, was the intellectual progenitor of our Manila conference. It was he who sketched the main areas to be covered in discussion and who suggested topics for the papers to be prepared in advance. As it was his initial memorandum, circulated well in advance of the conference, that provided a common reference point for both papers and discussions, it is perhaps advisable to introduce it at this point:

Memorandum on Scope and Purpose of Seminar

BY SOEDJATMOKO

In the course of the fifteen years in which the modernizing elite in the new states in South and Southeast Asia has had to deal with the question of economic and social development, it has become quite clear that the traditional value systems operating in this area pose a much more important problem in the modernization process than had been anticipated by most of these modernizers. If it was thought at first that the bonds of tradition impeding social and economic development could be broken in a frontal attack against tradition and as the result of the secularization accompanying the process of education, urbanization, and industrialization, the realization has come that the relationship between tradition and the modernization process is a much more complex one, requiring a clearer understanding and a more vigorous analysis. Especially in the field of economics a beginning has been made with such studies, and some cultural factors impinging upon economic behavior and upon the process of economic development have been identified. These studies, however, generally leave unanswered the questions that confront the modernizers—those who have dedicated themselves to the deliberate manipulation of political, economic, and social factors for the purpose of effectuating rapid progress and development.

It seems therefore that the time has come to face up to the general problem posed by the unsuspected strength and ubiquitous influence of traditional value systems in the modernization process, in order to see how the impetus for progress can be strengthened and sustained.

The welding together of disintegrating, smaller, and more primitive forms of social organization into larger, new, cohesive, and viable political units capable of effectuating economic development, which has been the main task of the political leadership in the new nations in South and Southeast Asia, has forced that elite, in varying degrees, to take into account and to harness traditional forces for that purpose, at least in those states that are unable to or that prefer not to use force or totalitarian methods. The problem faced by the modernizers among the political elite has been how to utilize these forces without being captivated by them and without losing the impetus for rapid social change.

Also, the existence of more than one concept of modernization among the modernizers themselves made a political struggle between them inevitable, leading the adherents of various concepts of modernization to secure some degree of political support from the traditional forces. The recent history of some of these new nations has shown that those modernizers who were unwilling to make such compromises with the more traditional forces soon found themselves on the sidelines of the political arena. The mobilization of the political strength of traditionalism in this way has become an important power factor, adding to the already formidable weight of social and mental inertia that keeps large parts of the population of these countries immobilized. Moreover, in the countries with Western parliamentary systems, as well as in those countries that are in the process of building new political structures in South and Southeast Asia, these modernizers have been compelled, for the sake of welding sufficient political power, to come to terms, though in varying degrees and forms, with traditionalism; and this, too, has strengthened traditionalist forces considerably more than many modernizers had anticipated—except of course in those instances where the modernizers are committed to the forcible destruction of traditionalism and its underlying social organization, with a view to releasing dynamic new social forces.

At the same time, the uncertainty and anxiety accompanying the

breakdown of traditional values and social structures without their
immediate replacement by new ones have, in several of these countries,
led to militant and fundamentalist reassertions on the part of the various traditionalist forces, endangering the possibilities for comparatively
smooth transition toward modernization.

These three factors, the requirements for political integration, the
power struggle among the modernizing elite and the fundamentalist
reaction of traditionalism, make it a matter of great importance for the
modernizing elite to prevent further hardening of the resistance against
modernization and make the question of how to link up at least some
elements of the traditional value system to the modernization process
an extremely important one.

In the economically more developed nations, economic growth is
a self-sustaining process of continuous innovation, change, and development. It is predicated on a particular view regarding the significance
of life on this earth, on the acceptance of the idea of progress, that is,
of a present better than the past and a future potentially better than
the present. It assumes the perfectibility of man and society as a continuous possibility; it assumes man's ability to control and improve his
natural environment, as well as the legitimacy of man's desire to do
so. The question now is whether or not such views and attitudes are
totally alien to the traditional value systems in South and Southeast
Asia. Are there elements or variants of these value systems that could
be harnessed for the modernization process; are there, on the other
hand, elements that inherently constitute impediments to modernization? And is secularization the only way to overcome these impediments to progress?

Essentially, the problem is, how elements of the traditional value
systems and the new values of progress can be integrated on the basis
of the present general desire for a better life.

Very little is known about these questions; very little is known
of the relationship between these traditional value systems and social
action in general; and even less is known about this relationship in
connection with the needs and desire for economic and social development. In fact, a clearer definition of these traditional value systems in
relation to the concept of progress is very much in order.

At the same time, a closer look at the modernization process in
general, as a historical phenomenon, is indicated, as is an attempt to
relate the generalizations that can be made regarding this process with
the specific value systems operating in South and Southeast Asia. A
clearer understanding of the function of ideologies, old or new, with
their particular perspectives on the future and their impacts on the will
and determination of a people, in this process of political integration
and social transformation, is also much needed. An inquiry into the
traditional value systems might also shed some light on the relative

receptivity for particular modern concepts of progress as embedded, for instance, in the liberal and in the Marxist outlooks, in the open or closed concepts of the future. The views on history and the historical process in traditional cultures are relevant in this connection.

Briefly, then, the questions these modernizers face—and for which they have had so far to find their answers by dint of their political instinct—are the following: What are the keys to the traditional and modern mainsprings of creative social action that could sustain the modernizing process? Should traditionalism be treated simply as an enemy? Is it possible to fight it in open battle without being crushed by it? Or without being isolated and reduced to political impotence? Is it possible to undermine traditionalism by an indirect approach? Is it possible to activate and mobilize those elements in traditional culture that would lead themselves to support for progress without encouraging at the same time other elements in traditional culture that would tend to impede progress?

There is also a host of more practical problems that are encountered on the operational level of economic development projects and that stem from the pervasiveness and strength of these traditional cultures. To mention a few: the attitude toward work, toward time, toward money; saving and spending habits; forms of decision-making and of the resolution of conflicts; functioning within large impersonal social organizations; forms and structure of economic enterprise; labor mobility and labor recruitment; questions of achievement orientation, of incentives and disincentives for economic activities. Many of these questions have already been discussed by economists; a few anthropologists have also entered the field. So far, however, the results have by and large been inconclusive and often contradictory. A more systematic consideration of these questions, from the point of view of their fundamental connection with the traditional value system as a whole, might therefore prove illuminating and might possibly provide us with some operational clues.

Such an inquiry would inevitably lead us—except possibly in the case of Confucianism—to consider the religions from which in large measure these traditional value systems stem. At the same time, an attempt to relate the ideas and values as expressed in the sacred books and similar texts to our problems—which certainly will have to be made at this seminar—would only very partially meet our needs. For we are also concerned with these religions in their historicity. None of these religions—or value systems—has been without change and development, without its alternating waves of reformation and stagnation, or without its periods of great social dynamism. Were any particular emphases or interpretations of the value system connected with these periods—to disappear with the onset of stagnation? We shall also have to consider the variants of these systems, existing side by side at any particular time in history, but also in the present. The aristocrat's frame of value reference has always been different from the lowly peasant's, and it would be foolish indeed in our search for keys to the release of dynamic social action in the traditional sectors of our societies to ignore these differences. Whatever the difficulties in defining the traditional value systems therefore, the desirability of at least probing the relationships between these religions and value systems, in their various historical and sociological transfigurations, and social action seems to me obvious. And our seminar should set itself at least to explore the heuristic possibilities of this approach.

This then is a sketchy and preliminary description of the general area with which our seminar should concern itself. It would require the co-operation of scholars who have made the modernization process as such the focus of their academic concern, of religious phenomenologists, of anthropologists and sociologists, but also of politicians and, in general, of representatives of the modernizing elites in these new countries in South and Southeast Asia. The area to be covered is a wide and various one; in it are to be found the Hindu, Confucian, Buddhist, Muslim, and Christian value systems, as well as their variants and admixtures. It is quite unlikely that a single seminar could achieve much more than a clearer delineation of the field of inquiry and possibly a determination of some fruitful approaches for the study of this field. It will be quite likely that a series of standing interdisciplinary seminars, extending over a rather prolonged period would produce at least some answers to the questions posed here. It seems to me, however, that the fundamental importance of this field of inquiry is so great and urgent that even such a preliminary seminar as envisaged here would be fully justified.

This memorandum, then, provided the common framework for the participants as they gathered in Manila in early June of 1963. It is worth noting that not only the place but also most of the participants were Asian. A list of the participants is appended to this volume so that the reader may see exactly who they were and from what countries they came. Of twenty-nine participants, only five were not Asians. The participants were not "representative" in either a formal or a statistical sense. Each "represented" only himself, yet it is evident that most of the Asians are members of what Soedjatmoko in his memorandum called "the modernizing elite." Although many of them are scholars trained in the highest standards of scientific objectivity, it is also obvious that their interest in the problem of our seminar was not simply "academic." Almost all of them are men and women dedicated to the social, political, and cultural development of their societies, some of them indeed engaged primarily in political and social pursuits rather than in scholarship. The nature of the majority of the participants gave an immediacy and a sense of drama to our deliberations that would be difficult to duplicate in a conference on "Asian development" organized by Western scholars in Europe or America.

The Asian context of our discussions was highlighted from the very beginning by the opening remarks of General Carlos P. Romulo, President of the University of the Philippines and our gracious host. He pointed out that for too long the West has considered Asia as a mere scene, arena, or landscape for the West as actor to play out its historical roles. This situation is characteristic even in the sphere of scholarship in which Western experts have for long studied Asia from the point of view of Western concerns and have developed research projects with mainly Western interests and needs in mind. But Asian scholars, thinkers, and statesmen are now capable of serious reflection, investigation, and research on the problems of their own development, as this seminar itself demonstrates. "The world may," he said in conclusion, "well know that Asia has ceased to be a mere stage, for it is the world which is the stage and all must play their individual roles. The age of prompters is gone. What we are witnessing is an Asia that acts and utters its own original lines."

The Papers

As the papers were all written and most of them circulated before the conference, it might be useful to introduce them briefly before summarizing some of the main lines along which the actual discussion developed.

Soedjatmoko's basic paper is clearly a development of the

preliminary memorandum already quoted. He sketches even more clearly what turned out to be the dominating concerns of the discussion. He discusses the problem of the "motivational structure of society," the "wider structure of meaning" that enfolds particular values and attitudes toward economic and social development but often eludes both social scientist and politician. Yet a reorganization at these deeper levels of motivation and meaning may be the critical prerequisite for more obvious kinds of development or at least a necessary accompaniment to them.

Instead of smooth reorganization Soedjatmoko finds, in many cases, a deep crisis, a crisis of identity that involves doubts not only about the value of the traditional past but also about the worth of the insistent new. In surmounting the problems of development, the formation of a new national identity may make crucial contributions, but at the same time may perhaps give rise to new problems. In a seminal passage, Soedjatmoko declares:

The idea of national identity is concerned with the self-awareness of a nation, its self-image, and its values. It springs from a nation's desire for fixed points of reference in the world, as well as from the hope of finding those points within one's own individuality as a nation. A nation's self-image then emerges from the way it perceives its history and is shaped by its aspirations, ideals, and purposes. The relevance of this self-image and national identity for our discussion becomes obvious when we realize that the sense of purpose derived from a clear self-image and the purpose itself as part of the self-image constitute motivational factors in the decision-making process that determine, to an important degree, the perception of the outside world, the nature and the order of priority of its problems, and the choices and responses of the nation to them.

In a sense, the introversion, the brooding preoccupation with the national self, that accompanies the search for national identity, commensurate in intensity with the depth of its identity crisis, is an unavoidable phase in a nation's adjustment to a changed environment. And until a clearer image of its own identity and of the broader purposes of its existence emerges, it will be difficult for a nation to define its place in the unfolding of world history or to set itself consistently and with determination to any major undertaking.

To this extent, this search for clearer definition may contain an important key to social cohesion and social action. Carried to the extreme, however, it may hamper the nation's capacity to view and act upon the new problems it faces rationally and dispassionately by focusing the national energies on a virtual image. For in the final analysis it is not from self-examination that national identity emerges. Instead it is defined and constantly redefined in the continuous flow of actions and choices in response to problems.

In overcoming the identity crisis in a way that will not foreclose but will actually stimulate further development, Soedjatmoko suggests, the articulation of traditional religious and modern secular values may be extremely strategic. To this end he advocates increased communication and understanding between modernizing and the traditional elites. Most desirable would be an inner reformulation of the traditional religious position to make it conducive to modernization, although Soedjatmoko emphasizes that such a reformulation cannot be made to order but must issue from the inner travail of religious experience itself. Failing that, at least better communication and understanding between modernizing and traditional elites may help to neutralize any negative effects of traditional religious and cultural values and may thus allow secular modernization to gain ground.

Soedjatmoko warns against the easy acceptance of the traditional-modern dichotomy, as did others in the seminar also. "Traditional" and "modern" are not only categories of people but also categories that exist within people. The modernizers are inevitably heirs to their own traditions. The most traditional man in the middle of the twentieth century shares many attitudes with the most modern. Finally, Soedjatmoko asks why modernization cannot simply be awaited as the inevitable accompaniment of industrialization. Because, he answers, industrialization itself has been so difficult to begin in many Asian countries and because time is so short. Concern with deeper problems of motivation and meaning may therefore be of direct practical significance in initiating changes that objective conditions insistently demand.

Father de la Costa's paper deals with several definitional questions of cardinal importance to our topic. First, he considers the various senses in which a society may be called a "Christian" (or by implication "Buddhist," "Islamic," and so forth) society. That is, how exactly is a religion institutionalized in a society, and how does institutionalization vary among societies in both degree and mode? Then Father de la Costa considers the concept of progress, its Christian origins, and its complex and ambiguous relation to religious values. Finally, he deals with another issue of general significance, the degree to which cultural contrasts between East and West, Asia and Europe, are really contrasts of historical epoch, that is, of preindustrial and postindustrial. Father de la Costa's clear delineation of these problems proved especially helpful in the discussions that followed.

Senator Manglapus's paper, coming as it does from a man actively engaged in political activities, provides a refreshing example of social change as it actually occurs. His discussion of the "Fiestas for Progress" movement, set in the context of general reflections about the relations of values to development in Asia, lent a stimulating concreteness to our deliberations.

Mr. Dube's paper relates a number of the seminar's concerns to the particular problems of India and Hinduism. Particularly interesting is his suggestion that, though the ultimate values of Hinduism may seem somewhat unfavorable to modernization, the proximate values, that is, the values that are actually operational are in many cases neutral or favorable to development.

Mr. Sayigh expresses in his paper the economist's doubt that cultural and religious factors are really major determinants of economic development in either a positive or a negative sense. Dealing with a number of the cultural obstacles to development that have arisen in the Arab world, he suggests that education and actual experience with industrialization rapidly erode these apparent hindrances. Aside from the operation of strictly economic incentives, however, Sayigh does recognize the importance of one extra-economic factor, political initiative, as of great importance, in many cases at least, in rapid development.

Mr. Coulson's paper concentrates specifically on the problem of legal development and change in the Islamic world. The close link between religion and law has threatened the legal flexibility that seems to be an important prerequisite of modern society. His remarks, both on how the traditional inflexibility was established and on how it is being circumvented in the modern Muslim world, are most instructive.

Mr. Geertz's paper is concerned with change in Islamic institutions in Indonesia. He argues persuasively that educational institutions are at the heart of Islamic life everywhere and are thus a key area in which to study change. He finds the shift from medieval to modern educational forms and orientations of profound significance in the gradual adaptation of Indonesian Islam to the realities of modern life.

Mr. Sarachandra discusses how Buddhism of the great tradition and at the folk level relates or fails to relate to the modernization process. He illustrates vividly, with the case of Ceylon, some of the problems of identity crisis of which Mr. Soedjatmoko wrote.

Finally, Miss Saniel, in her well documented and cogently argued paper, suggests some of the lessons, positive and negative, that the Japanese case holds for the more recently developing nations. The degree to which Japan is or is not a relevant example for other Asian societies proved to be a controversial point in the subsequent discussions.

The Discussion

The discussions at the Manila seminar lasted for six days and touched on a wide variety of topics. It is only possible to mention here some of the highlights and to deal with some of the most recurrent themes. For a better sense of the discussion, the reader is referred to the chapter of excerpts that follows the presentation of the papers in this book.

The salience of the notion of progress, as expressed in the

title of this volume, reflects the predominantly Asian origin of the conferees. A more "academic" Western gathering would perhaps have eschewed the word "progress" as smacking too much of value connotations and as not sufficiently scientific. But for many of those present, progress, defined by Mr. Soedjatmoko as "a present better than the past, and a future potentially better than the present," is not an academic matter at all but an urgent necessity. Progress was seen as not only desirable in itself, but also, in rather tangible form, as the indispensable precondition for avoiding a lapse into complete chaos in many Asian countries.

In terms of an operational definition of progress, the emphasis of most of the participants was on economic development and industrialization. Mr. Anwar quoted Barbara Ward to the effect that the aim of modernization can only be to raise living standards and to give people hope for a better life. Mr. Venkatappiah included democratization along with economic development in his definition of progress, and a number of others seemed implicitly or explicitly to consider the development of free political and social institutions as an important part of the desired modernization. Yet the degree to which economic advance necessarily implies democratization was very much open to question. The cases of Japan and some of the Communist nations were cited as evidence that the relationship between economic development and democratization is highly ambiguous.

The notion of religion also turned out to need some degree of definition. Although it was used mainly to refer to "the great religions," some of the sociologists present used it in a broader way to include such nationalistic movements as the Japanese emperor system of the late nineteenth century and the more obviously "secular" religion of communism. But even within the more conventional usage of the term it seemed useful to make several sorts of distinction. Mr. Geertz in his opening remarks stressed the distinction between religion as idea and belief system and religion as part of the continuing social structure. He argued that we cannot deduce social facts directly from doctrinal positions but that the social realities of a religion must be studied in their own right. This distinction between religion as culture pattern and religion as social institution was generally accepted, and the importance of research at both levels was recognized.

A second distinction that played a prominent role in the discussions is that between folk religion and the great tradition. Folk Buddhism in Ceylon, for example, or folk Catholicism in the Philippines was felt to be often very remote from normative scriptural Buddhism or Catholicism. Again, in understanding the social consequences of a religion, it was generally agreed that both folk and "orthodox" traditions had to be studied and their adherents located in the fabric of any particular society. Partially related to this distinction is the useful one introduced by Mr. Dube between ultimate and proximate values within a religion. An adequate assessment of the social implications of a religious position requires a careful analysis of the operational importance of proximate as well as of ultimate religious values.

In dealing specifically with the problem of whether or not religion is a barrier to progress, a variety of positions was taken. The folk-orthodox distinction was used to deal with this issue but in contrasting ways. The Catholics tended to argue that, whereas orthodox Catholicism is certainly no barrier, folk Catholicism often is. Conversely, the Indians and Mr. Sarachandra from Ceylon seemed to hold that, while scriptural positions within Hinduism and Buddhism might stand in the way of development, the actual folk religion has managed to adapt itself to the world sufficiently so that it can gracefully accommodate modernization. Although it was rather generally agreed that in principle all the religions represented in the conference can adapt to modernization, there was considerable diversity with respect to how far they had actually succeeded in adapting, how difficult adaptation is, and, indeed, whether or not adaptation is necessary or even important to successful modernization.

Mr. Qureshy of Pakistan felt that Islam in his country had been almost completely a positive force for modernization, stressing as it does the equality and dignity of man. Islamic ideology, he argued, had provided the justification for land reform and equality of opportunity in Pakistan. Mr. Majul of the Philippines felt that Islamic influence in the southern islands of his country is often retrogressive and a barrier to modernization, although younger and better educated Muslim leaders are often progressive. Mr. Castro of the Philippines seemed to believe that his country has learned to adapt to such an extent that it has already overcome the barriers holding back some of the other Southeast Asian countries. Mr. Soedjatmoko, looking at the Philippine situation from the point of view of Indonesia, doubted that all serious problems had been overcome. Mr. Wang of Malaysia was especially insistent that secularization is a major prerequisite for modernization and that reformulation in effect usually means the retreat of religion from positions of former strength and influence.

Even assuming that some coming to terms with traditional religion is an important part of the modernization process, a point that Mr. Sayigh, for example, never fully accepted, there was still considerable difference of opinion as to how easy such a coming to terms might be. Taking off from some remarks in Mr. Sayigh's paper, some of the participants saw a division between activists and scholars. The scholars, particularly the sociologists and anthropologists, it was argued, tend to emphasize the difficulties of cultural accommodation to modernization, to be "pessimistic" about the possibilities of reorienting the traditional religions. The activists, on the other hand, were said to move ahead more quickly, often discovering the scholars' fears to be illusory. This distinction between scholars and activists, it must be admitted, was considerably more attractive to those calling themselves "activists" than to those designated as "scholars," the latter category including the editor of this volume. Finally, leaving aside the question of whether accommodation between religion and socioeconomic change is easy or difficult, Father Doherty and Mr. Geertz asked whether or not any ultimate resolution of tension between religion and society is possible or indeed desirable. In other words, it was left open whether any total sanctification of "modernization" by religion would be possible without violating the integrity of religion, the world, or both.

At the social structural level, one of the most frequently utilized conceptions was that of the traditional and modern elites in the developing nations. Some degree of communication and understanding between the two was regarded as essential to a smooth process of modernization in the realm of motivation and values. Variations on this theme were suggested by a number of conferees. Some divided the modern elite into "problem-solvers" and "solidarity-makers," the former more interested in development, the latter in social integration. The solidarity-makers, it was maintained, sometimes become allied to or even merge with traditional elites and become susceptible to the latent antimodern orientations of traditional groups. When the split between problem-solvers and solidarity-makers within the modern elite becomes too deep, especially when the solidarity-makers are led to renounce modern values, the dangers to rapid development can become severe.

On the other hand, Mr. Wang and Mr. Sayigh indicated that in their respective lands, Malaysia and the Arab world, the emergence of a mediating element that shares modern values but has not lost touch with traditional culture and still has links to the traditional elite has provided an impetus to modernization and a basis of stability that neither the extremely modern nor the extremely traditional elite groups could have done.

Another area of strategic importance was indicated by Mr. Geertz, Mr. Sayigh, and others: the groups and individuals who link elites and masses. Especially important are those who communicate the orientation of the modernizing elite to the masses, the "cultural brokers," to use Mr. Geertz's term, or the "sergeant-majors of modernization," to use Mr. Sayigh's phrase. It is through such elements that new attitudes and ways of acting

permeate the people, and they were felt to be especially in need
of careful empirical study, as well as being an important locus
for policy decisions.

The degree to which the relationships between the modern
and the traditional on the one hand and the elite and masses on
the other is to be conceptualized in terms of manipulation,
mobilization, or the use of force was a matter of concern to some
of our members. Mr. Dube and Father Bulatao especially emphasized that communication between apparently opposed elements
should be a two-way matter, should involve listening as well as
telling, should have a quality of openness and respect. Most
agreed that the opening of multiple communication channels
among the various groups in the developing societies would in
itself do much to solve the problems with which we were concerned. This point takes us to suggestions for future work.

Suggestions for the Future

Two sorts of proposals developed as the conference neared
its end. The first involved ways in which the communication
channels could be opened or improved. The second dealt with
various sorts of study that might increase our knowledge of this
still largely uncharted field.

Father Bulatao offered the concrete proposal of follow-up
discussions in the Philippines between members of the traditional
and modernizing elites. He noted that the Filipinos present were
almost all members of the modernizing elite and that such a
conference as ours had not tapped the traditional groups. But, in
the spirit of respect and openness, he thought there would be
much to be gained by frank discussions on problems of mutual
interest between members of both elite groups.

Mr. Soedjatmoko argued that Asian intellectuals should take
a more active role in thinking through the problems of value
orientation that confront them and should share their thoughts

through some suitable means of communication. Various participants favored the idea of some sort of serial publication that would provide an outlet for Asian self-examination, as well as summaries and reprints of some of the best scholarly investigations in the area of religion and values in changing Asia.

Suggestions for particular studies were concentrated on elite groups and the intermediaries between elites and masses. Miss Saniel proposed a comprehensive multidisciplinary biographical survey of the modernizing elite in selected Asian nations as well as of samples of local elites from various areas, in order to understand the forces favoring the development of such modernizing elites. Father Doherty suggested that a study of the traditional religious elites would be most helpful. Mr. Sayigh and Mr. Wang proposed careful studies of the "sergeant-majors" of modernization, those who build bridges between the new ideas of the educated elite and the ordinary man in the village or city street. Mr. Geertz and the editor urged that conceptual problems be given further attention so that empirical studies can be as relevant and economical as possible.

Of course none of these proposals was meant to have any formal effect. They simply indicate the stage of thinking reached in the discussions and what seemed to us at the time the most likely avenues to pursue. They are, like most of the papers and discussion that came out of the conference, at the same time evidence of the state of mind of a portion of the Asian intellectual elite and indications of ways to analyze the Asian situation.

SOEDJATMOKO

Cultural Motivations to Progress: The "Exterior" and the "Interior" Views

The Identity Crisis

IN THE PREPARATORY MEMORANDUM,* I have tried to enumerate some of the values and attitudes that influence economic development. They bear more specifically on the questions of motivation, the saving-investment level, the family system, the class structure, and social mobility, all of which constitute important factors in the process of economic growth. The purpose of our discussions is to identify more clearly and fully these values and attitudes in their relevance to the economic development process and, where necessary, to discuss ways and methods for further study of them.

The identification and analysis of developmental values alone, however, is not enough. It is also necessary for us to con-

*See pp. x–xiv.

sider the dynamics of their operation. It is quite obvious, for instance, that many exhortations and admonitions from the political leaders have not always led to very impressive results in accelerating economic growth and that we shall have to reach more deeply into the motivational structure of society in order to achieve that goal.

The basic conviction underlying the preparatory memorandum is that, to this end, it will be necessary for the modernizers to increase their manipulative capacity with regard to the traditional sectors of their society and that more specific and even more basic motivations than those normally used by the politicians will have to be brought into play.

The developmental values and attitudes, once identified, come to life only if they become a part of a wider structure of meaning.[1] The difficulty is that the developmental process itself is not a self-justifying proposition.[2] The possibility of raising living standards and attaining greater material wealth may, in many cultures, not be sufficient enticement to make mobilization of the motivational forces in the traditional sectors of society very effective. In order to be sufficiently persuasive, it is necessary to relate the purposes of the development process to other worthwhile purposes of human endeavor and of society. The problem is that, in the period of transition when old value systems are breaking down and new ones are not yet sufficiently crystallized, no such wider structure of meaning presents itself. The progressive breakdown of traditional social structures, with their established customs, and the difficulty of relating to emerging new ones have left many in our traditional societies with great uncertainty and anxiety, leading in some cases to a genuine *crisis of identity*. The image of one's self, the answer to "who am I, and who do I want to be?" has become blurred and fragmented. Questions like to whom or to what to be loyal? after whom to model one's self? which pattern of behavior to adopt or adjust to? have all lost their obvious answers, and no satisfactory new ones are readily available. The problem is compounded by the fact that the modern world—rent as it is by schisms and itself in obvious crisis—into which these transitional societies are moving does not present a particularly attractive model of any obvious superiority to the traditional purposes of life and society. In fact we see that, even where the notion of economic development is accepted as a worthwhile objective, there is often a simultaneous rejection of what is felt to be the crass materialism and secularism of modern civilization.

I think we should not underestimate the reality of this identity crisis. It expresses itself in various ways and in varying degrees of intensity. I venture to suggest that the intensity is greatest in those countries where there is no significant indigenous commercial and entrepreneurial middle class or where the entire social structure has come into question, but it is present in all our transitional societies on the individual as well as on the collective level.

On the individual level we shall therefore have to consider which personality types as structures of integration of values and attitudes might be effective agents of social change and economic development. This point raises the problem of personality formation in our society and the requirements for an educational system that, aside from its other purposes, can also serve as an important tool and accelerator for economic growth. If I may be so bold as to say so, education in our transitional society is too important a matter to be left to the teachers, and I am sure that during our discussions several of us will want to address themselves to this problem.

The idea of national identity is concerned with the self-awareness of a nation, its self-image, and its values. It springs from a nation's desire for fixed points of reference in the world, as well as from the hope of finding those points within one's own individuality as a nation. A nation's self-image then emerges from the way it perceives its history and is shaped by its aspirations, ideals, and purposes. The relevance of this self-image and national identity for our discussion becomes obvious when we realize that the sense of purpose derived from a clear self-image and the purpose itself as part of the self-image constitute motivational factors in the decision-making process that determine, to an important degree, the perception of the outside world, the nature and the order of priority of its problems, and the choices and responses of the nation to them.

In a sense, the introversion, the brooding preoccupation with the national self, that accompanies the search for national identity, commensurate in intensity with the depth of its identity crisis, is an unavoidable phase in a nation's adjustment to a changed environment. And until a clearer image of its own identity and of the broader purposes of its existence emerges, it will be difficult for a nation to define its place in the unfolding of world history or to set itself consistently and with determination to any major undertaking.

To this extent, this search for clearer definition may contain an important key to social cohesion and social action. Carried to the extreme, however, it may hamper the nation's capacity to view and act upon the new problems it faces rationally and dispassionately by focusing the national energies on a virtual image. For in the final analysis it is not from self-examination that national identity emerges. Instead it is defined and constantly redefined in the continuous flow of actions and choices in response to problems.

The point of this discussion is to demonstrate that there exists a great gap between the way in which the development-oriented modernizer perceives the problems of his nation and the real preoccupations of the nation's political leadership in response to the ways in which the transition process and its accompanying problems are experienced and perceived by the majority of the nation. If, therefore, we want to succeed in linking the requirements for economic development in terms of values and attitudes to the deeper cultural motivations of the nation as a whole, we should know a great deal more of this view from the inside.

The Nationalist Solution

We should, in this connection, I think, also discuss the ways in which the major ideologies have tried, with varying degrees of success, to solve this problem. There is no doubt that nationalism has proved a potent force for national integration and for developing a new sense of purpose, helping to sweep away the anxieties and uncertainties resulting from the nation's shifting identity. In fact, the preoccupation with national identity itself is an inherent part of nationalism. The insistence on the uniqueness of one's own nation has occasionally, however, also led to the glorification of attitudes and values that were integral parts of the value system of the closed agricultural society from which it is emerging. Although the reconfirmation and elevation into permanent virtues of these values and attitudes undoubtedly contribute to greater self-confidence, they may at times make creative adjustment to the needs of modernization more difficult by prematurely freezing or fixing the self-image into a somewhat traditional cast.

There is another limitation to the effectiveness of nationalism as an agent of development. Although it is undoubtedly true that nationalism has greatly facilitated acceptance of the need for economic development and although nationalism has succeeded in linking much of the national energies to industrial and other development projects, it has by its very nature in a sense denaturized the growth process by emphasizing the prestige aspects, the physical plant, and the outward trappings of modern industrial society as symbols of national grandeur, without integrating the motivations and the inner dynamics of the growth process itself. Nationalism alone therefore can serve the development process as a motivational force only up to a point. For economic growth to sustain its momentum in its initial stages, other motivational forces will most likely have to be called upon. Increasingly therefore we see postindependence nationalism incorporating into its doctrine elements of either socialist or communist ideologies—both inherently more development oriented—in order better to cope with problems for which the nationalist response has proved insufficient.

The Challenge to Religion

Having briefly examined the ideologies as social mobilizers and integrators of development purposes with the wider purposes of society in our region, we cannot but note the limited success achieved so far. Some of the reasons I have mentioned in the preparatory memorandum, but this limited success also reflects the difficulty that secular ideologies have in communicating with the traditional sectors of our societies.

When we speak of the wider purposes of society, we are really speaking of the ultimate questions regarding man, society, and the significance of life in relation to the divine. The limited capacity of secular ideologies effectively to mobilize motivational forces in the traditional sectors of our society is conditioned by the inseparable connection of cultural values and attitudes in our societies with the complex of religious beliefs.

What is required then is the activation of more basic and more specific motivations for the acceleration of economic development. And these motivations in our societies are undoubtedly embedded in the cultural religious matrix. In part the problem is one of more effective symbol creation and symbol manipulation. A great deal more can and should be done in this respect.

It has, however, been the natural inclination of the modernizers to dismiss as unimportant the particular ways in which the leaders and literati of the traditional sectors view the present crisis of transition and their responses to it. Because of this dismissal, real communication has rarely been established, and the transmission of developmental values has remained defective. Much more serious attention will therefore have to be paid to the prevailing "interior view" within the traditional sectors. In this task, however, failure must be laid not only on the doorstep of the secular modernizers but also on that of the generally more secularized political leadership that has emerged from the traditional sectors of society itself or has adopted the religious and traditional sectors as its basis for political power. But even if more effective communication were established, we should have only partially solved our problem. The mobilization of the motivational forces embedded in the cultural and religious sub-soil is open to deliberate manipulation only to a degree. It is only fully possible when activated from the inside, from the well-spring of religious life itself.

We could for instance point to the need for legitimation of the purposes of economic development, as well as of the attitudes conducive to it, in terms of the traditional and religious value systems. Or we could say with Professor Shils that it requires the "dispersal of charisma"[3] to the economic sector and its activities. But even with effective communication, I do not think we could achieve this result, for we are now confronted with a question regarding the inner vitality and social dynamism of the religion concerned.

Essentially, for each of the religions in our societies, the problem is to relate itself to the great and pressing revolution of our time—the effort to abolish poverty, ignorance, and indignity; the striving for a better life on this earth; the emergence of a new social structure; and the continuous presence of change—in terms other than regret or wistfulness, fear, grudging acceptance, self-justification, or militant fundamentalist rejection. The intellectual exercise of apologetics, the attempts to vindicate one's religion in the face of significant departures in the new situation, are not enough for that purpose. Nor will any deliberate, and therefore synthetic, adjustment of the religious system to new social conditions do.

When everything has been said and done, it is only a new religious impulse from within the religion concerned that can give the process of reorientation and redirection a new and real vitality. But here we are entering the almost autonomous sphere of personal religious experience. It is, I think, only through the spiritual agony engendered by facing the crisis of the times and through reaching from the depths of one's own religious experience that it becomes possible to reaffirm and restate one's religion's essential relationship with society and to integrate the moral forces impelling the convulsive changes of our time into the living center of one's religion. Then it is possible to meet the "necessity of reinterpreting the unalterable, fundamental positions, without which a religion loses its self identity" and to achieve the "re-directing and re-inspiring of the religious will."[4]

I think most of the religions with which we are concerned at this seminar have in the past shown the capacity for such resurgence and renewed social dynamism in the face of new challenges. They have also shown the capacity to bring forth the leadership that is required. But if we can only hope for this response, we certainly cannot wait for it. It remains therefore incumbent upon the modernizers to try, as much as possible, to establish more effective communication with the traditional and religious sectors and to increase their manipulative capacity in that respect.

For where such religious resurgence fails to take place, leaving the traditional religious leadership outside or behind the mainstream of social change, it is still possible for new leadership to emerge that, although possibly moved by a deep sense of religious obligation, sets itself to the task of modernization in purely secular terms. The emergence of leaders from the ranks of the military in some Muslim countries to positions of national leadership in undertaking the task of economic development is, I think, a case in point.

Traditionalists and Modernizers

The wide divergence in frame of reference between the world of religious values and that of the modernizers clearly points up the need, on the part of the modernizers, for clearer understanding of and greater sensibility to the interior views of the religions in our region regarding man, society, and the contemporary situation. They should take more seriously than before the subjective ways in which these religions look at things, at their sense of crisis or its absence, and at the terms in which they perceive the present and its problems. Heightened self-awareness in relation to the many ways in which their nations' pasts continue to impinge upon their dreams of the future can only increase their effectiveness as modernizers by allowing them to cast their roots deeper and more consciously into the cultural subsoil, thus widening the reach of their empathic powers.

On the other hand, it becomes important that a better understanding be reached among religious and traditional leaders and the literati of the terms in which the modernizers define the problems of the nation and the legitimacy of the purposes they seek to serve through their commitment to development. Such understanding calls for a continuous dialogue between the two worlds, through which the one world can explain itself in terms of the other, in the hope that gradually a clearer understanding of each other will be achieved, from which might grow greater mutual recognition and willingness to co-operate in the modernization process.

This result would require the existence of a group of scholars and intellectuals willing to devote themselves continuously to this endeavor, who would take it upon themselves to bring the many often unconscious assumptions on which social action and decision-making in our transitional societies are predicated into the daylight of consciousness, to try to make them explicit and open them to rational examination. This function would clearly be of great importance for more effective communication and might facilitate fuller mobilization of human resources for the purpose of speeding up economic development. In this way also, these scholars and intellectuals might help to ease the painful confrontation in the traditional sectors of our societies of their changing social environment, the insistent demand for a better life that is now abroad. Eventually they might, when and if the traditional religions find it within themselves to respond positively and constructively to the new challenges, facilitate that adjustment. And possibly such an accommodation might even help to inculcate into the modernization process values that might help in shaping a uniquely new society.

I have raised these questions here in the conviction that, if we want the developmental values and attitudes we are going to discuss to become operational and effective, we shall have to link them with broader motivational forces. This problem brings us face to face with questions of existing views on the ultimate purposes of life and of the possibility of integrating new and old purposes into meaningful wholes. To this end, it will be necessary to take a closer look at the subjective, interior view prevailing in the traditional sectors of our society—as opposed to the modernizer's external view—of the challenges they face. This close look can be achieved through various foci. In this brief introduction, I have tried to focus on the identity and religious crises.

The Question of Time

I should like to raise another point here. The integration of new and old values into a value system more conducive to economic development is not only the result of the leadership and the manipulative capability of the modernizers on the one hand and of the capacity for adjustment and reorientation of the traditional frame of reference on the other. After all, this activity is taking place in a society already in motion. The modernization process is already inexorably under way. Urbanization, secularization, and education are advancing, and much greater social mobility is already visible, inducing in turn other changes in all sectors. The traditional sector, for instance, is certainly not so traditional as it was twenty years ago.

The modernization process is in fact a dynamic process involving a complex set of factors in continuous interplay. If we have discussed our problem here in terms of the tensions between the modernizers and the traditional sector, we have actually imposed a polarity on social reality that does not exist to so great an extent. None of the modernizers for instance is himself entirely free from the traditional value system. It shows up in sometimes surprising forms at surprising times, and I think that in our own environments, and in our own lives, we can point to sufficient instances of this kind. Similarly, as I have said before, none of the religious or traditional leaders or the literati has remained free of the compelling impact of some aspects of modern life.

There are also social conditions that by themselves facilitate the modernization process and the emergence of new value systems. As Nash[5] points out, for instance, if the prevailing distribution of wealth, power, and prestige is in some contradiction to the value pattern, then social change and new economic patterns are likely to find sanction among a sizable segment. He also suggests that the presence of conflicting religious systems, philosophies, and world views in a society may indicate the malleability of the value complex and in that way may make social change and the emergence of new patterns easier.

In any case, I think that we would benefit from looking at this particular aspect of our problem. And I am sure that in the course of our discussions other such conditions will emerge.

The question that inevitably arises at this point is, How important is all this? Are we not allowing ourselves to be overwhelmed by problems the magnitude of which is of our own making? Are we not overestimating the force of cultural factors and exaggerating their drag on the momentum of social change or their capacity to accelerate or direct it? After all, cultural values are not the sole determinants of social action, nor are they autonomous forces, although they of course constitute an important ingredient in determining the choice between alternative courses of action. Nor does any man live by a single value system alone. It is quite possible to function reasonably well with several simultaneous value systems that may not be consistent with and may even be contradictory to one another. Will not many problems therefore simply disappear with increased industrialization? I think the answer to the last question is yes. But at the same time our problem, at least in some countries, is how to get the industrialization process started at all. And once it is started, can we then leave the matter to a kind of natural expansion of effects? We should also ask ourselves, Can we afford the time? There is of course a wide range among our countries in the degree of urgency felt. There certainly are parts of our global area where there is not much time because of population pressure or because of the prevailing political dynamics. A high degree of mass participation in politics, with heightened popular expectations for material improvement as a crucially important political factor, is an example. In those places, rapid economic development is a *conditio sine qua non* for some measure of political stability. And if more coercion is to be avoided, the mobilization of motivational forces embedded in the cultural religious matrix becomes unavoidable.

Some Problems

The range of problems that our seminar has staked out for itself is quite formidable, and we can hardly hope to do justice to all of them. And while we speak about Hinduism, Islam, Buddhism, and Christianity we shall most likely be obliged to ignore the various forms in which these religions manifest themselves in our various countries. We can only regret this necessity, for the very differences among these forms might suggest interesting insights into various types of economic behavior. Also in several of our countries there are religious manifestations that cannot adequately be discussed under the heading of "dominant religion within the country." Javanese mysticism is one instance.

I think we should also be aware of another limitation, the fact that we all speak from different situations, from different histories, from different social structures, that we have been subjected to different pressures and priorities. Although we may be using the same terms and concepts, we may, initially at least, not really be speaking the same language. In fact, our own situations are often not entirely clear to us.

Most likely each of us knows only a few segments of the many-faceted complex of cultural reality in his own country. Still we are gathered here to talk about certain problems in the hope that we shall gain clarification, illumination, and encouragement from understanding how each of us grapples with these problems. I am sure that at least this much we shall be able to achieve. We may also hope for an additional result from our seminar: that it will help universities in our area to concentrate the developing intellectual and scholarly capabilities of our nations on these problems of national integration and economic growth, the principal pivots of the modernization process our nations are undergoing.

To that end, considerable reorientation will be necessary. The study of the social sciences as well as of Orientology, for instance, will have to free itself from the traditional preoccupations of its disciplines and to direct its attention and energy much more deliberately and especially much more imaginatively to these great problems of our nations.

Notes

1. The term is Reinhold Niebuhr's, although he uses it in a different context. Reinhold Niebuhr, *Faith and History* (New York: Charles Scribner's Sons, 1949), p. 19.
2. Manning Nash, "Some Social and Cultural Aspects of Eco-

nomic Development," in *Economic Development and Cultural Change*, VII, No. 2 (January, 1959), 147.

3. Edward Shils, "The Concentration and Dispersion of Charisma, Their Bearing on Economic Policy in Underdeveloped Countries," *World Politics*, XI, No. 1 (October, 1958), 12.

4. Hendrik Kraemer, *World Cultures and World Religions* (London: Lutterworth Press, 1960), p. 349.

5. Nash, *op. cit.*, p. 141.

H. DE LA COSTA, S.J.

The Concept of Progress
and Traditional Values
in a Christian Society

IN A SEMINAR LIKE THIS ONE, it is important to establish initially some common ground on which discussion can take place and, in fact, to ask ourselves whether or not such common ground can be established. Each participant must define as clearly as he can how he understands the key terms that are constantly being used in the course of the seminar, terms like "Christian society," "progress," "modernization." In this way, we can discover whether there is agreement or difference over the meanings of these terms.

Problems of Definition

THE CONCEPT OF A CHRISTIAN SOCIETY. It is quite true, as Mr. Soedjatmoko points out in the "outline" that was distributed during the planning stage of this seminar, that traditional value systems stem "in large measure" from the dominant religions of their societies. This close connection between religion and value system is what justifies our specifying societies by their dominant religions, calling this society "Christian," that one "Muslim," and so forth.

It is, however, equally obvious that there has been a plurality of Christian societies, both current and historic, and that these societies have not been Christian in exactly the same way. We are thus faced with the necessity for determining *in what sense* Christianity may be said to be the dominant religion of a given society. For it may prove, upon investigation, that Christianity is not really dominant but only seems to be—or that it was dominant in the past but is so no longer, although because of Christianity's historic role the society continues to be designated "Christian." France was once the "eldest daughter of the Church," and even today, if we select our indicators with some care, we can justify calling France a Christian country. Yet it is frequently asserted, not by foreigners but by Frenchmen, that France—or at any rate certain regions and social sectors of France—is mission territory, needing to be converted to Christianity all over again.

Or it may happen that what is dominant in a society may be called "Christianity" and may well have been Christianity at one time but has ceased to be so either wholly or in part. The regions and peoples of the later Roman Empire that adhered to one or another of the great heresies of that period continued to call themselves Christian, but, as they denied some of the most central teachings of Christianity, it is clear that this label can be accorded them only with the gravest reservations.

We must also pay particular attention to the *form* or *manner* in which Christianity is present in what is called or claims to be a "Christian" society. Is it present as personal conviction, strongly and widely held and active as a determinant of attitude and conduct? Is it present, furthermore, as an institution, prescribing and receiving adherence to certain external forms of organization, worship, ritual, and socially acceptable behavior?

Is it present in both these senses or in only one? Is it perhaps the dominant personal religion of large numbers, although prevented for various reasons, like hostility from the state, from expressing itself in institutional forms? Again the later Roman Empire is a case in point, for in this sense that Empire was already Christian and had been so for some time before Constantine accorded Christianity freedom of external worship and Theodosius made it the religion of the state.

Alternatively, is Christianity dominant not as a personal religion but merely as an official or social one, to which external conformity is given because it is safe or useful to do so and not necessarily from inner conviction or even from understanding of the implications of conformity? We may suspect that such is the case, at least initially, wherever Christianity has been imposed by force, as by Charlemagne among the Saxons, or wherever Christianity maintains a hollow dominance through social prestige or state authority, as in those modern nations still nominally Christian in which secularism has effected mass apostasy.

Finally, it is necessary to determine with some accuracy *to what extent* Christianity is dominant in the society in question. Granted that it is the dominant belief, to what extent does belief color attitude and condition conduct? What part has it played in the formation of the prevailing value system? How far have its implications been spelled out in the various concerns and activities of society: in education; in philosophy, letters, and the arts; in the organization of the economy; in the conduct of government? How deeply does it permeate family life, the customs and usages of the village, the multiple relationships of the town?

I therefore suggest that we cannot, for the purposes of this seminar, define a Christian society simply as one whose traditional value system stems "in large measure" from Christianity, for the measure of this "large measure" differs with each Christian society. It differs not only quantitatively, as the metaphor of "measure" implies, but also qualitatively, which is far more important and, incidentally, more difficult to determine. It differs not only by "how much?" but by "in what sense?" and "in what form?" The Philippines, by quantitative measurement, is a Christian society, but we should not get very far in our deliberations if we assumed that it is therefore the same *kind* of Christian society as Spain or Canada, for example.

THE IDEA OF PROGRESS. I note that the presence (or absence) of the idea of progress in Hinduism, Buddhism, and Islam is put down in the list of papers and sessions but not the relationship of the idea of progress with Christianity. This omission may be dictated merely by lack of time or by some other procedural necessity; or it may have been purposely made. I should like to assume the latter because I can think of a good reason for it. It is proper to omit discussion of "the concept of progress in Christianity" because the concept of progress is, after all, a Christian concept.

I am not claiming, of course, that the concept of progress is absent from Hinduism, Buddhism, and Islam. Much less am I claiming that, if it has been absent hitherto from these religions, it cannot be built into them without violation of their total context. I am merely pointing out that the idea of progress, as it has been elaborated in the West, has its origin in the Christian tradition and that we cannot account for its genesis without reference to that tradition.

I realize, of course, that most of the textbooks and manuals of history and sociology in current use attribute the emergence of the idea of progress to the eighteenth-century philosophers and that the eighteenth-century philosophers were most explicit in proclaiming that the idea of progress was their own invention, owing nothing to the Christian background of the society in which they lived. Nevertheless, they were mistaken. They owed a great deal to that background.

The idea of progress has been variously stated. Mr. Soedjatmoko's statement will serve as well as any. It is the idea of "a present better than the past and a future potentially better than the present." It is based on the assumption of "the perfectibility of man and society as a continuous possibility." It takes for granted "man's ability to control and improve his natural environment as well as the legitimacy of his desire to do so." Now it is curious, but a fact, that this idea as defined did not form part of the Greco-Roman legacy to Western Europe. What the Greeks and Romans believed was in fact almost exactly the opposite: a present worse than the past and a future that would almost certainly be even worse. For Hesiod in the eighth century B.C. as for Ovid in the first century A.D., what lay in the past was a remote golden age that had become successively debased into silver, bronze, and iron ages, and both the present and the foreseeable future were definitely of the iron age. True, the cycle would be repeated, as Plato taught; the golden age would come again. It might even be imminent, as Vergil at one time rather wistfully hoped. But the new golden age would represent not an advance but a return, not progress but recurrence. And, after the crest of the wave, there would come inevitably the plunge into the trough. So thought the ancient world of the Mediterranean, influenced perhaps by the philosophers of India.

If we now turn to the Judaeo-Christian view of life, which is the other major part of the cultural legacy of Western Europe, we shall immediately perceive it to be in sharp contrast to the Greco-Roman view. It is not cyclical but linear, and it is irreversible. The world had a definite beginning and will have a definite end, an end in two senses. An end is the last of a series, but it is also a goal, an objective to be attained. Man, individually and in community, attains his objective by his own activity, by the proper exercise of his God-given powers, and a significant part of that effort is the gradual domination of his environment. For God said to the first man and woman not merely, "Increase and multiply and fill the earth," but also "Make it yours; take command of the fishes in the sea, and all that flies through the air, and all the living things that move on the earth" (Gen. 1: 28).

There was thus really no need for the eighteenth-century

philosophers to invent the idea of progress, nor could they have done so. It had already been invented. Their contribution was to take the idea out of its Christian context and to transpose it into purely secular terms. There is no doubt that this transposition gave a tremendous impetus to the improvement of living conditions on this earth, to man's comprehension and control of the physical forces of his environment. For clearly the great achievement of secularism has been to divert tremendous human energies from the pursuit of spiritual perfection to the generation of material power, from the attainment of heaven to the achievement of heaven on earth. It may, however, be permitted us to wonder whether or not this gain in impetus and acceleration has not been accompanied by a corresponding loss in another and rather vital respect, in a loss, that is, of direction. We are certainly moving and moving fast. Or perhaps we should say that the West is moving fast and that we Asians are trying desperately to move as fast as the West. But where is it moving? Toward what? Westerners' forefathers knew where they were going or thought they did. Do Westerners today even think they know? And we—we Asians—are we quite clear about the direction of Western progress, and are we quite agreed that it is the direction we wish to take?

Whatever answers to such questions may be arrived at in the course of this seminar, it should at least be clear that what Mr. Soedjatmoko calls the "modernizing elite" in Asia has nothing whatever to fear and everything to hope for from Christianity. I refer, of course, to Christianity purely as a theological and philosophical system, as a set of beliefs and insights into the nature and purpose of the universe and of man's role and destiny within it. The traditional value systems that have developed in societies called "Christian" are quite another matter. Such systems are never the products of Christian belief alone but the resultants of many causes, of surviving pre-Christian beliefs, of ecological imperatives, of the psychological conditioning induced by long-standing social institutions and usages, of a host of other factors that we are only now beginning to appreciate or even to suspect.

If, then, the traditional value system of a given Christian society puts obstacles in the way of progress, we must ask ourselves whether it does so precisely because it is Christian or because of some other factor or factors that have entered into its formation. And if we are able to satisfy ourselves that it is the Christian element that is the source of the difficulty, then we must ask ourselves the further question, whether the Christian objection is to progress itself or to the direction that it takes, that is, to the particular orientation of a modernizing elite.

THE MODERNIZATION PROCESS. This term is employed by Mr. Soedjatmoko for the phenomenon of modernization, and it has an admirable precision that we shall do well to preserve in our discussion. In effect, modernization is a *process;* it belongs to the category of becoming not of being, to the realm of means not of ends. It is described by Mr. Soedjatmoko as being (at least in part) a process or a task of "welding together smaller and more primitive forms of social organization into larger, new, cohesive, and viable political units capable of undergoing economic development," economic development or growth being defined as "a self-sustaining process of continuous innovation, change, and development." Modernization is, then, partly a political process, partly a social process, partly an economic process. And we are asked to consider in this seminar, first, whether or not the traditional value systems of Asia hinder this process; and, second, if they do, how they can be prevented from hindering the process; and, indeed, third, how they can be made to subserve the process, how they can be "manipulated," "mobilized," "reoriented" to promote instead of hinder the process.

But surely, this formulation makes no sense. For values, unlike processes, belong to the category of ends. Values, in fact, *are* ends, and one does not adapt ends to means but means to ends. One may consider attending a symphony concert a thing of value, and he may consider riding a motor yacht an admirable way of reaching the symphony concert. But he does not first decide to go to symphony concerts in a motor yacht and then bend every effort to reorient, manipulate, and mobilize symphony concerts so that they should henceforth be held in places accessible by motor yacht. At least, we hope not.

I gather, therefore, that we are really meant to consider how traditional values can be rendered compatible not with the process of modernization itself but with those ends or purposes that the modernizing elite in Asia have decided are the proper objects of that process. We are to consider how traditional values can be brought into line with "modern" values. Put that way, the proposal begins to make sense. If the modernizing Asian can persuade the traditional Asian to want what he wants, then obviously he stands a better chance of persuading him to adopt the means or the process—the modernizing process—by which both can obtain what they want.

The question therefore arises, What exactly does the modernizing Asian want? What are *his* values? What is this new value system to fit which we must "reorient," "mobilize," and "manipulate" our traditional value systems? To be sure, there are hints in Mr. Soedjatmoko's "outline" of what the value system of the modernizing elite may be. For instance, he asks whether or not there are elements in the traditional value systems "that inherently constitute impediments to modernization" and, if so, whether or not "secularization [is] the only way to overcome these impediments to progress." The questions certainly suggest that, if it comes to a choice, the modernizing elite will prefer secularization with progress to traditional values without progress; and this suggestion in turn implies that, in the minds of the modernizing elite, a secularized society, a society in which the secular world view prevails, is certainly compatible with progress, whereas one that clings to its traditional value system is only doubtfully so. But what does secularization mean? What constitutes the secular world view *as the modernizing elites of Asia understand it?*

Again, a clue to the new value system may be embedded in the idea of progress itself, which, as Mr. Soedjatmoko puts it, is acceptance of "a present better than the past, and a future potentially better than the present." But what exactly does "better" mean? How to determine what is better and what is worse? Is an industrialized society better than an agricultural one? In what sense? Are the purposes to which a Buddhist monk dedicates his life inferior to the purposes to which a factory manager dedicates his? They may well be, but if we wish to convince the monk of the fact we must make it plain why his purposes are inferior, by what standards, norms, or measures they are wanting. And I take it that we do want to convince the monk; we do not want merely to analyze him.

In this connection, I believe it is pertinent to note that inquiries like the one in which we are presently engaged are most often not only initiated but also carried out by the modernizing elites. It could hardly be otherwise, as in Asia it is this group that contains the social analysts who are interested in this kind of inquiry and consider it important. It often happens therefore that what is considered traditionally or characteristically Asian is indeed analyzed but in the light of principles and norms that are simply assumed to be valid without themselves being subjected to analysis. It may even happen that the people to whom what is traditionally or characteristically Asian is attributed are "manipulated," "reoriented," and "mobilized" by a process known, I believe, as "social engineering" toward purposes and goals whose desirability is similarly taken for granted. In other words, the traditional Asian, the Asian unhappily burdened with a traditional value system, is dealt with consciously or unconsciously as object, not subject; as a fact, not a person; as a neurotic on a couch or a case history on a card; as a man whom one observes, not with whom one converses; as a man to whom one listens not for ideas but for symptoms; as something but not someone. I suppose analysis of this sort has its uses, but it certainly does not win friends and influence people. To do that, we must engage not only in analysis but also in dialogue, and dialogue involves not a person-object but a person-person relationship. It implies a readiness to analyze and, if necessary, to "reorient" not only the other but oneself.

From these considerations, the following propositions emerge:

First, Christian societies are not uniform but differ greatly from one another in the manner in which Christianity is present in each, in the depth of penetration of Christian belief in the society it dominates, and even in the sense in which Christianity can be said to be dominant at all.

Second, as the idea of progress derives, historically, from the original Christian insight into the nature of the universe and the destiny of man, the process of modernization in Asia ought not to encounter any impediment on the part of Christianity as such. In fact, it may reasonably expect aid and support.

Third, if, then, the efforts of the modernizing elite do encounter opposition from the traditional value system of a Christian society in Asia like the Philippines, this opposition may be due either to elements in the value system that are not Christian at all or are insufficiently penetrated or dominated by Christianity or to Christian opposition not to modernization itself but to the aims and objectives, that is, to the value system of the modernizing elite.

Attitudes or Institutions?

We may now consider what Mr. Soedjatmoko calls the "more practical problems that are encountered on the operational level of economic development projects." Mr. Soedjatmoko suggests that these problems arise from the "pervasiveness and strength" of the traditional cultures of Asia. That is, if I interpret his thought correctly, they arise from the opposition presented by traditional Asian attitudes and values to the operations, methods, and institutions necessary for modern economic development. He then offers an extremely helpful list of the areas in which such problems have arisen or are likely to arise: "the attitude toward work, toward time, toward money; saving and spending habits; forms of decision-making and of the resolution of conflicts; functioning within large impersonal social organizations; forms and structure of economic enterprise; labor mobility and labor recruitment; questions of achievement orientation, of incentives and disincentives for economic activities."

It is frequently argued that there are typically Filipino attitudes toward these various forms and aspects of economic activity that hinder or act as brakes upon rapid economic development. Doubtless there are, as so many experts say so. I should like to suggest, however, that they may be fewer than they are sometimes made out to be.

There is, for instance, the so-called *mañana* habit, compounded of roughly equal parts of shiftlessness, indolence, and procrastination. There is the lack of punctuality and in general of a sense of the value of time. There is the improvidence and lack of thrift that are at the bottom of widespread peasant indebtedness and debt slavery. There is the tendency in those who do manage to accumulate savings to squander them on merry-making, ostentation, and luxuries instead of employing them in the further production of wealth. There is, finally, the inclination to look down on manual work and to give a high social rating to the white-collar worker. All of these attitudes have at one time or another been put forward as typically Filipino.

But are they really typical? Would it not be almost true to say that the *mañana* habit has always been attributed to one-half the human race by the other half? Certainly it has been attributed to Central Americans by North Americans; to Latins by Anglo-Saxons; to Africans by Europeans; to Arabs by Jews; and to Greeks by Romans. Furthermore, it is not only instructive but also amusing to read a whole series of Spanish writers of the eighteenth and nineteenth centuries as they deplore the congenital indolence of the Filipino and then to take up a parallel series by foreign observers who visited or resided in the Philippines at the same time—among them the American Bowditch, the Frenchman La Pérouse, and the Scotsman MacMicking, to mention only a few—and to find them deploring with the same superior air the congenital indolence of the Spaniard.

As for the sense of time (or lack of it), the absence of thrift, and the tendency to conspicuous consumption, analysts of Asian societies would do well to read what their colleagues have written about medieval Europe. We might suggest, for a start, Marc Bloch. If we strip away from our picture of medieval Europe the technicolor trappings with which Hollywood has obscured it, we Filipinos find much that is not only familiar to us but also much that we are continually told is peculiar to ourselves.

Why is this so? Surely it is because similar historical situations tend to develop similar attitudes and patterns of behavior among human beings placed in similar contexts. Such, at least, is the explanation that the simple-minded historian arrives at. If it is too simple an explanation, I nevertheless do not think we can altogether rule out the possibility that the shortcomings (and of course the virtues as well) of precapitalist Asia are less Asian than precapitalist.

And if, after all, this observation should turn out to be correct, then the Filipinos' attitudes toward work, time and money, saving and spending habits, and the rest may not stem from a traditional value system peculiarly their own, much less from the religion specifying that system, but may simply reflect the stage of economic and social development they have reached. These attitudes may change of themselves as Filipinos pass into another stage. This change occurred in Europe with the organization of trade, the rise of a middle class, and industrialization, and there is no reason to think that it will be any different in Asia.

Indeed, such changes are already taking place. Members of

this seminar have doubtless already met Filipinos who are fairly punctual, who dress and live soberly, who invest their savings in textiles or food processing, and who read *The Economist*. Many have been told that these Filipinos are "Westernized." We shall have something to say about Westernization before we finish.

We must, of course, pay attention to Boeke's influential thesis that the Asian—more specifically, the Southeast Asian—is not *homo oeconomicus*, that he does not have the (theoretically) unlimited economic desires that provide the mainspring of Western capitalist society because his world view imposes social limits on his economic needs. I gather, however, that more and more economists are tending to attribute the narrowness of our economic horizons less to world views than to world trade. Given the opportunity, as Father McPhelin has pointed out, the Southeast Asian is quite as capable as the next man of "high living and plain thinking" and of taking the necessary steps to reach that happy state.

Westerners today are devoting a great deal of time, money, and even thought to trying to understand Asians. This effort is very good of them, and we could wish that Asians would devote a proportionate amount of effort to trying to understand the West, instead of simply aping it or, alternatively, cursing it. In this process of mutual understanding, the tendency is naturally enough to look for contrasts rather than similarities. You are you, not I. How different are you from me? The sharper the contrast, of course, the better; it makes you so much more clearly and definitely you. But there is a danger of falsifying reality, for nature abhors contrasts even more than it abhors vacuums. There is, for instance, the danger of taking some quality that is fairly strongly present in me and less strongly present in you and insisting that its presence in me is permanent and absolute and its absence in you total and irrevocable. The quality in question, which may be merely an accident of history or circumstance, is thus made to seem essential: an attribute of race, nationality, or

culture. The contrast is sharp and clear, as in a retouched photograph, and, as in a retouched photograph, false.

Something of the sort seems to have happened to the idea of
impersonal organization and impersonal authority. The ability to
operate within an impersonal organization under an impersonal
authority is conceived as an attribute of Western culture; the
inability to operate except within a person-oriented (or a family-
oriented) organization under a personal authority is conceived as
an attribute of Asian culture. And because economic growth
demands impersonal organization and impersonal authority, we
have here a neat explanation for Asian economic backwardness.

But then the theory comes up against the case of Japan.
How many interpretations of Japanese society, before the war,
heavily underscored the personalism of the Japanese ethos, the
inability of the Japanese to conceive of authority except in terms
of kinship or vassalage, the lengths to which they would go to
make even a cartel look as much like an extended family as
possible! Yet postwar Japan does not seem to find much difficulty with the kind of economic organization that enables it to
deal on equal terms with Western capitalism. What has happened
to the contrast?

The standard answer is, of course, that Japan has been
"Westernized." And, in a sense, it has been Westernized, in
precisely the same way that the West itself was Westernized.
For impersonal organization and impersonal authority, far from
being constants of European culture or character, were developed in much the same way that they were developed in Japan,
by a process of economic and social change. Surely Westerners
cannot have forgotten that, before the revival of trade in the
thirteenth and fourteenth centuries and in many parts of Europe
long afterward, Western society was a *feudal* society? And what
is feudalism if not the very apotheosis of personal organization
and personal authority? It began with the Merovingian concept
—or rather the Merovingian inability to conceive of the authority
of the state, the Roman *res publica*, except in terms of private

property, divisible and inheritable—and it developed to the point where a noble Austrian family of modest means and attainments, the Hapsburgs, could acquire by a series of strategic marriages almost half of Europe.

From this point of view, it surely would be more accurate to argue that Japan has experienced not "Westernization" but simply those economic and social changes that, some three hundred years earlier, transformed the West itself from a feudal to a capitalist society. And this argument is not merely *lis de verbo*, a question of appropriate nomenclature, or, as the Chinese say, "a rectification of names." It affects the very terms of reference of the present seminar. In effect, we must ask ourselves whether the question posed is primarily a problem of changing attitudes or one of changing institutions. Is it primarily a problem of reorienting, mobilizing, and manipulating values or one of institutional innovation in order to get the economy off the ground, trusting that Asians will have as much intelligence about and adaptability to flight as Europeans, even as they begin to enjoy its advantages?

RAUL S. MANGLAPUS

Philippine Culture
and Modernization

The Culture of Poverty

TWO FORCES—fear of catastrophe and hope of prosperity—have led men and nations, particularly the powerful among them, to be more than ever concerned with the economic conditions of others, specifically with the poverty of nations, and with some very basic questions: Why are nations poor? Why are some nations poor and others rich? What are the forces retarding progress in the poor nations? How can such forces be overcome with the least pain?

In an admirable and widely reprinted article originally written for the October, 1962, issue of *The Atlantic*, John Kenneth Galbraith analyzed the differences between the Marxian and the non-Marxian views on the poverty of nations (the title of the article, incidentally, is "The Poverty of Nations"). As analyzed by Galbraith, the Marxian view blames national poverty on certain retarding institutions like feudalism, colonialism, and capitalism. The non-Marxian view is that poverty is self-perpetuating and is caused by the lack of capital necessary to catalyze growth. Accordingly, the Marxian and the non-Marxian approaches to the solution of poverty are as widely divergent as are their views on its causes. The Marxian approach is to abolish the retarding institutions by exporting revolution, while the non-Marxian way is to relieve the hunger for capital by exporting capital and technology.

Galbraith criticizes the Western, non-Marxian view as inadequate and incomplete for not paying enough attention precisely to that dimension of the problem on which the Soviets concentrate.

I come now to the principal disadvantage of Western development. The Marxian alternative, I have noted, emphasizes the destruction of the bonds that tie the economy to the past. Our emphasis is on capital, education, technical assistance, and the other instruments that allow of change. Until recently, at least, we have been tempted to suppose that any society is a platform on which, given these missing elements, development can be built.

In fact institutions do chain economies to the past, and the breaking of these chains is essential for progress. The promise of such drastic reform is a valid and appealing part of the Marxian case. There is no chance of agricultural development in the underdeveloped (and hence agricultural) country under such systems of absentee landlordism where the workers or sharecroppers are confined by law and tradition to a minor share of a meager product. These feudal agricultural systems, moreover, extend their corrupting influence to government, to the provision of public or military sinecures to those who lack a claim on the land, to the milking of industrial enterprise, and to the destruction of the morale of the society itself. . . . Progress does require the radical elimination of retarding institutions. . . .

The essay lucidly dissects the problem of poverty and how to combat it from the points of view of the two power blocs. It discusses the foreign-aid policies of the Western bloc as opposed to those of the Soviet bloc and how assistance under these policies can be improved. Galbraith necessarily confines himself to the point of view of the "giver" nation; he is, after all, a citizen of the biggest dispenser of foreign aid in the world.

What remains to be discussed is the point of view of the "recipient" nation. What can and must be done by the recipient nation to render the aid given her effective and fruitful? What can and must be done by the developing nations of the world to launch themselves on the road to progress? For clearly it is not enough for capital to be received or institutions to be demolished for prosperity automatically to follow. Surely it is theoretically and historically unsound to expect a nation to take off to progress merely upon the infusion of capital goods and the destruction of certain institutions.

Perhaps the duty of the giver nation ends with the exportation of capital or of revolution (depending on which side of the Curtain one is on). It can do no more. The recipient nation must take up the work from there. Progress ultimately depends on what the recipient nation does with the aid capital and how it reacts to the elimination of old institutions, decisions that cannot be made by the giver nations or even by the governments of the recipient nations but only by the people of these recipient nations themselves. Capital and the abolition of retarding institutions are indispensable to progress, but by themselves they are insufficient.

There are many places where capital imported from non-Marxian nations has been found adequate and where the governments have undermined retarding institutions sufficiently to make the importation of Marxist revolution unnecessary. Yet the people in those places have remained poor. In this country (the Philippines), for instance, there are places where social overhead capital is not wanting—beautiful concrete roads, kilometers of power lines, adequate irrigation. Yet the masses of the people remain poor and continue to live the way their forefathers lived before the invention of electricity and before the discovery of steel.

Share tenancy, together with the feudal society based on it, is generally recognized as one of the institutions that most effectively hold back economic progress. Galbraith himself singles it out as one of those institutions that must be abolished by orderly means if it is not to be destroyed violently. The Philippine government officially bowed to this reality when it committed itself to the abolition of share tenancy and submitted a bill to Congress that would completely wipe out this institution by legislative fiat. It is true that such a measure has been long in coming, and its enactment should do much good, not only in those places where tenancy thrives, but also in all sectors and on all levels of the economy and of society. But during the course of the Senate hearings on the bill, it became quite clear that even in areas where tenancy does not exist, where the farmers own the land that they till—even, I might add, where all the necessary social overhead is present beside—there the masses have remained poor.

While land reforms and social overhead are necessary conditions for progress, they are not *guarantees* for progress. It all depends on what man decides to do with his land and with the facilities at his disposal. As long as he looks at roads merely as avenues by which to see the sights or go to the cockpit and not as arteries of trade by which to market his produce and therefore as added incentive for ever greater production, as long as he uses power merely to light up his festivals and not to bring forth industries, so long will he remain as poor as his father and grandfather before him. If the farmer looks to his land merely for security and bare subsistence and not for capital to use in more and more intensive production, indeed for profit, he will remain as destitute as any tenant.

In brief, while capital goods and the abolition of certain institutions are preconditions for progress, the attainment or even the beginning of progress ultimately depends upon the people, upon their minds, upon their outlook on life. The struggle for progress transcends all competition between Marxism and capitalism; its main arena is in the minds of men. The main protagonists in the fight for progress in the developing countries are not the Russians or the Chinese or the Americans, or England, Germany, Italy, or France, but the people of the developing nations themselves.

I submit, at the risk of gross oversimplification, that the key factor in progress is the particular people's outlook on life, its set of attitudes, its system of values, its whole way of thinking— its culture. This factor is why the general theme of this seminar, "cultural motivations for progress," is very much to the point. For I am convinced that the most powerful forces retarding progress are to be found among the elements of a people's culture. In culture, perhaps, can even be found the answer to the question of why some nations are rich and others poor. It may well be the key to the solution to the poverty of nations.

The Filipino *Fiesta*

If these premises are valid, what is it in Philippine culture that has placed this country in its present economic condition? What is it in this Christian—specifically, this Catholic—society that has retarded progress or, in less harsh terms, that has made it lag far behind the economic advance of the United States, Australia, Western Europe, and Japan?

The identification of a society or a culture in religious terms, as when one refers to a "Christian society," is not irrelevant or accidental. For religion constitutes one of the strongest forces that shape the culture of a people. This seminar has recognized this fact and has related religion in South and Southeast Asia to the "cultural motivations for progress."

If religion—meaning a set of beliefs, attitudes, values, and norms of behavior in reference to man's relationship with God —is at the core of culture and if it is granted that a people's culture is the key to its economic progress, then a people's religion must at least influence its economic development. One of the first and most famous thinkers to see a direct link between religion and economic development was the pioneering German sociologist Max Weber. In his celebrated work, *The Protestant Ethic and the Spirit of Capitalism*, as well as in the essay "The Protestant Sects and the Spirit of Capitalism," Weber advanced the theory that the "spirit of capitalism" emerged where and when it did because of certain qualities developed by the beliefs and practices of the Calvinist and Puritan versions of Protestantism, those qualities being individualism and self-reliance, rational orderliness, industry and efficiency, and discipline.

Taking off from Weber, Thomas McHale, an American who has done some studies of the social causes and effects of Philippine economic development, ascribes the beginning of a "spirit of capitalism" in certain sectors of Philippine society to the Protestant orientation of American colonial and educational policy. McHale also argues in favor of the obverse of this thesis, namely, that Hispanic Catholicism, which, according to him, fostered qualities opposite to those embodied in the "Protestant ethic," contributed to the economic stagnation of the Philippines through its doctrines and policies and the behavior it encouraged.

While the economic progress of Japan, of Italy, and of the Catholic areas of France and Germany, as well as cases like that of the Medici of Renaissance Florence, precludes the universal application of the Weberian thesis, the McHale proposition derived from it bears examination on its own merits. Is the undeveloped state of the Philippine economy indeed largely due to the country's Spanish Catholic heritage? Or is it, as I suggest, to a great extent due to the pre-Spanish and largely Asian beliefs and traditions of the Filipinos, which persisted through, were indeed encouraged by, the Spanish Catholic dispensation? For one of the features observed by anthropologists and historians in Latin Catholicism is its fusing quality, its ability to merge Christian doctrine and practice with indigenous beliefs, rituals, and traditions. This ability has been the source of both its strength and its weakness. For while it smoothed the way for rapid conversions, it helped preserve beliefs and practices not only irrelevant but sometimes contrary to Christianity.

One of the most telling illustrations of this fusing quality in Latin Catholicism is the Philippine institution of the *fiesta*. When the Spaniards began their colonization of the Philippines, they came upon certain habits and traditions of the people, among them the practice of throwing lavish feasts on certain days of the year and on such occasions as births, weddings, funerals, harvests, departures of raiding parties, and their victorious returns. In the subsistence economy then prevailing, those feasts were means of sharing the bounty of the "haves" with the "have-nots" and of consuming produce that might be in excess of what was necessary for bare subsistence. These feasts not only were occasions for relieving the monotony of rural society but often also took on the quasi-religious nature of ritual feasts in petition or thanksgiving to the gods. And because they were also occasions on which the people engaged in communal activity, the Spanish missionaries took advantage of them to preach, baptize, and dispense the sacraments, first taking care to consecrate those days to Roman Catholic saints. But they also took care not to do away with the people's cherished traditions, thus avoiding opposition. This policy and the absence of opposition accounted to a great extent for Catholicism's spectacular success in the conversion of the Filipinos.

The result was that, while the trappings and certain external observances of Catholicism have been superimposed on the indigenous traditions, the *fiesta* retains the essential character of the pre-Spanish festivals. One indication is the fact that the *fiesta* in rural areas is home-centered rather than church-centered. (The images of saints that are venerated and carried in procession in the *fiesta* are kept in the homes of the well-to-do rather than in the parish churches.) *Fiesta* activities are less often focused on church ceremonies than on preparation of food and drink for the invariably lavish feasts that are open to all comers, feasts that are direct descendants of the ritual feasts and food offerings to the gods of old. (It is actually believed that the heavily laden banquet table at the *fiesta* is pleasing to God and the patron saint.)

The secondary role that Roman Catholic rites play in the Philippine *fiesta* is indicated by the fact that the *fiesta* is not necessarily held on the feast day of a saint, as prescribed by the liturgical calendar of the Church, but is usually held in April or May. The non-Christian aspects of the *fiesta* are also manifested in the folk rituals usually performed in connection with it, which are closely related to similar rituals in other parts of Asia, places where Christian influence has been negligible—river processions (called *pagodas*, a Buddhist term), fertility dances, water festivals, flamboyant street decorations, rockets and fireworks. The Christian ingredients of the Philippine *fiesta* are often submerged under these elements.

What does this indigenous survival have to do with economic progress and the cultural motivations for it, the theme of this seminar?

The answer is that, although culture and religion are cardinal factors in economic development, what I think has most retarded progress in this country is not Hispanic Catholicism itself but those non-Christian and pre-Spanish practices, traditions, and attitudes that Spain's missionaries failed to eradicate and even encouraged for the sake of apostolic efficiency.

First, the *fiesta* itself, those elements carried over in its present observance from pre-Spanish times, represents a huge waste of funds that could be diverted to industrial and other productive uses. The funds squandered on food and drink alone, for the consumption of acquaintances and strangers alike, are estimated at an annual total of about ₱200 million. This figure does not include the funds devoted to arches that are torn down the next day, to fireworks, to bands. And this extravagance is indulged not only by the wealthy but also and even more by the poor in the rural areas, where the pre-Christian traditions are strongest.

It is the usual practice for a family to spend for the *fiesta* one-half its annual income. This amount most often must be borrowed and paid back at usurious rates, a process repeated year after year and also on several occasions throughout the year, so that the borrower is forever doomed to virtual slavery to the moneylender. Good land is often sold to raise the funds for these ritual feasts. The education of children is forgone.

But the *fiesta* is not only in itself a tremendous waste of resources; it is also indicative of a whole outlook on life, of a set of attitudes and values. It is a symptom of a culture that is not Catholic, that is not even Christian. Filipino parents will not have a child baptized until they have saved or borrowed enough money for a lavish baptismal feast, in spite of Church injunctions to have infants baptized as soon after birth as possible. A Filipino couple will cohabit without benefit of Christian marriage until there is money for a big wedding feast. It is not the Christian sacrament that is of value but the non-Christian ritual feast.

Filipino welcome and farewell parties take on the extravagance of similar festivals of pre-Spanish times, and this habit has spilled over to birthday, graduation, and anniversary celebrations. In this culture, there are thoughts only for today and none for tomorrow. The entire culture is wrapped up in extravagant consumption, consumption in occasional spurts, and lolls in the torpor of poverty the rest of the year. There is no room here for savings and investments and the drive to ever greater production, which are all so vital to economic growth.

The Cyclical View of Life

This culture of improvidence is not confined to the Philippines but has manifestations in the rest of Asia, except Japan.

There are the lavish feasts given in Theravada Buddhist countries in petition or thanksgiving for a recovery from an illness, in prayer for a good voyage and in thanksgiving for a safe return, and for a host of other occasions. There are the expensive burial rites for the dead at the cost of further poverty to the living. There are Chinese festivals characterized both by lavish feasting and by riotous and extravagant merry-making. There are fabulous festivals amid general poverty in India and Ceylon.

There are the food offerings to the spirits, the tremendous wealth consumed in funeral pyres.

Perhaps the key to the question of why some nations are poor and others rich, of why the Asian is poor and the European, for example, is rich, can be found in this point: that, while the European looks upon wealth as a tool to produce more wealth, the Asian looks upon the goods at his disposal merely as commodities to consume and enjoy. This Asian attitude toward wealth, toward consumption and investment, toward the present and the future has its roots in the age-old Asian philosophies, which originated on the Asian mainland and were wafted by the trade winds to the very edge of Europe and down to the villages of Indonesia. It is dominated by a fatalistic, cyclical conception of life.

The doctrine of the transmigration of souls is a primary plank of belief in Asia's traditional religions. The cycle begins with the soul inhabiting the lowest animal form, progressing after each death to a higher form until it infuses the body of man, after whose death it returns once more to the lowest form. According to this doctrine, "most souls have no hope of full salvation; they will go on transmigrating indefinitely. This is inevitable, for the number of souls is infinite and however many pass to the state of ultimate bliss an infinite number will still remain bound in the toils of matter, for infinity remains infinity, however much is subtracted from it." The process of transmigration continues eternally, and the universe passes through an infinite number of phases of progress and decline.

Then there is the Indian succession of the Sovereigns of the Golden Wheel, the Silver, the Copper, and the Iron Wheels, each presiding over 20,000-year periods of rise and decline. There are the Chinese Sovereigns of Heaven, Sovereigns of Earth, Sovereigns of Man and Fire Dragon, followed by many kings over a period of 10,000 years in fate-dictated cycles.

Only in Japan did the royal succession not come in cycles. There were no uncontrollable recurrences of good and evil kings, of good and bad times, of rise and decline. There was only one line, one continuing national life, one destiny, one imperial house descended from the goddess Amaterasu. The thirteenth-century Japanese political historian Kitabatake Chikafusa wrote, "Only in our country has the succession remained inviolate, from the beginning of heaven and earth to the present. This is due to the ever-renewed Divine Oath and makes Japan unlike all other countries." Japan, indeed, was and is unlike all other countries in Asia. With the infusion of capital and of Western technology and the abolition of feudalistic institutions, the Japanese were prepared for their unique economic take-off, for Japanese tradition was nurtured by a philosophy that did not go round in circles but made room for progress.

But in the Philippines and in the rest of Asia, the cyclical outlook on life remains. Just as the soul transmigrates from lower forms to higher forms of life and back again to the lower forms in a never-ending process, just as the Sovereigns of the Golden, the Silver, the Copper, and the Iron Wheels and the Sovereigns of Heaven, of Earth, of Man, and of the Fire Dragon succeed one another in eternal cycles, the life of man turns inexorably in a fate-determined cycle of good and evil days. If times are good today, we should relax and enjoy them, for bad times are sure to come again. If times are bad today, we must suffer and endure them, for surely good times will come again. So it is that one consumes and spends everything he has on those days of the year that the Wheel of Fortune assigns for release and merry-making. It is useless to provide for the future. The future is in the hands of fate and the gods. Life and natural environment are therefore to be submitted to and never to be mastered. Nature is to be feared and obeyed, never to be controlled.

This culture and mentality are those the Spaniards found in the Philippines. They were swept into that all-embracing fusion that the Spanish missionaries found it convenient, indeed necessary, to forge between the indigenous culture of the Filipinos and the doctrines and rituals of Roman Catholicism.

As I have tried to show, the fate-dominated and consumption-oriented mentality of the Filipino is an integral part of his essentially Asian culture, and the fact that this mentality remains strong today is due to Hispanic Catholicism's compromise with that culture rather than to the inner nature of Catholicism itself.

For it was precisely Christianity that snapped the Asian-born fate-dictated cycle that it found in Greco-Roman philosophy and culture and gave it a beginning and an end. Man, Christianity taught and teaches, has his origin in God and his destiny in Him. But this destiny can be attained only by the free exercise of his will and the development of all his faculties. Man has the capacity and the duty to perfect himself on all levels of his being. He must no longer be bound by fate but is to work out his own spiritual and material well-being, his own salvation, with diligence.

Summary

In this cursory examination of the problem of poverty and its relation to culture and religion, I have tried to make the following points:

1. Culture is a crucial factor in the economic progress or stagnation of a nation.

2. Religion, as an important facet of culture, has some influence on economic development.

3. The economic sluggishness of the Philippines can be traced in large part not to the Spanish Catholic heritage but to the indigenous culture and the qualities and attitudes it fostered, with which Hispanic Catholicism found it convenient and necessary to compromise.

4. This indigenous Filipino culture is rooted in the same cultural soil as the rest of Asian culture.

If any practical conclusion can be derived from these points, it is that leadership in Asia—beside mustering capital from abroad and from the government, beside imposing five-year programs on the people, beside initiating institutional reforms—must address itself to the infinitely more difficult task of social change, of changing the minds and psychology, the attitudes and values of the people.

S. C. DUBE

Cultural Problems in the
Economic Development of India

CONTEMPORARY INDIA illustrates the many paradoxes and complex problems of a society in the process of transition from a traditional to a modern way of life. Her modernizing elite has prepared ambitious blueprints for national development and is seeking to bring about, at an accelerated pace, the transformation of her backward economy and preindustrial technology. The experience of the first phase of this experiment in planned change has increasingly brought home to the planner the realization that traditional values and institutions play a vital role in determining the direction and rate of economic growth. In consequence, there is evidence of a growing concern for scientific appraisal and evaluation of the human element and the value factors that influence economic development and technological change. Increasing attention is now being given to the structural context and the institutional framework within which the plans for economic development must be implemented. The associated value system is also being explored, with a view to the possible utilization of some of its elements for the smooth and speedy im-

43

plementation of the development plans. The inadequacy of mechanical economic determinism is now generally recognized. The contemporary trend is toward comprehensive planning that takes note of the entire complex of ideological, motivational, and institutional factors that significantly condition and govern the process of economic development.

Traditional Cultures and Economic Development

Economic development involves making critical decisions and choices at various steps in the different stages of the process. The decisions of the planner are often determined by anticipation of the likely reactions and the possible preferences of those for whom he is planning.

All efforts at planned change must be initiated and implemented on an existing social base. It is safe to assume that no culture will be initially receptive to the entire range of innovations offered by a development program; along certain sensitive frontiers it is bound to be resistant to changes. But it would be wrong to start with the assumption that traditional cultures resist all modern innovations, for even the most conservative among the tradition-oriented societies have certain "neutral" cultural frontiers along which resistance to change, if any, is symbolic rather than real. In fact they may also have certain "change prone" frontiers, which actually welcome innovation. In large measure, acceptance depends also on the actual content and the phasing of the specific program of modernization and economic development. In this connection, it is necessary to examine the various elements in the development program severally and individually, first from the point of view of culturally perceived need and then from the point of view of compatability with and adaptability to the ethos and idiom of the traditional culture.

Cultural factors affecting programs of economic development can be divided broadly into two classes: *ideological-motivational* and *institutional-organizational.*

The ideological-motivational framework includes, among others, the following elements: cultural orientations to life, time, wealth, work, experiment, and innovation; a minimal consensus on such social goals as higher standards of living, education, and health; and a system of incentives, rewards, sanctions, and controls.

The main components of the institutional-organizational framework are structural units and their articulation; stratification, status system, and mobility; patterns of authority and leadership; reference groups and patterns of identification and communication; structure and articulation of major institutions, especially economic, political, religious, and educational institutions; and systems of resource mobilization and role assignment.

The need, desirability, adaptability, and compatibility of new items are assessed and evaluated according to the norms implicit in these frameworks. Cultural values determine these norms and set the standards of judgment.

A value in this context may be described as a preference quality in action. Organized round the major themes of culture, values set the parameters of action by ascribing *most desirable, desirable, neutral, undesirable,* and *most undesirable* qualities to possible choices in a given situation. They are a series of explicit or implicit culturally sanctioned guides to action that set the direction and limits of behavior in specific situations within the framework of a given culture.

A culture is essentially an adaptive mechanism. No culture is static; at any given point in time it has elements of both continuity and change. Cultural values reflect both these kinds of element. While some emphasize stability and persistence of certain components of the culture, others encourage adaptation and change. Cultural change is invariably preceded, accompanied, or followed by value change. It is therefore erroneous to attribute a static quality to cultural values.

In relating cultural values to economic development, it is essential to distinguish between different types of value and to assess their meaning and significance for the culture. A theoretically oriented and comprehensive typology of values is perhaps out of place here, and only brief comments will therefore be made on the more important operationally significant types.

First, it should be borne in mind that all values are not equally important. Between the core values and the peripheral values of a culture there is often a wide zone of subcultural and alternative values. The core values are built around the central emphases of the culture and ramify into its different aspects. They integrate the culture by providing it with a system of meanings and a logic of choices. These values invariably apply to all subcultural groups encompassed within the culture and demand a rigid conformity. They are universal values and permit only limited, if any, choice of action. In addition, subgroups within a culture may have their own core values that provide indices of legitimation to special forms of subcultural behavior. These alternative values permit much greater choice in action in a given situation, although they too can often be graded hierarchically in terms of their preference quality. Peripheral values are not rigid in their demands.

Second, a clear distinction between ethico-religious values and structural values is essential. There is a general tendency to exaggerate the importance of the former without going sufficiently deep into their structural implications. In reference to economic development, the significance of structural values should not be underestimated.

Third, an attempt should be made to distinguish between statement of formal positions and the empirically observed reality underlying these values. Through a process of interpretation and rationalization, the content of values often assumes certain forms that are remarkably different from those implied in formal positions.

Finally, it is most essential to differentiate between ultimate

CULTURAL PROBLEMS IN INDIA 47

and proximate values. Many critical choices in the general area of economic development are made in reference to proximate values rather than to ultimate values.

Cultural problems involved in the process of modernization and economic development in Hindu society will now be considered within this general framework.

Hinduism and Economic Development

The formal outlines of Hinduism are fairly clear and simple, but its empirical content is infinitely complex. Hinduism as it is practiced in daily life is not quite the same as the Hinduism of the sacred texts. Variations in regional and subcultural forms of Hinduism are considerable. The differentials in the application of its norms to the different levels and classes in the society are also significant. Acceptance of modernization in different degrees in different aspects of life further confuses the issues. What makes the analysis difficult is the fact that Hinduism cannot be considered without reference to its many divergent forms. In point of fact, Hindu society is a complex of many societies. The differences that can be ignored in a broad conceptualization of Hindu society are meaningful and relevant to the promoter of modernization and economic development.

In our discussion only Hindu society in general can be considered. This kind of treatment can take account of certain broad features only. For diagnostic and operational purposes, an examination of local, subcultural, and regional variations is essential.

The ideological-motivational framework of Hindu society can be understood in reference to the culturally defined goals appropriate to different stations in life, as well as to the different stages of life, to the doctrines of *karma* and cosmic causation, to the ideals of selfless action, and to the cyclical view of time.

The goals of life, as defined in both classical and popular

Hinduism, are *dharma* (conformity to the "prescribed way" or adherence to "appropriate action"), *artha* (acquisition of wealth and attainment of material welfare), *kama* (satisfaction of the cravings of the body), and *moksha* (liberation of the soul from the continuous chain of birth, death, and rebirth). While they are generally accepted as applicable to all sections of the society to a certain extent, these four major goals of life differ in their emphases and applications among groups occupying different stations in life and among persons at different stages of life. *Varna* and *asrama* concepts elaborate the themes of "station" and "stages." Hindu society is divided broadly into four divisions called *varna*, which are hierarchically graded. The Brahman (priests), the Kshatriya (warriors), the Vaisya (traders), and the Sudra (service-rendering groups) constitute the four levels, with the Brahman at the top and the Sudra at the bottom. In addition to these four, there is a fifth level, consisting mainly of the untouchables, who have the lowest social and ritual status, which cannot be fitted into the fourfold division of society. Membership in the *varna* (and also in their subdivisions called *jati* or "castes") is ascribed, and vertical mobility in the scale is barred. Each *varna* has its own divinely ordained norms of conduct, which constitute its *dharma*. Ideally life evolves through four stages or *asramas*. In the first, the stage of celibate life, one is expected to acquire discipline and prepare for the responsibilities of life. Thus prepared one enters the second stage and as a householder assumes the manifold worldly responsibilities appropriate to his station in life. This stage is followed considerably later by the stage of resignation. During this period, one should ideally start detaching oneself from one's multifarious worldly involvements. This stage is a preparatory step for the final stage of renunciation, when one gives up all of one's worldly ties and accepts a life of contemplation. The *dharma* for the four stages is also different. Even the stages do not apply uniformly to all the *varna* levels. The goals of *artha* and *kama* have to be subordinated to and pursued according to the norms of *dharma*. Together the three should lead to the final and supreme goal of life—*moksha*.

In broad outlines, this scheme of life is comprehensive and attractive. It recognizes the interdependence of economic pursuits, pleasures of the body, and a higher spiritual quest. The three are integrated in a way of life that is guided and controlled by the norms of *dharma*.

To a great extent, this scheme of life is sustained and supported by the doctrines of *karma* and of cosmic causation. The *karma* theory assumes the phenomenon of rebirth and transmigration of soul and holds that the quality of a man's actions in past lives or life determine his present life and that his actions in the present life will determine the character of his future life or lives. The iron law of retribution is believed to control the course of human life. To this belief can be added the doctrine of cosmic causation, which attributes many events in human life to supernatural powers that control human destinies.

The ideals of *artha* and *kama* are generally secular in content, but they too are not without important sacred overtones. We observed earlier that the pursuit of *artha* and *kama* must be guided by *dharma* and that all three must be oriented to *moksha*. This point brings in the concept of selfless action. Nonappropriation and noninvolvement are expected to characterize activities of this order. The ultimate reality lies not in this world but beyond. The pains and pleasures of life are *maya* (illusion), and involvement in them blocks the realization of the ultimate goal. Through selfless action alone can one look forward to the attainment of the supreme goal of life.

The time orientation implicit in Hinduism is cyclical. Inevitably the society moves from epoch to epoch, each successive epoch being characterized by progressive decline. Four such epochs are postulated. Standards and values differ from epoch to epoch. When decline reaches its lowest ebb, divine intervention restores order, and the cycle starts over again.

Viewed as a scheme of life motivated by a system of values,

this ideological-motivational framework contains several elements that can be successfully utilized for promotion of economic growth. It should be borne in mind that *dharma* or "appropriate action" is also viewed as contextual; its content and interpretation are related not only to particular stations in and stages of life but also to specific situations in *desa* (space) and *kal* (time). Viewed historically, its interpretations and emphases have changed. In the context of the requirements of economic development, which is a new manifestation of *artha* and *kama*, the norms of *dharma* can be adopted to the new ethos. Similarly, the doctrine of *karma* does not rule out individual volition completely. In fact, it encourages it, within certain limits, to improve the prospects of an individual's future. The emphasis on steadfast devotion to duty regardless of its consequences provides a base for determined and disciplined action that can be effectively utilized for realizing the goals of economic development. Contrary to views commonly expressed on the subject, the doctrine of selfless action can be a help rather than a hindrance in economic development. The early decades of planned economic growth require a considerable degree of sacrifice by choice and demand high standards of discipline. The successful emergence of the desired pattern depends upon a new social conscience and social character; both these elements do in fact require a great deal of selfless action. On the other hand, it should be added that there are also some inconvenient elements within this framework. The view of life as illusion, the doctrine of cosmic causation, and the cyclical view of time can hinder programs of economic development.

But the ideological-motivational framework cannot be considered in isolation from the institutional-organizational framework. In fact, the main argument of this paper is that the latter is the more important of the two and that the structural expression of values and goals influences programs of modernization more meaningfully than do formal positions in regard to them.

There is an unfortunate tendency to equate the conceptualization of Hindu society in classical texts with contemporary Hindu society. In point of fact, there is a considerable gap between the two. The Great Tradition has doubtless influenced the regional and local traditions, but the last two are still vital and empirically relevant for the purposes of economic development. The lofty cultural ideals and the deeper metaphysical implications of Hinduism can be comprehended only by the select in the elite; the common man's understanding of them comes through mythology and legends. His interpretation and rationalization largely determine the character of Hinduism as it is practiced by the common people. Naturally therefore in considering Hinduism in relation to economic growth, we cannot be overly concerned with its philosophical implications alone. Its living form is more important.

This point brings us to the structural expression of the ideological-motivational framework discussed above.

The linkage of *dharma* with *varna* has resulted in a segmented society with five major divisions (four within the *varna* framework and one outside it) and countless *jati* or castes within each *varna*. Complex considerations of ritual pollution and purity keep these segments distinct and apart through rules governing intermarriage, commensality, occupation, and other patterns of interaction. The socioeconomic system of the village integrates them to a certain degree through an organized pattern of interdependence, but the fact still remains that narrow and segmental loyalties hinder the growth of a true community view of problems. Stratification and a status system based on ascription limit not only the levels of aspiration but also the avenues of achievement. Caste is a hindrance to occupational mobility and to freedom of enterprise. Authority tends to be oriented toward kin and caste. The choice of reference groups is restricted; identification with one's own caste or subcaste is encouraged and is rarely expected to extend beyond groups of comparable or slightly higher status. Communication is also restricted in consequence. Institutional forms and their articulation bear the impact of the social system; divisive rather than unitary tendencies prevail. Under these conditions kin and caste orientations obstruct the emergence of true interest orientation toward larger community perspectives. Resource mobilization and role assignment follow the traditional ascriptive segmentation of the society rather than a rational pattern that might be more in harmony with the desired model. Conformity, often of a ritualistic order, convenient rationalization, and fatalism as justification of failure and of absence of more effort characterize the value system. Innovation and experiment, in consequence, can find encouragement only to a limited extent.

The consequences are obvious. Even the organized efforts of the elite have not been able to produce and articulate a minimal consensus on broader social goals. Inadequate incentives, a restricted system of rewards, and weak sanctions and controls pose problems of the cultural order that block economic development.

Four Aspects of Economic Development

As background for this discussion we shall now review briefly cultural problems observed in land reform, community development, the industrialization process, and the family concept in Hindu society.

The progressive ideology of the elite notwithstanding, the program of land reform has made little headway. The legislative efforts of the government have in many ways proved self-defeating because of opposing pressures within the political organizations seeking to bring about these reforms. Vinoba Bhave's ethico-religious approach of *bhoodan* has produced more barren land than fields that are cultivable. Nothing perhaps reveals the yawning gap between verbalized values and concrete realities more strikingly than these failures. The results very convincingly show that the doctrines of nonappropriation and selfless action are theories divorced from reality.

The experiment of community development in India has

indeed been comprehensive and imaginative. Experimental and flexible in nature, it has refused to adopt a doctrinaire approach. In terms of conveniences extended and production increased, its record is impressive, but in achieving the true ideals of community development it has experienced difficulties almost at every step. First, there is the relative absence of community consciousness in the Indian villages. Evolving a community perspective out of the multiplicity of narrow and segmental loyalties is proving a task of great magnitude. Secondly, beyond the recognition of certain minimum needs in terms of the immediate present, there is no consensus on short-term and long-term economic and social goals. Third, orientation of the people to kin and caste rather than to identifiable larger interests is another major obstruction. This orientation blocks the emergence of a unified leadership capable of giving the community a sense of direction and of taking over the program as a continuing process. Fourth, the ascriptive order, with its numerous taboos and injunctions, limits occupational opportunity and mobility. The development program cannot thus plan beyond the limits set by the social structure. Fifth, as an indirect consequence of the social structure, a considerable section of the people has extremely low levels of aspiration, and even in its wildest dreams the horizons of its ambitions are constricted. The margin at the disposal of these people is at any rate too narrow to encourage them to undertake uncertain and possibly risky experiments. Additional earnings made by these people through adoption of new techniques promoted by the community development program are often used to discharge traditional obligations. This use of resources obviously obstructs the continuity of economic growth. Finally, religious beliefs interfere in the acceptance of certain programs. Reluctance to castrate scrub bulls and refusal to slaughter useless cattle on religious grounds may be cited as two of numerous examples to illustrate this point.

The industrialization process is also affected by many of the factors mentioned in reference to the community development program. Limited mobility, taboos on occupational choice and social interaction, and the tendency of the extended kin group to absorb a great deal of disguised unemployment are factors that impede industrialization. Such culturally determined attitudes toward saving and expenditure as seeking security in the ownership of gold, rather than making possibly risky investments in productive pursuits, and excessive expenditure in ceremonies and rituals may be cited as additional factors. It may, however, be noted that, where entrepreneurial skills exist in a group, the extended kin group supports the risks taken by individual members. Many personal fortunes and industrial empires of India have been built in this way.

A word about the family concept: To a degree, larger kin groups do not have the same integrated structure and solidarity today as they had when the traditional order prevailed, but it is wrong to suggest that the traditional forms have broken down or that they are anywhere near the breaking point. Their form has changed, but the functions of the family and the extended kin groups remain largely the same. Individuals migrating to urban areas or to industrial centers support and sustain the village-based family as a ritual and social unit. Patterns of influence and communication among the kin are still strong and can be utilized for certain aspects of the program of development and modernization. It is true that the family and the extended kin group often obstruct the acceptance of new modes, but at the same time we should bear in mind that they effectively exert sanctions against the spread of normlessness, which can become an ugly feature of a transitional society.

Summing Up

The ascriptive order; emphases on the sacred, conformity, and ritualism; and the segmentary nature of the social structure are the major cultural problems affecting India's economic development. Her basic value system has several elements that could encourage and stimulate economic growth, but her structural inadequacies stand in the way of modernization and development. If a strategy for the removal of these inadequacies can be devised, it should not be difficult to adapt many of the traditional values to the new ethos. At the same time, an effort will have to be made to resolve the contradictions within the traditional value system. Problems of conflict and accommodation between traditional and modern values will also require attention. Many of the ultimate values are still respected but as remote ideals, and the proximate values of the society do not bar acceptance of several elements of modernity. This sign is a hopeful one. If the old and the new can be synthesized, the stresses and strains involved in the transitional phase will automatically be minimized.

YUSIF A. SAYIGH

Cultural Problems and
the Economic Development
of the Arab World

THE ECONOMIST is severely handicapped when attempting to assess the power of cultural problems in economic development. His training is too narrow to permit him adequately to investigate a question that goes deep into the territory of psychology, sociology, anthropology, political science, and the humanities.

This limitation besets the economist anywhere, but it is particularly drastic for the Arab economist. The Arab world, from which my observations are drawn and to which they are meant to apply, poses other limitations. There is, for instance, the painful scarcity of empirical studies that investigate the nature and power of cultural problems in development. Indeed, most Arab students of the relevant sciences have satisfied themselves with restatement of the hypotheses and propositions that Western scholars examine in the context of their own or of other societies but not of Arab societies. The obsessive drive for speedy development that the Arab world has been experiencing since the late Forties is pursued on so wide a front that it allows neither the resources nor the skills, nor even the time, that research into cultural problems would require. In consequence, my inquiry must be, on the whole, impressionistic and speculative.

The examination of cultural problems is usually dominated by one of two attitudes: that of the scholar who, in his greater familiarity with the cumulative nature of culture and with its subtle power, tends to overstate the case for the prohibitive aspects of the cultural factor; and that of the activist who tends, if he gives the matter adequate thought at all, to underestimate the weight and power of the cultural factor or alternatively to overstate the promotive aspects of this factor. The first attitude is probably characteristic of the sociologist, the anthropologist, the historian, the institutionalist, the second, of the political decision-maker who sets the pace for the planner and for the economist. Neither is a "pure type" attitude; nonetheless, the combination of the two types rarely produces a neat balance of emphasis but usually a predominance of one or the other.

In the view of the scholar, the cumulative weight of the cultural factor is decisive in the behavior of people in a society driving hard for economic development—as it is, indeed, in a stagnant society. This view finds support in the justifiable contention that development is more than economic growth in terms of rising incomes, that it involves radical change in the "state of the arts," in political and social institutions, in organization, in attitudes toward work and saving and the inevitability of any given situation. Such a broad view of development brings into relief a poignant confrontation between cultural values and systems associated with the "old" situation and those values that, even though tentatively and hesitantly, *seem* to be necessary for the "new" or approaching situation. The change in cultural values turns out to be one of gentle accommodation or one of mutation and hurried and conscious grafting, depending on the particular society considered—the temperament of its people, its resources, its level of development and that of its neighbors or of those other societies it tries to emulate, the urgency of change, and the type and power of its leadership.

The activist's or decision-maker's attitude in poor countries striving hard for development—and that of many intellectuals who at times suggest the attitude in advance, at times rationalize it *ex post facto*—stems from the conviction that development is a revolutionary process spreading over several fronts of social and individual action. According to the activist's view, when society seeks development—or when it allows a ruling group to seek development without serious obstruction—then it must allow its value system to be shaken to the roots. Acceptance of radical change in economy and technology and in social and political institutions amounts, in this view, to acceptance, or toleration, of change in the value system without unduly harsh reaction.

Which of the two attitudes predominates in the Arab world today? The answer can be meaningful only in those countries seriously attempting development in the broad sense. It is only in those countries that we can watch the confrontation between values that allow the acceptance of radical change and values, sanctified by time and tradition, that resist the onslaught of the new. The answer can be sought in three areas of inquiry: land reform and community development, the industrialization process, and the family concept. It is useful to consider the problems (or clashes) that are likely to arise (or that are known to arise) as a result of the confrontation, as well as the accommodation of the two forces in confrontation. To this task we now turn.

Land Reform and Community Development

We combine land reform and community development in our analysis because of the belief that a far-reaching land reform must be linked to community development if it is to be meaningful. What is involved in this joint process is much more than the elimination of large land-holdings, through land redistribution and the provision of cheap credit, of clean drinking water, and of a few other things. It involves appropriate changes in the organization of production and distribution, of financing, and of marketing and, more generally, changes in the locus of ownership and decision-making in the rural sector. The community-development aspect of reform involves road-building, improved housing, public health and sanitation, education, and the development of ancillary activities to go with agricultural activity proper.

This wide range of change cannot be brought about without a change in attitude of appropriate direction and dimensions. I single out here two instances of this change: willingness to accept new tasks and roles and power to behave in a manner consistent with these tasks and roles.

Before we attempt to examine some of the cultural problems arising from the process of land reform and community development in the Arab world, we ought to point out that this process has been launched on a large scale only recently and only in one Arab country: Egypt. We cannot therefore apply a full-fledged test to general Arab reaction to the changes in tasks and roles, in technology, and in organization.

Egyptian agriculture is wholly irrigated; it is centrally controlled and has been for many centuries. It is intensive and enjoys an elaborate system of crop rotation. Consequently, it cannot serve as an ideal testing ground. Nevertheless, vast changes have taken place in Egypt, which are worth examining in the context of our inquiry into cultural problems. The large landlord has disappeared, whether as owner of the land, planner of agricultural operations, source of finance, political boss, or patriarchal figure. His functions have been taken over by the co-operative society, the former tenant or wage-earner or small proprietor, the government official, the agricultural bank manager. Piped drinking water has come to almost all villages. Sanitation and social and health services have reached hundreds of villages through social centers. Land rent has been noticeably reduced. Sharecropping arrangements have been changed in favor of the tenant. Education has been expanded. Birth control is being both preached and attempted, in order to contain the population explosion.

How has the fellah reacted to this transformation, which has come all in one decade? The disappearance of the large landlord created a temporary vacuum. Becoming one's own master seems indeed to have baffled and worried some peasants—but not for long. The successors to the authority of the landlord have largely succeeded in filling the vacuum. By and large, the peasant's dependence on the landlord and loyalty and obedience to him have not held long as a "cultural defense line" in the face of change in the system of authority arising from the re-distribution of land. Individualism and freedom of action have never been uncurbed in the Arab world, especially in Egypt and Iraq, with their central irrigation systems. The entry of the government agent—as co-operation adviser, bank representative, or machine operator—does not amount to a large measure of added infringement on individualism.

Other aspects of reform and community development—like improvement in living conditions, reduction in land rents, provision of improved seeds or of cheaper credit, piping of drinking water, or establishment of clinics—do not seem to meet with noticeable, if any, resistance. Nor do expansion in public works, public health measures, and educational facilities seem to have saddened or shocked the peasant. In brief, cases of resistance have proved rare when benefits have been demonstrable. The urge for betterment in one's conditions seems to be much stronger than the resistance of old habits and attitudes. Judging by available reports, the peasants adjust rather quickly to new situations when the monetary incentive is large enough. As Egyptian agriculture has been mainly market-oriented for long generations, pecuniary incentives are understandably potent.

Yet this evaluation ought to be qualified in at least three ways. First, after generations of submission to powerful landlords bent, on the whole, on personal enrichment and determined to keep their financial and political control, the fellahin tend to be suspicious of the motives of the landlords' successors in authority. The government is not at all immune to this suspicion, as it did not enjoy the confidence of the underprivileged in pre-revolutionary Egypt. The growth of confidence is further slowed by the modest size of the tangible, material benefits of land reform and community development spread over a relatively large and fast-growing population.

The second qualification is the greater sensitivity of the fellah to the example of his neighbors than to the preachings of an outsider, especially if the outsider is the representative of officialdom. This phenomenon prevails in the Arab world generally, as it does in India, Greece, and Turkey. It is here that the co-operative society, properly guided and advised, can render considerable service, for it can be a more effective transmitter of change than can a government official acting directly.

Third, responsive as the fellah has been to pecuniary incentives and acknowledging as he does the usefulness of the co-operative, he is still slow to take the initiative in forming and running co-operatives. (The initial failure of the Liberation Province in Egypt is a case in point.) When these co-operatives have been formed "from above," they have been demonstrably more active and effective than when they have been encouraged to emerge from below. The contradiction between the fellah's suspicion of government authority and his greater readiness to accept co-operatives formed through governmental initiative is undeniable. The disappearance of this contradiction (and of suspicion) is, I submit, a function of time and the continued devotion of government.

The Process of Industrialization

Cultural resistance to change is probably greater in the process of industrialization than in the process of land reform and community development. Even though the latter process involves remarkable change in the economy of Egypt, it is in the process of industrialization that Egypt, and Arab society in general, encounters wider departures from the pattern of life with which it has been familiar. Manufacturing is radically different from traditional activities, and industrialization, which embraces manufacturing but is wider in significance, involves newness in technology and organization and in attitudes and concepts, as well as in the nature of products and in the mode of production.

The prestige attaching to industrialization turns it into a modern-day fetish. And, like any other fetish, it arouses awe and commands respect. Indeed, it is less appropriate to talk of resistance or reluctance to accept change than to discuss fear of an altogether new mode of life. Hence the inconsistency between strong desire for industrialization and insufficient mental preparation for it—an inconsistency arising from the novelty of industrial activity and from the novelty of the organizational patterns and the attitudes and success symbols that attach to industrialization. I submit that this inconsistency is manifest not only in the Arab world but also elsewhere in the underdeveloped world.

More than any other economic activity, manufacturing requires a reasonably high level of literacy. It is true that the Arab countries or centers that have long-standing mercantile traditions have proportionally larger literate populations than do the other parts of the Arab world and that literacy includes familiarity with bookkeeping and business correspondence. Yet manufacturing, which also requires bookkeeping (even cost accounting) as a tool of calculation and account analysis, calls in addition for a general level of literacy that would enable the foreman and his skilled laborers to read specifications and understand the operation of machinery. Industrialization, furthermore, calls for a developed banking system, an efficient transport system, and a number of ancillary activities like research and design, none of which can operate properly without a minimal level of literacy beyond the basic requirements of agriculture and trade. The inadequacy of educational standards in the Arab world today, particularly of vocational training, constitutes a serious problem for the process of industrialization, especially outside Egypt.

But is there basically any factor in the cultural heritage of the Arab world that can be assessed as promotive or inhibitive in the process of industrialization? Although I shall touch on this question, I wish here to express my doubts about the existence of any clear-cut influence either way. It seems more correct to say that the supporter of any position can find evidence in literature, in the Qur'an, in current proverbs, and in the value system generally that supports his position. Whatever is promotive or inhibitive in the cultural heritage of the Arab world is more subtle and less obvious than explicit injunctions, which are most frequently the reflections of deeper cultural attitudes. It therefore becomes the duty of the social scientist to explore the depth of these attitudes in order to determine the extent to which they are the product of social conditioning or of deeper and more permeating cultural forces.

We shall not attempt, however, to go into the roots of cultural problems that can be observed to beset the process of industrialization. We shall identify instead the problems and assess their effects. Eight or nine of these problems will be discussed here as they manifest themselves in the Arab world today.

Earlier in the process of industrialization in the Arab world, we saw or heard of instances of hesitation to accept change in locus or grounds of authority—from the patriarchal or the hierarchical within a blood kinship to the professional or the hierarchical within an industrial structure. This reluctance was the stronger the closer the labor force was to tribal or village society. Today, however, the shift in the locus of authority has been successfully accomplished in most industrial centers. It seems to us a remarkable sign of human adaptability that two decades of movement along the course of industrialization should witness so great a shift. This movement is no less visible in the labor force of the oil industry in Saudi Arabia than in the

Mehallat al Kubra in Egypt, the textile industry in Syria, or the refining industry in Iraq. And, if I may reveal myself as a sympathizer with the "activist's" rather than with the "scholar's" or the "historian's" interpretation of the power of cultural problems in development, I add that the speed with which the shift has occurred is evidence that the degree of stickiness of cultural patterns is not so high as the conventional sociologist—with anthropological overtones—wants us to believe.

Another problem to be faced is shyness of the new organization necessary for industrialization, of the corporate form of business, factory organization and discipline, and labor unions that perform mainly professional—rather than political—functions. Along with this problem runs a preference for the partnership, especially with one's brothers or cousins. But having made this statement, I must hasten to qualify it. This shyness is probably not so much the product of deeper cultural forces as of expedience. The corporation (or its counterpart in English usage, the limited company) cannot emerge in a vacuum: in the absence of adequate legislation, before audit services and an audit law have emerged, before business ventures of large size begin to multiply and to call for the corporate form of association, before people of modest means begin to be able to afford saving, before the acceptance of the divorce (or at least the separation) between ownership and control of capital becomes widespread. That the prerequisites have not been satisfied is due in turn to historical accident (like the influence of French commercial law and practice in much of the Arab world) and to suspicion of large associations of people in business undertakings (due in turn to unsettled political and economic conditions making narrowly based ventures safer, to the adequacy for most purposes of small ventures in countries not yet developing fast, to the insufficiency of protective legislation for the interests of small savers, and so forth).

In a study of entrepreneurship in Lebanon that I conducted during the period 1958–1960, I saw clear acceptance of manufacturing (in a society renowned for its mercantile tradition) combined with hesitancy to accept the organizational forms that go with efficient manufacturing activity. Underlying this ambivalence is the reluctance of business leaders to part with some of their authority and their decision-making power, either horizontally to their peers (directors and associates) or vertically to their subordinates. Equally noticeable is the greater readiness of the more educated and the more widely traveled business leaders to adopt nontraditional activities and nontraditional organization. The ambivalence is probably characteristic of the present stage of entrepreneurial development and will probably be overcome in due course. Indications of a greater shift toward the corporation and away from the family partnership already abound.

A third problem is the sloppy or cavalier attitude toward time that upsets industrial organization and adds to its burdens. This attitude is partly the product of traditional agricultural activity and perhaps partly a leftover of life in the desert, where man feels he has all the time in the world. Industrial organization and activity require strict adherence to timetable, punctuality, co-ordination. Arab character in this respect shows an endless capacity for patience, manifest in the ability to wait; people who can wait are not exigent about punctuality. The sloppy attitude toward time shows itself in, among other things, inadequate rationalization of movement, overstaffing, or featherbedding. The generally low level of wages for the unskilled probably explains why the problem is not yet very pressing in the Arab world.

We next come to a cultural problem that relates to the quality of entrepreneurship: the slowness of movement from rule-of-thumb to rational (sophisticated) business calculation. This slowness is the product of a number of factors combined, factors like suspicion of the unfamiliar processes of calculation, belief that elaborate data collection and calculation are not really needed, traditionalism, and hesitation to surrender still one more area of action to the expert in the business establishment. Here again my impression is that the slowness represents not so much an innate refusal to make the shift as a characteristic of the present phase of development. My study of entrepreneurship in Lebanon revealed that certain nontraditional sectors and businessmen with college educations were, on the whole, readier than the rest to make the shift in the basis of decision-making.

One further cultural problem from which industrialization suffers is the slowness of Arab society to change from a fatalistic attitude toward events to acceptance of technical and economic causality. Fatalism characterizes agricultural activity. The explanation of this phenomenon must probably be sought partly in the influence of Islam, with its great emphasis on the need to submit to God's will, which controls all our lives and actions. In part, the explanation lies in the fact that the link between man's actions and their results is clearer in industrial than in agricultural activity. Man is even more at the mercy of natural forces if his agriculture is rain-fed than if it is irrigated. The spread of education, especially in the fields of natural and physical sciences, the noticeable weakening of religious ideas and shrinking familiarity with the Qur'an, and the growth of manufacturing industry have in combination led to growing awareness of causality within man's power. With this change there must emerge a greater sense of economic responsibility.

As in all cases where industrialization has merely begun, the industrial worker is not far from the experience of close association with the end product of his work. As industrialization proceeds, the separation between worker and product becomes more marked. Industrial activity becomes more repetitive, more steady, more monotonous, even though more advanced mechanically. It therefore requires greater discipline. Only in a small number of large, highly mechanized industries has the Arab industrial worker reached the stage at which his reactions to the rigor of factory discipline are put to severe test. By and large, it seems that many more years will have to pass before he becomes used to the new pattern of work without loss (or rather with gain) in efficiency. One factor that will probably shorten this period of transition is the attraction of higher industrial wages and steadier employment than exist in the agricultural sector.

This last point raises the question of the strength of money rewards as incentives. There is an ambivalence toward such rewards, characterized by strong acquisitiveness combined with inability or unwillingness to link reward and effort closely. I do not quite mean here the "backward-sloping supply curve of labor." This curve probably slopes backward in any society, though at different points along the wage scale. What I mean, however, is the inconsistency of the expectation of higher and higher rewards without the realization that more effort is expected in return. The inconsistency is partly due to the noticeable rise in income levels in Arab economies at large—a rise that has boosted expectations unreasonably and blurred the distinction between worthy and unworthy cases.

Associated with this confusion is one related to the sanctity of contracts. Viewed group by group, most economic groups behave as though they believe that their contractual relations with other groups impose certain obligations on the other groups but not on them. There is widespread failure to recognize that rights and duties are the two inseparable sides of a coin. This failure characterizes the behavior of the domestic maid, as it does that of the industrial laborer or the business manager. But it is perhaps more noticeable among the laboring classes than among their employers, owing to the growing strength of laborers and to their growing awareness of this strength. The spread of social ideas among them—ideas stressing their rights and perquisites—is faster than the rise of their productivity, a discrepancy in the rates of speed that can only lead to unrealistic expectations. This generally prevailing lax attitude toward the sanctity of contracts is in no small part also due to the deterioration in public morality over the last three or four decades and to the breakup of the traditional system of authority. The war and postwar periods have been a major factor in the deterioration.

In summing up these observations on cultural problems and

the industrialization process, we can say that, on the whole, resistance in the areas of behavior suggested is weakening, and adaptability to the behavior pattern necessitated by industrialization is quite marked, especially in Egypt, Lebanon, Syria, and the Maghreb. Where the benefits are observable or demonstrable, people undergo the subtle transformation in views and values comparatively readily—entrepreneurs, managers, technicians, and laborers alike.

Two factors have been instrumental in bringing about this speedy and rather painless transformation. The first was the initiation of industrialization after a major world war, which in itself prepared people's minds for drastic change and upset people's values considerably, especially through increased emphasis on monetary incentives, reduced emphasis on nonmaterial values, and cynicism. The second factor was the emergence of the state as engineer and executive of development *par excellence*, enjoying as it does immense authority and the prestige of exceptional knowledge and power. In a sense, much of what we are witnessing today is a surrender to the will of the state instead of the traditional surrender to the will of the father and of Allah. We do not yet have a usurpation of power by the common man himself, for himself.

The Concept of the Family

A great deal of importance is usually attached to the concept of the family and to the role and status of the family by sociologists and other scholars interested in the history of culture and by economists interested in the way institutions further or hinder the process of development. More specifically, attention centers around four areas:

size of family (the extended *vs.* the "nuclear" family); the degree of readiness for family planning; the position of the patriarch; and how the prevailing view of the size and structure of the family projects itself into the question of industrial structure;

family solidarity; the family's value and usefulness both as an agency
  of social insurance and as an arena for gregariousness; and how all
  these uses retard the emergence of associations not based on kinship;
effects of family cohesiveness on mobility of attitude, as well as of
  occupation and location;
reactions to family authority and solidarity.

The family is getting smaller, judging by the few studies
that have so far been undertaken in Egypt, Lebanon, Syria, and
elsewhere where population censuses have collected information
on the size of the family. The change in size is more the result
of the gradual disappearance of the extended family than of the
drop in the size of the nuclear family itself. Education, the dawn
of industrialism, the realization that obligations toward one's
children extend far and that Allah (though all-loving and able to
provide for His creatures) expresses His attention through the
means and efforts of parents have all been influential in the split-
ting up of large families and acknowledgment that smaller
families are more manageable.

At the peak of this growing recognition is the acceptance
that "family planning" is not a sin, that it may even be in line
with God's will. The Azhar itself has condoned family planning
—indeed it did so as early as 1938 or 1939. Many more people
believe in some form of birth control than are willing to admit
it, and the striving for social and financial improvement is so
strong in much of the Arab world that we may witness an early
containment of the population explosion.

All this progress has direct relevance to development. But
above all there is now a growing awareness that the family can
improve its means much faster through improvement in the
quality of its working members than through increasing the
number of working members at a low level of education and
training. The endless examples of laborer or peasant parents who
today have engineer or doctor or electrician sons with vastly
greater earning power than the parents ever had cannot be lost
on the parents themselves or on other uneducated Arabs.

With the decline in the frequency of the extended family,

the spread of education and the rise in its level, the shift in the industrial structure of Arab economies, and the widening of work opportunities in urban centers, the position of the patriarch has also undergone drastic change. Respect for the father (or the elder male in the family) is still prevalent. But quite often only lip service is paid to the position of the patriarch—simply to keep him happy in his last days. One might say the father now reigns but no longer rules. It is not rare nowadays for children to put their parents in their places when the latter try to give advice beyond their competence. This behavior would have been unthinkable as recently as the interwar period.

In fact, what we are witnessing is neither a complete preservation of the authority of the father and of the family hierarchy nor an open rebellion against it. This state of affairs projects itself into the industrial structure and into the relations between employer and employed. For there are at present only the beginnings of a new hierarchy based on professional competence; almost invariably one suspects that kinship and social status, in addition to professional competence, have determined the placement of men in positions of command. The reactions of the employees and laborers are mixed: They neither accept authority fully and readily, unconvinced as they are of the grounds for such authority, nor do they rebel against the heterogeneity of these grounds and thus bring about a speedier shift to professionalism in the locus of business authority.

The change in the size and structure of the family and the weakening of family authority over its junior members have been reflected in family solidarity and in the degree of mobility of family members. Family solidarity has not, however, been weakened to the point where the family has stopped providing some form of voluntary social insurance to its poorer and weaker members. This solidarity still provides a certain measure of identification and satisfies the need for gregariousness, particularly in view of the slow emergence of associations not based on kinship (associations like political parties and professional or vocational societies). On the other hand, useful as it is, solidarity itself retards the emergence of such other associations by weakening the need for them. From the purely developmental point of view and in recognition of the developmental significance of certain forms of social organization that cut across creeds and family ties, we cannot but admit that family solidarity as it exists now is probably a retarding factor in development and a discouragement rather than an incentive for greater effort by the labor force.

The effect of change in the size and structure of the family has been greater mobility, especially among younger members of the family. This greater mobility is a mixed blessing. On one hand, it helps to distribute the pool of labor more effectively and provides flexibility in the use of productive resources, thus spurring economic activity. On the other hand, it drains the countryside of some of its enterprising elements and encourages migration to the city when neither the pull of the city nor the push of the village justifies the volume of migration that takes place. To this disadvantage must be added the city's unreadiness to receive, serve, and employ more than a portion of the newcomers. One benefit that can be seen in this uninvited influx is the pressure for greater development that it creates—a pressure that cannot remain unheeded for long.

The reaction to family authority and solidarity can, in conclusion, be said to have been one of *discreet* rebellion: rebellion *outside* the family circle coupled with consideration for the structure and authority *within* this circle. This attitude is projected into everyday life. We see neither general open revolt nor complete submission, but a system of co-existence and accommodation.

As an over-all conclusion to this paper, I should like to suggest that cultural problems have not been very powerful in retarding development in the Arab world. Regardless of country and of social-political system, in most Arab countries, especially those bordering on the Mediterranean basin or near it, the cultural heritage has not been sticky. It is also legitimate to say that the cultural problems have on the whole been the products of social conditioning rather than of innate characteristics, with the result that changing social conditions—the changing framework of the economy—have eroded the cultural problems. The permissive attitude toward interest, readiness to shift to non-traditional sectors, acceptance of new patterns of economic organization, the shift in the basis of calculation toward more rationality, and the loosening of family structure and authority are some cases in point. True, these shifts have not yet gone far in all instances, but then the process has not been in operation for very long.

The scholar who worries that the body of literature or of religious beliefs or of attitudes toward the family weighs heavily on the process of development—as many scholars do—thus commits two mistakes. First, he overlooks the fact that part of the literature and beliefs and attitudes point in favorable directions, and, second, he overlooks the power of the drive for development in bringing about transformation, if not in the components of the cultural factor, then at least in the degree of attention given to them.

In brief, I suggest three reasons why cultural problems have not weighed heavily enough in the Arab world to menace seriously the drive for development. First, the Arabs are going through what must be considered a revolutionary period in their history—revolution not only in the political area but also in society, technology, and attitudes. In revolutionary periods, people pull free of the long-standing cultural ties that link them to their past, even if only briefly. Once the ties are shaken, however, they can never be as strong as before. Second, there is a strong sensitivity to incentives, and the experience of the past few decades has brought with it tangible monetary and welfare incentives. It is remarkable how easy the choice is between a poem or a Qur'anic verse denouncing liquor and a business deal in liquor promising a lucrative profit to the businessman. The fact that incentives include not only direct monetary profit but also all kinds of material and social improvements in status strengthens our point. Third, the Arabs have proved able to achieve accommodation between traditionalism and open revolt. We can almost call it a hypocritical adherence to the cultural heritage and an effective estrangement from that heritage, occurring side by side. (Whether this attitude reflects receptivity to change or simply a "split personality" remains an intriguing question.) Tradition is humored while modernization is accepted. I submit that, within this framework, much of what is happening in the Arab world, both in the cultural and economic realms, can be understood and interpreted.

NOEL J. COULSON

The Concept of Progress
and Islamic Law

"ALL INNOVATION is the work of the devil." These alleged words of the founder Prophet of Islam, Muhammad, do not merely reflect the innate conservatism and the deep-seated attachment to tradition that were so strong among the Arab peoples who formed the first adherents of the faith. They also express a principle that became a fundamental axiom of religious belief in Islamic communities everywhere—namely, that the code of conduct represented by the religious law, or Shari'a, was fixed and final in its terms and that any modification would necessarily be a deviation from the one legitimate and valid standard.

Among Muslim peoples, therefore, it is what we may call the traditional or classical Islamic concept of law and its role in society that constitutes a most formidable obstacle to progress. Western jurisprudence has provided a number of different answers to questions about the nature of law, finding its source variously in the orders of a political superior, in the breasts of the judiciary, in the "silent, anonymous forces" of evolving society, or in the very nature of the universe itself. For Islam, however, this same question admits of only one answer, which the religious faith itself supplies. Law is the command of Allah, and the acknowledged function of Muslim jurisprudence from the beginning was simply to discover the terms of that command.

The religious code of conduct thus established was an all-embracing one, in which every aspect of human relationships was regulated in meticulous detail. Furthermore, the law, having once achieved perfection of expression, was in principle static and immutable, for Muhammad was the last of the Prophets, and after his death in A.D. 632 there could be no further direct communication of the divine will to man. Thenceforth the religious law was to float above Muslim society as a disembodied soul, representing the eternally valid ideal toward which society must aspire.

In classical Islamic theory therefore, law does not grow out of or develop along with an evolving society, as is the case with Western systems, but is imposed from above. In the Islamic concept, human thought unaided cannot discern the true values and standards of conduct; such knowledge can be attained only through divine revelation, and acts are good or evil exclusively because Allah has attributed this quality to them. Law therefore precedes and is not preceded by society; it controls and is not controlled by society. Although in Western systems the law is molded by society, in Islam exactly the converse is true. The religious law provides the comprehensive, divinely ordained, and eternally valid master plan to which the structure of state and society must ideally conform.

Obviously the clash between the dictates of the rigid and static religious law and any impetus for change or progress that a society may experience poses for Islam a fundamental problem of principle. The Muslim countries of the Near and Middle East have sought the solution in a process that may be generally termed "legal modernism." It is the purpose of this paper to appreciate in broad outline the nature and efficacy of that solution. I propose that we focus our attention upon one particular

legal reform introduced in Tunisia in 1957: the outright pro-
hibition of polygamy, which represented a complete break with
the legal tradition of some thirteen centuries. I have chosen this
particular case not because polygamy is one of the most pressing
social problems in Islam today—it is generally not so—but because, first, it involves the status of the family, where the influence of the traditional religious law has always been strongest;
second, it highlights various issues in legal reform that are common to Muslim communities the world over; and, finally, it is one
of the most extreme and significant examples of the process of
legal modernism, which not only may radically alter the shape
of Islamic society but also may affect the very nature of the
Islamic religion itself. Our approach to the subject must be essentially historical, for it is only in the light of past tradition that the
significance of legal modernism and its potential role in the future
development of Islamic peoples may be properly assessed.

Traditional Muslim jurisprudence is an example of a legal
science almost totally divorced from historical considerations.
Islamic orthodoxy views the elaboration of the law as a process
of scholastic endeavor completely independent of and in isolation
from considerations of time and place, and the work of individual
jurists during the formative period is measured by the single
standard of its intrinsic worth in the process of discovery of the
divine command. Master architects were followed by builders
who implemented the plans; successive generations of craftsmen
made their own particular contributions to the fixtures, fittings,
and interior decor until, the task completed, future jurists were
simply to serve as passive caretakers of the eternal edifice. This
elaboration of the system of Allah's commands lacks any true
dimension of historical depth. Recent researches by scholars,
however, have shown that the genesis of Islamic religious law lay
in a complex process of historical growth intimately connected
with current social conditions and extending over the first three
centuries of Islam.

The first steps in Islamic jurisprudence were taken in the

early years of the second century of the Muslim era, around
A.D. 750, by scholars working in various centers, of which the
most important were Kufa in Iraq and Medina in the Hijaz. For
these scholar-jurists, the fundamental axiom of Islam—that of
total submission to Allah—meant that all human relationships
were subject to regulation by the divine command. Their aim,
therefore, was to elaborate a system of law that would express, in
terms of the rights of men and their obligations, the will of Allah
for Muslim communities, a system to be called the Shari'a. But
for these loose fraternities of legal scholars, which we may call
the "early schools of law," this activity entailed nothing more
than the assessment of existing legal practice in the light of the
principles embodied in the Qur'an. The Qur'an does not contain
a code of law in any sense. It sets out merely to reform, in a
limited number of particulars, the existing customary law by
precepts that often suggest rather than command, are predominantly ethical in tone, and amount in all to about 100 verses. The
Qur'anic legislation, in fact, amounts to little more than the
preamble to a code of conduct for which succeeding generations
were to supply the operative parts.

Accordingly, there was wide scope for the use of reason—
or *ijtihad*, as it came to be called—in the formulation of the
doctrine. And it is not surprising that this freedom to speculate
led to considerable divergence of doctrine among different localities. For outside the limited field covered by the Qur'anic precepts, the thought of the scholars was naturally influenced by
the particular social conditions prevailing in their localities, and
local customary practice was accepted as part of the ideal scheme
of things unless some explicit principle of the Qur'an was fla-
grantly violated. We may take one outstanding example of such
divergence.

The law of Medina held that every woman, minor or adult,
could contract a marriage only through her guardian (for this
purpose, a close male relative like the father or the paternal
grandfather). If the guardian did not conclude the contract on

her behalf, the marriage would be a nullity. Furthermore, the guardian possessed the power to give his ward in marriage regardless of her consent or lack of it—and again this law applied whether the female concerned was minor or adult. These rules were natural enough in the traditionally tribal and patriarchal society of Medina, where the inferior status of women and the tribal pride in marriage alliances combined to place the power to contract a marriage in the hands of the male members of the tribe. But in Kufa the rules were fundamentally different. There the adult woman was completely free to contract marriage for herself without the intervention of any guardian and could never be given in marriage without her free consent. These rules were conditioned in turn by the particular social climate of Kufa, where the cosmopolitan atmosphere, resulting from the very mixed population of a new town in a predominantly Persian milieu, naturally allowed women greater freedom and higher legal capacity.

For the greater part of the eighth century, therefore, Islamic law was represented by a number of different legal systems built by human reason around the common stock of the Qur'anic rules —systems designed to fit the varying conditions of the different localities.

This practical approach, however, was not to remain for long unchallenged. The opposition materialized in the form of a group who sought to enlarge the area of law specifically regulated by the divine command. They did so by appealing to the authority of the Prophet of Islam. Such legal decisions as the Prophet himself had given, they argued, must be regarded as divinely inspired, and it was these Prophetic precedents, positive manifestation of the divine will, rather than the custom of a particular locality that could form the only acceptable supplement to the Qur'anic revelations. So formulated, the appeal of this thesis was irresistible, and the zeal of its exponents resulted in the discovery and collection of a great mass of reports and alleged rulings by the Prophet, which were termed *hadith* and which, modern research suggests, represented not what the Prophet actually did say or do but what this group was convinced, in all good faith, that he would have said or done in the circumstances envisaged. Prior to that time, all indications suggest, the "establishment" in the early schools of law had regarded the Prophet as a human interpreter of the Qur'an, a *primus inter pares* because he was the closest in time and spirit to the Qur'an, but nonetheless a human and therefore fallible interpreter. Members of the "establishment," however, could no longer maintain the validity of their own human reason in the face of what was asserted by the doctrinaire opposition group to be divinely inspired conduct, and they reacted by gradually expressing their own doctrines in the form of *hadith* from the Prophet.

From this point onward, Muslim jurisprudence evolved a legal theory that expressed to perfection the notion of Shari'a law as a divinely ordained system. This theory asserts that there are two material sources of law and two only. The primary source is, naturally enough, the very word of Allah himself as expressed in the Qur'an, and the second source is the body of precedents established by the Prophet and recorded in the *hadith*. Known collectively as the Sunna of the Prophet, these precedents represent material divine in its content if not in its form, the function of which is to explain, interpret, and supplement the general Qur'anic precepts. Questions that are not specifically answered in these two sources and new problems that may arise are to be solved by a disciplined form of reasoning by analogy known as *qiyas*—that is to say, by deducing from parallel cases regulated by the Qur'an and the Sunna the principles to be applied to these new cases. This theory therefore achieves a synthesis of the roles of divine revelation and human reason in law, but before it came to be generally accepted, the basic conflict of principle involved produced further schools of law in addition to those that already existed.

The first systematic exposition of this novel theory of the sources of law was the work of the great jurist al-Shafi'i, who died early in the third century of Islam. Initially there was strong opposition to his thesis in the established schools of law in Kufa and Medina, which both continued to support far wider use of human reason in the formulation of the law than al-Shafi'i's insistence upon the restricted method of analogical deduction allowed. Accordingly, the immediate and convinced disciples of al-Shafi'i formed a group apart from the Shafi'i school and, on the basis of his teachings, elaborated a body of doctrine that differed considerably from that recognized by the schools of Kufa and Medina. On the other hand, there were extremist elements who refused to accept the validity of any kind of human reason at all in law, rejected the use of analogical deduction, and purported to rely exclusively upon the Qur'an and the Sunna as sources of law. In the late third century of Islam, this group formed the Hanbali school, taking its name from the founder of the movement, Ahmad b. Hanbal. Their particular jurisprudential principles are responsible for many distinctive and individual features of positive law that stand in sharp contrast to those of the other schools. One such feature calls for consideration here, as it is highly relevant to the question of polygamy.

Contract law in general, according to the views of the majority of Muslim jurists, consists of a series of individual and strictly regulated types of contract. Once a person enters into one of these defined contractual relationships, certain rights and obligations must result, and it is in general not permissible for the parties to modify or avoid these results by mutual agreement in the form of a stipulation in the contract.

As applied to contracts of marriage, this principle means that the marital relationship, the result of the contract, is defined by the law in terms of the rights and obligations that accrue to the husband and wife respectively. One of the rights that the law ascribes to the husband is the right of polygamy, the right to take additional wives up to the maximum of four concurrently. Should the parties agree by stipulation in the contract that the husband will not take a second wife during this marriage, they attempt to deny what the law regards as an essential right of the husband. This they cannot do. The stipulation is void and does not bind the husband. If he breaks it and takes a second wife, the first wife has no remedy. This approach, which largely negates any concept of contractual freedom, does not arise from any dictates of the Qur'an. It is simply the result of the liberal *ijtihad* of the early jurists, based upon local practice and influenced strongly by the concepts of Roman law current in the former provinces of the Roman Byzantine Empire. For the early Hanbali lawyers, such juristic speculation was, as we have seen, devoid of any authority. Relying exclusively upon the Qur'an and the *hadith* and in particular upon the Qur'anic text, "Muslims must honor their stipulations," they held that the courts must give effect to any stipulation that the parties to a contract might mutually agree upon, provided only that such stipulation did not involve anything expressly forbidden by the law and was not manifestly contrary to the particular contractual relationship in question. The effect of this principle in contracts of marriage is obvious. It is not expressly forbidden, nor is it manifestly contrary to the institution of marriage that a man should have only one wife. If then the husband makes an agreement not to take a second wife, Hanbali law regards this stipulation as enforceable—not in the sense that the husband will be prevented from marrying a second wife but in the sense that, if he does so, the first wife can claim a dissolution of her marriage.

In contrast to the Shafi'i and Hanbali schools, whose law was formally derived from the sources laid down in the legal theory, the early schools of Medina and Kufa had already developed a corpus of positive law before the legal theory was formulated. These two schools now became known as the Maliki and Hanafi schools respectively, taking these names from outstanding representative scholars, and, although they eventually adopted al-Shafi'i's theory of the sources of law, they retained this pre-established body of positive law and simply harmonized it, by devious means, with the dictates of the legal theory. For the

Malikis and Hanafis, the legal theory was a formal and *post facto* rationalization of existing doctrine, and the result was that doctrines that had in fact originated in particular local customs and individual juristic reasoning came to be represented as expressions of the divine command. The same is true, as a matter of fact, of Shafi'i and Hanbali law, for the purported prophetic precedents that were their cornerstones were in reality largely expressions of local precedents and the views of particular scholars. For example, we referred previously to the fact that Medinese law required every woman to be given in marriage by her guardian, while the law of Kufa allowed an adult woman to contract her own marriage without the intervention of her guardian. Hanafi law preserved the Kufa tradition and Maliki law the Medinese tradition, and, as the latter came to be expressed in the form of a *hadith* from the Prophet, it was taken over by the Shafi'i and Hanbali schools. Accordingly, wherever the Hanafi school prevails in Islam today, as it does in the Indian subcontinent, an adult woman has the capacity to conclude her own marriage contract. But a woman has no such capacity where the Shafi'i school prevails, as it does in Southeast Asia—a distinction that has grown from the particular social circumstances obtaining in Kufa and Medina in the seventh century A.D.

The final stage in the historical evolution of the classical Islamic concept of law was perhaps the inevitable result of this idealistic identification of every term of the law with the command of Allah and the growing rigidity that such identification entailed. The material sources of the divine revelation, the Qur'an and the Sunna, were fixed and final in their form. There were obvious limits to the exploitation of this material by way of interpretation and analogical deduction, and, by the beginning of the ninth century, the belief had gained ground that this task had been completed and that nothing further remained to be done. Perhaps the chief factor contributing to this process of ossification was the development of the principle of *ijma,* the consensus of the legal scholars. In the effort to ascertain the will of Allah, which is the essence of Muslim jurisprudence, the *ijtihad* of individual scholars was a human and therefore fallible process. Its results could constitute only probable interpretations of Allah's will. But jurisprudence asserted that, when a rule was the subject of general agreement by the scholars, its acceptance was proof of its correctness, and that it thus represented an incontrovertible expression of the divine will. This principle obviously precluded further discussion on any point so settled. Furthermore, where differences of doctrine between the various schools persisted, the notion of *ijma* was carried to the point where it was held to cover these differences as equally possible and equally legitimate interpretations of the law but at the same time to deny the right to adduce any further solution. And it was because the jurists had thus agreed to differ that the four schools of law were regarded as equally orthodox definitions of the will of Allah. In each school, therefore, the current body of law embodied in the authoritative legal manuals written in the early medieval period came to be regarded as the final and perfect expression of the system of Allah's commands. The role of future jurists was to be confined to the consolidation of this doctrine. There was no longer any need or scope for *ijtihad*, and ultimately this attitude was expressed as an infallible consensus of opinion that "the door of *ijtihad* was closed." Thenceforth all jurists were known as followers or imitators, bound by the doctrine called *taqlid* to follow the law expounded in the authoritative manuals.

As part of this body of crystallized law, the doctrine of polygamy was fundamental to all the schools. In permitting polygamy the Qur'an had stressed the desirability of the husband's being able to provide for his several wives and of his treating them impartially. But, naturally perhaps under the prevailing social conditions, the import of these precepts had been minimized by interpretation, and they were generally regarded as imposing merely moral obligations upon the polygamous husband. For their breach, the law did recognize certain limited sanctions. The wife might be relieved of her duty of cohabitation, or the husband might be subject to minor forms of punishment. But the obligations were not construed as restricting in any way the exercise by the husband of his undisputed right of polygamy. In this as in all other respects, the law was artificially set in a rigid mold—not, we may suggest, as the result of any incontrovertible axiom of the Islamic faith but as the outcome of a complex historical process springing from the desire to set upon each and every detail of the law the stamp of divine approval.

So it was, then, that the classical Islamic concept of law finally emerged as that of a law totalitarian in its terms and immutable, its authenticity guaranteed by the infallible *ijma*. It was a concept of law that was to dominate Muslim thought until the past few decades of our own century.

In modern times, the problem presented by the clash between the dictates of a legal system based upon a society of early medieval times and allegedly unchangeable and the demands of contemporary Muslim society naturally became acute. By the present century, the criminal and commercial law of the Shari‘a had been almost entirely abandoned in the Middle East in favor of codes of law based upon Western models. In the realm of family law, which was always regarded as a particularly vital and integral part of the religious faith, however, such an extreme solution was not acceptable. Turkey, it is true, abandoned Shari‘a family law outright in 1927 and adopted in its place the Swiss Civil Code. But it is a significant fact that, over the past forty years, when such intense thought has been given to this problem, no single Muslim country has as yet seen fit to follow this example. Instead, conscientious endeavors have been made to adapt the Shari‘a to the needs of modern society. This process of legal modernism we shall now attempt briefly to outline in its principal features as they have developed in the Middle East.

Because of the strength of the classical concept of law, the reformers strove at first to remain within the bounds of the traditional doctrine of *taqlid*, or imitation, and to base their reforms upon juristic principles recognized as legitimate by classical jurisprudence. The basis of their work was the doctrine of *siyasa*, which defines the position of the political authority vis-à-vis the Shari'a law. This doctrine asserts that, although the political authority has no legislative power to modify or supersede the Shari'a, it nevertheless has the power, and indeed the duty, to make supplementary administrative regulations to effect the smooth administration of law in general.

Two main types of such administrative regulation attracted the attention of the reformers. First, there was the power of the sovereign to define the jurisdiction of his courts. In general, the reformers argued, this power allowed him to codify the Shari'a and, in particular, when there was a conflict of opinion among the jurists on a given point, to adopt and embody in the code that particular opinion among the existing variants that he deemed most suitable for application. Conflict of opinion within the Shari'a is, as we have seen, reflected by the existence of four distinct schools of law whose varying doctrines are regarded as equally legitimate expressions of Allah's law. It was therefore open to a Hanafi ruler in the Middle East to select, and to order his courts to apply, the doctrine of one of the other schools on a given point. It was on this juristic basis that the Ottoman Law of Family Rights took a first step toward the limitation of polygamy in 1917 by "selecting" the Hanbali doctrine governing stipulations in marriage contracts as better suited than the Hanafi doctrine to the needs of the time. The Hanbalis, as we have noted, were the only school that allowed a wife to claim dissolution of her marriage if her husband married a second wife in breach of a prior agreement not to do so.

The widespread use of this principle since 1917 has resulted in many changes in the law as traditionally applied in the Middle East. Peoples who are officially Hanafis are now governed by codes of law that represent eclectic amalgams of the doctrines of all the four schools.

The second limb of the doctrine of administrative regulations successfully utilized by the reformers was the recognized right of the sovereign to confine the jurisdiction of his courts, in the sense that he might set limits to the competence of the Shari'a tribunals by forbidding them to entertain certain types of case on procedural grounds.

For an example of the subtle application of this principle in legal modernism, we may turn to a sphere of the family law other than that of polygamy—to legitimacy. The one aspect of legitimacy in Shari'a law that concerns us here is its importance in regard to succession. For the legitimate child is by law indefeasibly entitled to the bulk of the deceased father's estate, while the illegitimate child is barred from any right at all. When a child is born to a widow, whether or not he is legally regarded as the legitimate child of the deceased husband depends upon whether or not the law presumes that the child was conceived during the husband's lifetime. The law therefore lays down a maximum period of gestation—which it presumes may possibly elapse between the conception of a child and its birth. If a child is born to a widow within this period it will be presumed to be the legitimate child of the deceased husband. This maximum period of gestation laid down in the authoritative manuals was two years according to the Hanafis, four years and more according to the other schools. From the point of view of modern medical knowledge of gestation, the harsh and inequitable results of this rule were obvious. In particular, the bulk of a deceased Muslim's estate might pass to a child who could not be his own child.

An Egyptian law of 1929 therefore declared that no disputed claim of legitimacy would be entertained by the courts if it could be shown that the child concerned was born more than one year after the termination of the marriage between the mother of the child and the alleged father. The jurisdiction of the courts in matters of legitimacy was confined to hearing cases in which the factual situation involved was in accord with modern medical opinion. The rule of traditional Shari'a law was not contradicted or denied as such, but by a procedural device the courts were precluded from applying that rule.

By such methods, far-reaching modifications were effected in the Shari'a law as traditionally applied. And formally at any rate the reforms had been accomplished within the framework of the doctrine of *taqlid*, for it was the law as expounded in the medieval texts that was still accorded exclusive and binding authority. The limitations of such methods, however, are readily apparent, and eventually the desired reforms could not be supported by any shadow of traditional authority. At that stage, the reformers had perforce to abandon any pretense of *taqlid*. They came to challenge the binding nature of the medieval manuals of law and the interpretations of the original sources recorded in them; they claimed the right to step beyond this corpus of juristic speculation and to interpret the Qur'an afresh in the light of modern needs and circumstances. They renounced the duty of *taqlid* and claimed the right of *ijtihad*.

This approach was, of course, met with the argument from traditionalist elements that it contradicted the infallible *ijma* and as such was tantamount to heresy. But its supporters argued with some force that either such *ijma* did not exist at all—it being manifestly impractical to ascertain the views of each and every legal scholar throughout the far-flung territories of Islam in the ninth century—or, alternatively, that if it did exist it was not binding, for it amounted to the arrogation by a self-constituted human authority of a legal sovereignty that belongs only to Allah. Although scholars like Muhammad Abduh in Egypt at the turn of this century and Iqbal in Pakistan had already advocated a dynamic reinterpretation of the Qur'an as the basis for comprehensive legal reform, the reformers were very conscious that their activities constituted an outright break with the practical legal tradition of ten centuries standing, and so their first steps in this novel direction were hesitant and tentative.

Their approach to the problem of polygamy centered upon

the Qur'anic suggestions that a husband should be financially able to support his several wives and that he should treat them impartially. In 1953, the Syrian Law of Personal Status interpreted the requirement of financial ability as a definite condition limiting the exercise of the right of polygamy. With this interpretation was coupled an administrative regulation requiring all marriages to be registered and further requiring permission of the court as a preliminary to such registration. The result was that a court would not give its permission for a second marriage unless it was satisfied that the husband was financially able to support two wives.

It may of course be argued that the only practical result of this reform was to make polygamy the privilege of the rich. Yet the real importance of the Syrian reform lies in its juristic basis and in the fact that a novel interpretation had been given to the text of the Qur'an. Once unlocked, the "door of *ijtihad*" was swung fully open by the Tunisian Law of Personal Status of 1957. This law interpreted the Qur'anic injunction regarding impartial treatment of cowives in the same way that the Syrians had interpreted the requirement of financial ability—as a legal condition precedent to the very exercise of the right of polygamy and one that would naturally apply regardless of financial standing. But it is no longer within the discretion of the court to permit a polygamous marriage on the ground that it is satisfied that the financial condition will be fulfilled. For the law goes on to state that in the circumstances of modern society it is impossible for a husband to treat several wives impartially to their mutual satisfaction; in technical language, there is a conclusive or irrefutable presumption of law that this essential precedent condition is incapable of fulfillment. Polygamy was therefore prohibited outright.

Such is the current evolution of an allegedly immutable law in the Muslim countries of the Middle East. Two considerations must be borne in mind. In the first place, these reforms are not put forward as deviations, occasioned by practical necessity, from the ideal Islamic law, that is, as *hila* but as contemporary expressions of that ideal law. And, in the second place, there is no uniformity in the method of legal modernism or in its results throughout the Middle East, and it is apparent that the process will tend, initially at any rate, toward a growing diversity in Islamic legal practice conditioned by the varying reactions in the different areas to the stimuli of modern life. This point is made quite clear, even on the one question of polygamy, by the three most recent modernist enactments of Islamic law. The Moroccan law of 1958 merely gives the court the power to intervene retrospectively, by way of dissolution of the marriage, when a polygamous husband has failed to treat his wives impartially. The Iraqi law of 1960 goes only a little further than the Syrian law in decreeing that the permission of the court is necessary for a second marriage and that such permission can be granted only when the husband meets the necessary financial criteria and when "no inequality of treatment is to be feared." Finally, the Muslim Family Laws Ordinance, promulgated in Pakistan in 1961, requires the permission of a duly constituted arbitration council for a second marriage, under pain of penal and other sanctions, and states that such permission can be given only when the Council is satisfied that the "proposed marriage is necessary and just." As for when a second marriage will be considered "necessary and just," it is obvious that the consent or dissent of the existing wife is extremely relevant, but such factors as the sterility, physical infirmity, or insanity of an existing wife are also specifically cited as relevant.

We are now perhaps in a position broadly to appreciate the significance of the Tunisian reform in the context of the phenomenon of legal modernism.

In its simplest forms, the problem facing Muslim jurisprudence today is the same problem it has always faced, one that is inherent in its very nature—the need to define the relationship between the standards imposed by the religious faith and the mundane forces that activate society. At the one extreme is the solution adopted by classical jurisprudence, a divine nomocracy under which religious principles were elaborated into a comprehensive and rigid scheme of duties to form the exclusive determinant of the conduct of society. The other extreme solution is that of secularism, adopted by Turkey, which relegates religious principles to the realm of the individual conscience and allows the forces of society unfettered control over the shape of the law. Neither of these solutions, it appears, can be acceptable to contemporary Muslim opinion generally. For, while the former is wholly unrealistic, the latter must inevitably be regarded as un-Islamic. Obviously the answer lies somewhere between these two extremes in a concept of law as a code of behavior founded upon certain basic and immutable religious principles but, within these limits, responsive to change and permissive of such new standards as may prove more acceptable to current Muslim opinion than does indigenous tradition. Law, to be a living social force, must reflect the soul of its society. And the soul of present Muslim society is reflected neither in any form of outright secularism nor in the doctrine of the medieval textbooks.

In its efforts to solve the problem of the clash between the dictates of traditional law and the demands of modern society, legal modernism, as it appears in its most extreme stage, the Tunisian reform, rests upon the premise that the will of Allah was never expressed in terms so rigid or comprehensive as the classical doctrine maintained but that it enunciated broad general principles that admit of varying interpretations and varying applications according to the circumstances of the time. Modernism, therefore, is a movement toward a historical exegesis of the divine revelation and, as such, can find its most solid foundation in the early historical growth of Shari'a law that we have described. For recent scholarship and research have demonstrated that Shari'a law originated as the implementation of the precepts of divine revelation within the framework of current social conditions, and in so doing they have provided a basis of historical fact to support the ideology underlying legal modernism. Once the classical theory is viewed in its true historical perspective, as only one stage in the evolution of the Shari'a, modernist activities no longer appear as a total departure from the one legitimate position but preserve the continuity of Islamic legal tradition by taking up again the attitude of the earliest jurists of Islam and reviving a corpus whose growth had been artificially arrested, that had lain dormant for a period of ten centuries.

It cannot be said, however, that legal modernism has yet reached the stage in which it provides a completely satisfactory answer to the problems of law and society in present-day Islam. Traditionalist elements condemn some modernist activities like the unwarranted manipulation of the texts of divine revelation to force from them meanings in accord with the preconceived purposes of the reformers. This manipulation, argue the traditionalists, is, in substance if not in form, nothing less than the secularization of the law. Modernist jurisprudence does in fact often wear an air of opportunism, adopting *ad hoc* solutions out of expediency, and does not yet rest upon systematic foundations or principles consistently applied. "Social engineers" the modernists certainly are, inasmuch as their activities are shaping the law to conform with the needs of society. Yet if Islamic jurisprudence is to remain faithful to its fundamental ideals, it cannot regard the needs and aspirations of society as the *exclusive* determinants of the law. These elements can legitimately operate to mold the law only within the bounds of such norms and principles as have been irrevocably established by divine command.

Looking to the future, therefore, it appears to be the primary task of Muslim jurisprudence to ascertain the precise limits and implications of the original core of divine revelation. And this task will perhaps come to involve a reorientation of the traditional attitude toward the reported precedents of the Prophet, not only in terms of their authenticity, but also in terms of the nature of their authority once authenticity is duly established. And it seems axiomatic that, when the precepts of divine revelation have been so established, they must form the fundamental and invariable basis of any system of law that purports to be a manifestation of the will of Allah.

It cannot be denied that certain specific provisions of the Qur'an, like the one that commands the amputation of the hand for theft, pose problems in the context of contemporary life for which the solution is not readily apparent. But generally speaking the Qur'anic precepts are ethical norms broad enough to support modern legal structures and capable of varying interpretations to meet the particular needs of time and place. And, on this basis, it seems that Islamic jurisprudence can implement, in practical, realistic, and modernist terms, its basic and unique ideal of a way of life based on the command of Allah. Freed from the notion of a religious law expressed in totalitarian and uncompromising terms, jurisprudence could approach the problem of law and society in a different light. Instead of asking itself, as it has done since the tenth century and still generally does today, what concessions must be wrested from the law to meet the needs of society, it can adopt new terms of reference, precisely opposite in intent, to determine what limitations religious principles set upon the frank recognition of social needs.

But however considerable the problems that still face Islamic jurisprudence may be, legal modernism has at least infused new life and movement into Shari'a law and freed its congealed arteries from a state fast approaching *rigor mortis*. The era of *taqlid*, of blind adherence to the doctrines of the medieval scholars, now appears as a protracted moratorium in Islamic legal history. Stagnation has given way to new vitality and potential for growth.

CLIFFORD GEERTZ

Modernization in a Muslim Society: The Indonesian Case

AS A PHRASE, "modernization in a Muslim society" begs more conceptual issues in fewer words than almost any other I can think of: Only the preposition seems straightforward. First, there are the much discussed difficulties implicit in the notion of "modernization." The relationships between "modernization" and "Westernization," the usefulness of sorting cultural patterns and social practices into pigeonholes labeled "traditional" and "modern," the "progressive" roles certain "reactionary" institutions like the extended family, ascribed status, or personal clientship seem to play in some modernizing situations—all these elements have become recurrent concerns in the scholarly literature on the new states. Second, with respect to "a society," considered as a total bounded unit, the question has been raised whether or not it can be a proper object of scientific study at all. Or must we not instead resign ourselves to investigating particular ranges of social institutions—family, class, religion—and the specific relations obtaining among them, without attempting to talk about society "as a whole"? Some have gone so far as to

suggest that such entities as "Indian society" or "French society"
do not even exist in any recognizable sense, that these terms are
merely misleading names for political units—for states. But of
the three main concepts in my assigned title it is the third—
"Muslim"—that, somewhat surprisingly, conceals the most radical difficulties, for there the sheer possibility of scientific analysis
threatens to disappear. Some Orientalists, at least, are coming, as
a result of deepening awareness of the disparate character of
"Islam" as it is practiced from place to place and of the varying
nature of the modern world's impact on different "Muslim"
countries, to doubt "whether *in the religious realm* there is either
in empirical fact or in theory anything to which the name Islam
can meaningfully be given":[1]

There is the Islamic tradition which the historian can reconstruct and
which is, both in practice and in principle, an accumulating, evolving,
observable actuality. For some centuries this was sufficiently stable for
an abstraction called "Islam" to be reasonably significant and academi-
cally serviceable. But this was not true in the earliest centuries of Islamic history, and is again not true today. . . . The scholar, if he
is historically erudite, can report the accumulating tradition, and if
he is sensitive and imaginatively perceptive as well as disciplined, he
can report the actual faith of living persons. But can he tell what
Islam as a religion "is"? Should he not rather [say] . . . that he has no
access to such a thing, in either Heaven or earth?[2]

Like some ancient parchment kept as an heirloom, our very
problem thus threatens to crumble in our hands as soon as, ceas-
ing simply to affirm its importance, we attempt actually to
grasp it.

In countering this kind of stultifying historicism, which
every significant increase in scholarly realism about social matters
seems to bring with it, the anthropologist's response is always
to turn again to the smaller canvas, for what seems vague and
orderless may then take on more precise and regular outlines.
One can overcome many of the apparent failings of "modernization," "society," and "Islam" as abstractions by applying them

within the context of a concrete example. The value of such an example does not lie in its typicalness, in the possibility of assimilating other cases directly to it. Rather, it lies in the fact that, by viewing social and cultural processes in limited and specific terms, one can isolate some features that are truly general, features that, when suitably adjusted to special circumstances, are relevant to the analysis of a whole family of cases. Whether or not they are in heaven, Islam, modernization, and society exist on earth: The problem is to know where to look for them.

I shall look for them in Indonesia and most particularly in the religious school system there. This may seem an exceedingly odd choice, one that threatens to reduce serious intellectual problems to matters of mere pedagogy—and scholastic pedagogy at that. But, in fact, the Muslim educational system is the master institution in the perpetuation of Islamic tradition and the creation of Islamic society, as well as the locus of the most serious present efforts to modernize that tradition and that society.

Islam in Indonesia

As in India, Persia, and, to a lesser extent, in Morocco, Islam was intrusive in Indonesia, in the sense that it came late into an already well-established, non-Arabic civilization, which it, slowly and with great difficulty, only partly replaced. There are a number of results of this fact, of which perhaps the most important is that even the essentials of the Muslim faith—the Pillars, the acceptance of Qur'anic authority, the perception of Divine Majesty, and the acknowledgment of the Prophet—had always, and still have, to be maintained in the midst of a number of competing, even hostile, religious orientations of no mean strength, most of them also going, since the conversions of the thirteenth to sixteenth centuries, under the general name of "Muslim." Neither supported by the society and culture within which it grew up, as were Christianity in the West, Hinduism in India, and Islam in Arabia, nor unchallenged by other "great traditions," as were Buddhism in Burma or Thailand and Islam in Nigeria or the Sudan, Indonesian Islam had to secure its integrity entirely, so to speak, by its own efforts. It had to draw from within itself, from its own organizational and intellectual resources, the power to maintain continuity with its origins, to sustain contact with the distant heartlands of Islamic civilization, and to establish a clear and positive identity on the spiritually cluttered Indonesian scene. In this struggle, never wholly won and never wholly lost, the Muslim school played and still plays an absolutely critical role. Without the *pesantrèn*, and later the *madrasa* and *sekolah Islam*, Indonesia would not have become even a nominally Islamic society from the simple circumstances of contact.

But beyond this "acculturational" aspect, there are at least two other interrelated reasons why Southeast Asian Islam has been so dependent upon the school. These reasons, deriving as they do from the nature of the Islamic tradition itself, make the Indonesian case relevant to a larger area. First, there is the highly doctrinal, legalistic, scriptural—basically literary—quality of at least the mainstream of the tradition; second, there is a general absence of other social institutions within the religion capable of transmitting this sort of tradition effectively. The school has been important because, even on its mystical side, Islam has leaned heavily toward the scholastic; it has leaned heavily toward the scholastic because the other great institutions of scriptural religions—the priesthood, the sermon, even (despite the Friday prayer) collective ritual—have been comparatively speaking weak, undeveloped, or, in the case of liturgy, thoroughly simplified.

The typical mode of Islamization of an individual or of a group has thus been, like all educational processes, painfully gradual. First comes the Confession of Faith, then the other Pillars, then a certain degree of observance of the Law, and finally, perhaps, especially as a scholarly tradition develops or takes hold, a certain amount of learning in the Law and in the Qur'an and *hadith* upon which it rests. The intricate norms, doctrines, explications, and annotations that make up Islam, or at least Sunni Islam, can be apprehended only step by step, as one comes to control, to a greater or lesser degree, the scriptural sources upon which they rest. For most people, such control never goes beyond accepting, at second hand, the interpretations of those who control or seem to control those sources directly. But that learning, however crude, and access to scholarship, however shabby, are central to becoming a Muslim, in anything more than a formal sense, is apparent virtually everywhere in the Islamic world. That is why al-Azhar, the great Islamic university in Cairo, is, from some points of view, a better epitome of Islam than Mecca. Islamic conversion is not, as a rule, a sudden, total, overwhelming illumination but a slow turning toward a new light.

Certainly gradualism has been the case in Indonesia. Spread first by foreign traders (Gujeratis, Malabarese, Kalings, Bengalis, Persians, Arabs, and even a few Turks) and then by indigenous ones (Malays, Bugis, Makassarese, North Javanese), Islam found its initial foothold in the various spice-trade ports that grew up around the Straits of Malacca and the Java Sea after the thirteenth century. Very little is known about this formative period, at least on the cultural side, save that the creed as implanted had a distinctly Indian, thus mystical, cast centered around certain "semihistorical" itinerant teachers regarded as saints. After the Dutch conquest, which began at the turn of the sixteenth century and was reasonably well established, at least in Java and selected points in the Outer Islands, by the turn of the seventeenth, Indonesian Islam became more autonomous, spreading out from its coastal beachheads and developing a solider, more deeply rooted institutional structure in interior towns and, even more important, in the countryside. With the establishment in the middle of the nineteenth century of more direct relations with Mecca through the Hajj (by about 1850 transport facilities had progressed to the point where more than 2000 people could make the pilgrimage each year), more orthodox practices and ideas began to penetrate the Indonesian *umma* (Islamic community) and transform it into something less completely Indic. By the beginning of this century, nearly 7500 pilgrimages were being made annually, and in the great boom year of 1926–27, 52,000 Indonesians, comprising more than 40% of its foreign population,[3] journeyed to the Holy City. By that time reformist ideas, mostly flowing out of al-Azhar and based on the teachings of Muhammad Abduh (1849–1905), were prevalent in the Hijaz— particularly after the triumph in Mecca of Ibn Saud—and a few Indonesians even found their way to Cairo and studied at the great university itself. As a result, an Indonesian version of reform Islam—a reading of the ideals of nineteenth-century liberalism and humanism into primitive Islam, as Caskel has characterized it[4]—grew up in the archipelago in opposition both to the orthodox stream and to the popular syncretism of the peasant masses. Finally, since Independence, there has been an almost desperate search for a way to relate Islam—orthodox and reform alike— to the modern world in general and to the secular Indonesian state in particular. And at each of these stages of Islamization, one or another form of the Muslim school has been the social structural foundation upon which the entire seven-hundred-year-old development has rested.

The Indonesian Schools

The generic name for the traditional Muslim school in Indonesia is *pesantrèn*—"place of religious students" (*santri*)—and, historically speaking, it grew not out of the classical Islamic academy, the *madrasa*, but out of the Hindu-Buddhist monasteries of medieval Java, secluded compounds in which monks or other adepts studied and composed holy writings, where religious pilgrims rested, sometimes for years on end, on their sacred journeys, and where local youths were instructed in their faith.

Except that the scriptures involved were later Qur'anic rather than tantric and the permanent residents *ulama* rather than monks, the traditional *pesantrèn* was—and in some places still is —essentially the same institution. A walled compound of student dormitories centered on a mosque, usually in a wooded glade at the edge of a village, it consisted of a religious teacher, usually called a *kijaji*, and a number of young, in most cases unmarried, male students—the *santris*—who chanted the Qur'an, engaged in mystical exercises, and seem generally to have carried on the pre-existing Indic tradition with only a slight and not very accurate Arabian accent. The student notebooks—the so-called *primbon*—that have come down to us from this period are permeated with a heterodox mystical monism directed toward the same sort of personal release as were the explicitly Hindu-Buddhist writings that preceded them. And in such documents as we have, for example the late eighteenth- or early nineteenth-century didactic poem *Serat Tjentini*, that describe life in these schools before the growth of orthodoxy, the atmosphere seems far more reminiscent of India or Persia than of Arabia or North Africa.

But even by the time of the *Serat Tjentini* a more orthodox tradition, demanding a closer observance of the Law as written, was appearing, stimulated by the improvement of communications—direct in the case of the Hajj, indirect in the case of religious publications and Arab immigration—with the Near Eastern heartland of Islamic civilization. The *pesantrèn* (or at least many *pesantrèn*s) became a much more proper Qur'anic school, usually headed by a returned pilgrim and supported by a religious foundation of the local well-to-do. Although mysticism hardly disappeared, especially in Java, it came to be more rigorously contained within the bounds laid down by al-Ghazzali and by the orthodox Sufi orders. The *pesantrèn*'s form changed little, but the content of its teaching changed significantly, as knowledge, or half-knowledge, of the classical Islamic subjects—*fiqh* (jurisprudence), *tafsir* (Qur'an commentary), *tarikh* (history), *tawhid* (theology), and so forth—increased. The orthodox revival, which took place in the Middle East in the eleventh and twelfth centuries and which, as Gibb has noted, "marks the turning point in the history of Islamic culture,"[5] the creation of its still unbroken medieval synthesis, thus began to take firm hold in Indonesia only six or seven centuries later in the guise of a gradual educational reform that turned the *pesantrèn* into a mediator of that durable amalgam of Shari'a legalism and *tariqa* mysticism that Ghazzali had legitimized.

Although, as time passed and shipping schedules improved, the scholastic side of the *pesantrèn* grew rather stronger and the antinomian side rather weaker, it was not until the launching of the reformist attack upon it and upon the intellectual tradition for which it stood that this descendant of the Hindu hermitage and the Buddhist monastery became at least a reasonable facsimile of an orthodox *madrasa*. The content of the reform movement is familiar from frequent description—a "back to the Qur'an" fundamentalism mixed with an "Islam is entirely up-to-date" modernism. But what is less familiar, because less often described, is the profound social effect reformism, abortive though it turned out to be, has had on the mainstream of Islamic orthodoxy. In Indonesia at least, the ultimate importance of reformism is to be measured not so much in terms of its own success as a social movement, which was local and momentary at best, but in its transforming impact upon the force it opposed and seems ultimately to have been unable to dislodge: the *pesantrèn* tradition. If the counterreformation has triumphed, at least for the present, the social changes in religious pedagogy that it necessitated mark perhaps another turning point in the history of Islamic culture. And, as developments in the archipelago no longer trail those in the rest of the Muslim world, perhaps not in Indonesia alone.

In these terms, the main achievement of the reform movement in Indonesia was the introduction of the modern, graded, partly secularized, formally organized—in a word, rationalized—

school into the established Islamic educational tradition. The modern school was not, of course, introduced into Indonesia by the Islamic reform movement, for Dutch government and Christian missionary schools, on a rather small scale, preceded them and in fact served as added local stimuli to and models for the reformers' innovations. But the direct impact of these schools was largely confined, so far as the Indonesian population was concerned, either to the uppermost levels of the aristocracy or to the very small confessional minorities, and even when it was not so limited the orthodox distrusted and shunned these schools as infidel. For them, the *ulama* and the *santris* who (both at the *pesantrèn* and after leaving it for more ordinary peasant or tradesman existences) were the *ulama*'s followers, it was the reform movement that, however bitterly they at first resisted it, made secular learning, modern modes of teaching, and in fact the whole drift toward a less medieval world outlook legitimate. Like the Sufi brotherhood before it, the modern school has become absorbed into the body of the Sunni tradition, and its effects, though as yet limited, may ultimately prove to have been as fateful.

The reformers called their schools *madrasa*, intending to stress the fact (as they saw it) that the *pesantrèn* had been seriously compromised by too intimate contact with heterodox local and Indic traditions and that thoroughgoing purification of these "backward" or "old-fashioned" institutions was essential before they could qualify for the title of "genuine" Muslim schools. The major innovations the *madrasa* introduced included the teaching of secular subjects (arithmetic, Latin characters, national history and literature, geography, and so forth); a curriculum organized along a strict subject, grade, and textbook pattern, complete with class hours, examinations, marks, diplomas and so on; the employment of teachers who, though believing Muslims, made no claims to be *ulama* or even especially learned in the scriptures and the law; a day-school rather than a boarding-school pattern; and, perhaps most radical of all, the education (sometimes even the co-education) of girls. Religious instruction continued, of course, occupying anywhere from one-third to three-quarters of the curriculum, but even it was conducted in a novel manner. Rather than the chant-and-echo pattern of the *pesantrèn*, in which the *santri*, ignorant of the meaning of the Arabic words he was repeating, gained his little understanding of the text from cryptic annotations offered ex cathedra by the *alim* (whose own Arabic was often enough hardly more than rudimentary), in the *madrasa*s an attempt was made either to understand the Arabic text directly or to work with vernacular translations. Religious knowledge, such as it was, was thus democratized to some extent, and the *hajjialim*'s role as privileged adept was seriously undercut. As by 1954 there were about 12,000 *madrasa*s with about a million and a half pupils, compared to 53,000 *pesantrèn* with nearly two million pupils[6] (before the first decade of this century, there were virtually no *madrasa*s in the modern sense at all), the impact upon Indonesian Islam of this most recent transformation in the country's most venerable educational system can hardly have been trivial. The precise nature of that impact is much more difficult to assess, but that it has been in the direction of loosening the grip of mindless ritualism and empty legalism seems certain. Secular political leaders and intellectuals, as well as Western scholars, who despair of the narrow confines within which the thought and feeling of the more pious sector of the Indonesian population seem to move might do well to consider what that thought and feeling would have been had the *madrasa* revolution not occurred. Whether or not the *madrasa* has made Indonesian Islam modern, it has surely made it, for what must be the first time in its history, critically, even painfully, self-reflective.

The initial reaction of the orthodox to the appearance of the *madrasa* was, as one would expect, sharply hostile. The new pattern of education struck at the very foundations of *ulama* power. It was no longer so important to have made the pilgrimage or to be able to chant the Qur'an from memory as it was to be able to communicate something of the intellectual content of the Islamic tradition and modern learning in general, and to relate, in some plausible way, the one to the other. But the orthodox reaction, though severe, was surprisingly short-lived. From the very beginning, some *ulama* saw the direction in which they must move if they were to maintain their position as spiritual leaders of the more pious element of the Indonesian population. And by 1926, the number of such more perceptive and flexible Qur'anic scholars had grown to the point that a counter-reform organization, called Nahdatul Ulama ("The Renaissance of the Ulama"), could be formed and could adapt the reformer's pedagogical innovations to the purpose of the *pesantrèn* tradition. *Madrasa*s began to appear, led by *ulama* but assisted and actually directed by some of their more modern followers, first independently of the *pesantrèn*s and then finally within their very walls. For their part, the reformers, exhilarated by success and supported by the times, pushed the evolution of their own schools forward, developing the so-called *sekolah Islam*, "Islamic schools," which, rather like Catholic parochial schools in the United States and much of Europe, are essentially secular schools with a place reserved for religious instruction and not *madrasas*, where secular learning has no autonomous justification but is a mere handmaiden to sacred teachings. The battle thus shifted from simple opposition between the *pesantrèn* ("monastery" or "hermitage") pattern and the graded-school pattern to one between graded schools of varying religious tempers, and arguments came to be centered around the proper relations between religious and nonreligious learning, rather than around the legitimacy or even the reality of the latter. The *pesantrèn* persists, as the figures I have quoted indicate. But few now are without some secular classes, offered either on their grounds or in a village *madrasa* nearby, which the *santri*s are allowed, sometimes even required, to attend. The few institutions that have maintained the older tradition intact and have continued to exclude modern learning entirely have great difficulty attracting *santri*s and are slowly fading—relics of an earlier stage of the evolution of Islam in Indonesia—from the scene.

In fact, in the distribution of types of Islamic educational institution in Indonesia, we can see reflected the whole development of the religion in this, its most distant, outpost. The orthodox synthesis of medieval Islam persists in the *pesantrèns*, usually slightly modified by some fairly weak modern influences, sometimes not. There are even a few examples of the older mystical pattern still to be found in remoter regions. The reaction of this synthesis to the reformist attack, an absorption of a limited amount of basic secular instruction—"reading, writing, and arithmetic"—into orthodox study organized along somewhat more systematic lines, is found in the *madrasa* that nearly every pious village now contains. And the reformers' concept of an Islam at once purified of medieval accretions and adjusted to the modern world finds its expression in the *sekolah Islam*—"parochial" elementary, middle, and normal schools—found mostly in the towns. In the larger cities, there have even appeared a number of Islamic "universities." The school—far more even than the mosque or prayer house, whose importance is almost purely ritualistic—is thus the social structural core of Indonesian Islam, now as in the past. And in the changes in its form is written more clearly than in the development of religious thought, legal, moral, or theological (which in Indonesia has always been more derivative than creative and not especially profound), the nature of the modernization process that Islam has undergone and, beneath the clamor of radical nationalist politics, is still undergoing.[7]

The fact that the renovation of "Islam" as a religious system tends to find its center of gravity in educational reform, rather than in reorganization of an ecclesiastical hierarchy or alteration in liturgical practice or even, at least initially, in reorientation of theological speculation has some important implications for the whole process of "modernization in an Islamic society," not only in Indonesia but fairly generally.

One of the difficulties Islamic reform faces and, perhaps

everywhere in the Sunni world except Turkey, has always faced, is the absence of easily identifiable targets against which to direct its attack. There is no pope whose supremacy can be rejected; no priestly hierarchy whose mediating powers, special privileges, isolating celibacy, or symbolic fatherhood can be dispensed with; no synthesis that, like Thomism, can be philosophically undermined. There are only the *ulama*—a loose collection of rather individualistic legal scholars and teachers without any formal status, any special perquisites, or, at least until recently, any particular internal organization—or the even more elusive and individualistic Sufi *shaikhs*. In such a sociocultural framework, there is no point at which a radical breakthrough, a sudden overturning of the whole system, can be accomplished, or at least if there is such a point no one has yet been able to find it. All that seems possible is a step-by-step attack on the multiple strongholds of traditionalism, mystical and scholastic alike. The great intellectual and sociological dramas of the Christian Reformation are exceedingly difficult to stage in such a setting of dispersed and rather uncertain religious authority, and attempts to do so lead almost inevitably to fruitless sectarian schism.

It is perhaps for this reason that so many Western scholars of Islam seem to be so disappointed, even personally put out, with the reform movement and have, at times anyway, rather underestimated its transformative effects upon the Islamic tradition. Expecting Luthers and Calvins, they have found instead a collection of, for the most part, rather cautious pedagogues; instead of a few great thinkers of surpassing boldness, there has appeared a cloud of not terribly distinguished and usually rather unoriginal academicians. This fact makes history—and history writing—less colorful; but, in the same way that Islamization in the past has been a gradual process, a slow accretion of minor changes rather than a series of spectacular quantum jumps, so too, and for the same reasons, may its modernization be. Sixty years ago the Dutch Islamic scholar, Snouck Hurgronje, warned his colleagues in the Netherlands East Indies civil service that In-

donesian Islam, which seemed so static, so sunk in torpid medievalism, was actually changing in fundamental ways. But these
changes were so gradual, so subtle, so concentrated in remote
and, to non-Islamic minds, unlikely places that, "although they
take place before our very eyes, they are hidden from those who
do not make a careful study of the subject."[8] Today, after four
decades of thoroughgoing and quite obvious upheaval in the
Indonesian *umma* have rendered these words prophetic, the
warning they contain is no less apposite. The tendency to underestimate the dynamism of Islam is as apparent both among the
governing elite and among learned scholars as it was a century
ago, a characterization that holds, by and large, for the leaders
of Islamic countries and students of Islam generally.

As far as the topic of this session of our seminar—"reorientation and mobilization of traditional values in the modernization
process of a Muslim society"—is concerned, the picture I have
given of the Indonesian case has, if it is accurate, some important
policy implications for the elites of the new states of South and
Southeast Asia, who have found, as Soedjatmoko remarked in
his outline paper, that traditional value systems growing out of
long standing religious commitments represent "a much more
important problem in the modernization process than had been
anticipated by most of these modernizers."

By far the most important of these implications is that the
continuation of a vital school tradition, and especially its renovation, is essential to what Soedjatmoko calls "a comparatively
smooth modernisation." And this point leads in turn to what
may seem a curious paradox: that a strong and active parochial
school system (if I may adapt this Catholic Christian term to
Muslim uses) is not, in an Islamic country and certainly not in
Indonesia, an enemy but an ally of the secularist modernizing
elite. It is an ally not because it promotes the ideals of a militant
and totalistic secularism (ideals that only a small minority of
these elites themselves hold) but because it allows, and in fact
encourages, an established religious tradition with a powerful

hold on the minds of the population to come to terms with the modern world, neither simply rejecting nor simply capitulating to it but becoming part of it. More paradoxically yet, it is not a rigid separation of education from religious influence that will make it possible to render unto Caesar the things that are Caesar's in an Islamic society but the further integration of secular and religious learning in modern schools. It is through such schools that Islam, on the sociological level and in consequence on the intellectual level as well (for ideas cannot develop in a social vacuum), will be able to enter the modern world. To cut the *umma* off from this critical regenerating institution in its midst by a strict adherence to a state-supported and -directed secular school system and by vague hostility to "Qur'anic" schools as "backward," "feudal," or "fanatical" is to ensure the rigidification of Islamic institutions generally and, in consequence, of Islamic thought.

Today, as in the past, the school is the lifeline of the Islamic tradition, and the reformed school is that tradition's path to the present. It is essential that this path not be blocked by shallow and short-sighted "modernization" policies that attempt to catch up with the West by mindless imitation of its external forms.

Notes

1. W. Smith, "The Comparative Study of Religion in General and the Study of Islam as a Religion in Particular," Colloque sur la Sociologie Musulmane, *Correspondance d'Orient*, No. 5 (Brussels: Publications du Centre pour l'Etude des Problèmes du Monde Musulman Contemporain, 1962), pp. 1–15.

2. *Ibid.*

3. J. Vredenbregt, "The Hadj: Some of Its Features and Functions in Indonesia," *Bijdragen tot de Taal-, Land- en Volkenkunde*, 118 (1962), 91–154.

4. W. Caskel, "Western Impact and Islamic Civilization," in G. von Grunebaum, ed., *Unity and Variety in Muslim Civilization* (Chicago: The University of Chicago Press, 1955), pp. 335–60.

5. H. A. R. Gibb, *Studies on the Civilization of Islam*, S. J. Shaw and W. R. Polk, eds. (Boston: Beacon Press, 1962), p. 22.

6. *Indonesia*, Subcontractor's Monograph, Human Relations Area Files, II, (New Haven: 1956), 422. As these figures were reported to the Ministry of Religion, the *pesantrèn* figures reported (where no subsidies are involved and a lingering suspicion of the intentions of government is lodged) are almost certainly much too low.

7. A full review of recent experiments in Islamic education in Indonesia would be out of place here, but attempts to set up new forms of religious schools continue and have perhaps even accelerated. One pattern—started before the Revolution in Gontor, a village in South Central Java, and attempted afterward in Jogjakarta and elsewhere—is to divide the curriculum into thirds: one-third instruction in secular subjects, one-third in religious subjects (taught in a more modern fashion), and one-third practical work in fields, crafts, shops, and so forth. This system was a revision of the old work-your-way pattern of the *pesantrèns*. The proponents of these schools argue that, not only will they help to bring Islam "up to date," but that, with their practical work orientation, they will provide a more suitable education for Indonesian children than do the clerk-oriented government schools. The future of these experiments, most of which have been encouraged and supported by the Ministry of Religion, is uncertain, but that they are even planned and attempted shows the vitality of the Qur'anic school tradition. In addition, of course, a great number of ordinary primary and secondary schools have been set up, by Muhammadiyah (a modernist social-welfare society), Nahdatul Ulama, and other Islamic organizations, and modeled on the state-run school system but with additional teaching in religious subjects. For a detailed description of the range of religious schools existing in one region of Java in the period 1952–1954, see C. Geertz, *The Religion of Java* (New York: The Free Press, 1960), pp. 177–98.

8. C. Snouck Hurgronje, *The Achehnese* (Leiden: E. J. Brill, 1906), p. 280.

EDIRIWEERA R. SARACHANDRA

Traditional Values and the
Modernization of a Buddhist Society:
The Case of Ceylon

ALTHOUGH THE OBSERVATIONS in this paper consist largely of conclusions drawn from an analysis of the Buddhist society of Ceylon, I view Ceylon as a representative instance of a society in which the form of Buddhism known as Theravada has been the major influence in the evolution of social institutions and the determination of moral values and ideals of life. I expect, therefore, that a good number of these observations should also be applicable in some measure to the other societies in which the Theravada Buddhist tradition prevails, namely those of Burma, Cambodia, and Thailand. I hope others will point out those instances in which the observations made here either need to be amended or are invalid in respect to these other countries, to help clarify our notions of the roles of Theravada Buddhism in the different contexts in which we find it.

At the same time, it is perhaps useful to point out at this stage that, although Buddhism is generally believed to be one religion, there is such a vast difference between its two forms, Theravada (more commonly known as Hinayana) and Mahayana, that we cannot talk of a "Buddhist society" as if it were a homogeneous entity or of "Buddhist values" as if they were uniform or even basically similar in the various societies of the world that can be called Buddhist. In fact, a Ceylonese Buddhist would be reluctant even to give the name "Buddhism" to the form of religion that predominates in Japan, for example. To the Ceylonese Buddhist, the Buddhism of Japan would appear as an instance of the corruption or decadence of the original doctrines. Such an attitude is not to be wondered at, for the Ceylonese Buddhist would find in the Japanese Buddhist a vast difference in his conception of life and the goal of existence. We may say that the manner in which the Japanese Buddhist translates the ideals of Buddhism into practical aims and purposes would seem to the Theravada Buddhist of Ceylon almost a violation of the spirit of Buddhism. Nevertheless, we cannot deny Japanese Buddhism the right to call itself "Buddhism," any more than we can deny the same right to Chinese and Nepalese Buddhism. For the present, we have to recognize at least the two broad categories of Theravada Buddhist society and Mahayana Buddhist society, although in the ultimate analysis we may be dissatisfied with these two categories and be forced to recognize that there are as many different categories of Buddhist society as there are countries that claim to be Buddhist.

These considerations indicate the importance of approaching our problem from the angle of sociology rather than from that of religion, although we are dealing with religion. The difference lies in the fact that religion, as it permeates society and molds social institutions and social attitudes, often departs from the doctrines in their pure forms preserved in texts or in theoretical tradition. It is particularly important to bear this point in mind when we discuss the Buddhism of a country like Ceylon where, not only in the present day, but also throughout history, there has been a gap between the Buddhism of the *religieux* and the lay elite, on the one hand, the Buddhism of the ordinary man, today's Sinhalese villager, on the other. This gap has sometimes led to open conflicts that have reflected themselves in literature and history. The Ceylonese intellectual of today is faced with the challenge to reconcile such conflict because, unless it is done, cultural and intellectual life, as understood in the context of modern society, seems impossible.

But I must first attempt to describe the traditional Buddhist society of Ceylon before proceeding to discuss how the values of this society stand in need of reorientation today.

Ceylon has always claimed and still claims to be the most important country in the Buddhist world, not only because its form of Buddhism is nearest to the original doctrines of the Buddha, but also because, even within the tradition of Theravada, it preserves the religion in its most authentic form. This claim is substantiated by the texts, and it has never been disputed that Buddhism has been preserved in Ceylon in its pristine purity. The historical reason is probably the fact that when Buddhism was first brought to Ceylon it did not meet with any strong opposition from organized primitive cults, as was the case in China, Nepal, and Japan. The result was that Buddhism in Ceylon was able to remain aloof from the primitive cults, which it treated with disdain and which were, in any case, not powerful enough to influence the new religion. The Buddhism that established itself in Ceylon was thus not the outcome of a compromise with a pre-Buddhistic native religion as was the case in China, Nepal, and Japan.

This explanation, however, is only partial, for, although Buddhism in Ceylon did not have to face strong opposition from organized cults, there were other factors, springing from the very nature of the religion itself, that caused the Buddhism that took root in Ceylon to differ ultimately from the pristine Buddhism that was brought to the island and is still preserved there in theoretical form. The original Buddhism was a religion that eschewed cults and ritual, had as few forms of prayer and worship as possible because it did not believe in a divinity, and was altogether an individualistic and intellectual approach to the problem of salvation. The earliest Buddhist literature gives us a picture of lone forest-dwellers, very much like the Upanishadic seers, who lived in contemplation of the vanity of life, seeking to eradicate desires and attachments in their final quest of the goal of nirvana. These men (and women too) exemplified the true ideal of Buddhism. Later, although still in the lifetime of the Buddha, came the organization of monks. The monks practiced a kind of community living and had certain congregational rituals, but they were kept to the very minimum necessary for community life. Their attainment of salvation was the result of individual effort and lonely contemplation. The layman came last of all. For him there was a lay ethic, which was but a concession to his needs. As for the higher life, which he must aim at as a final goal, he could never achieve it unless he put behind him all attachments to family and kin, all duties and cares that could act as hindrances, and devoted himself entirely to contemplation and the quelling of passion. The way of salvation, therefore, was in a sense not a continuation on a higher level of the worldly life but something that lay in the opposite direction. One could not attain intrinsic purification through love of one another or through the performance of one's duties and the leading of a moral life. Those ideals did not possess ultimate worth because they could not lead to the goal of beatitude. They were, in fact, temptations to pull one down. One had to give them up and practice a different kind of discipline in order to attain salvation.

With these ideals, Buddhism was obliged to relate itself to the community in a manner different from that of most if not all other religions. At the level of practical living, religion seems to perform very much the same functions, whether the communities are those we call "civilized" or those we call "primitive." Religion steps in where man is more or less helpless, where his efforts seem to be of no avail. It is true that the range within which man must invoke the supernatural narrows as he gains greater knowledge of the workings of nature. What was once regarded as supernatural is subsumed under the natural. But with the necessary limitations of human knowledge and human resources, man still finds himself in situations in which he has been defeated, and it is then that the theistic religions seek to bring him comfort by holding forth hope for an afterlife or faith in the over-all benevolence of a deity whose ways are incomprehensible to the frail human mind.

This function Buddhism, in its faithfulness to the hard truths of life and its relentless insistence that man has no savior but himself, that he must save himself by knowledge alone and by facing that knowledge courageously, was not able to perform or did not attempt to perform. The Buddha did not believe in comforting people by what he regarded as false hope. It was better to face one's own hopelessness and thereby to gain the more permanent satisfaction that realization of the ultimate truth gives. Kisa Gotami, who had lost her only infant child, was not comforted by the Buddha with vain hopes that the child could be brought back to life or that she would be united with her child in life after death. She had to attain the realization that death is a common phenomenon to which everyone is subject and that *she* was not particularly singled out for such suffering. From the world view of countless births and deaths that a human being experiences, *sub specio sansarae,* so to speak, the span between one single birth and death is but a speck of sand on the limitless shores of time. The contemplation of such vastness and one's own littleness in the face of it cannot help but reduce the intensity of one's suffering.

But a religion of this sort can be of little help to the common man, who is not by temperament contemplative and who seeks some kind of solace in the crises of his day-to-day existence. It is this difficulty that Buddhism had to face in establishing itself in the life of the layman and in the organized life of the lay community. What would be its attitude toward secular activity?

It would expect the layman to approximate as closely as possible to its ascetic ideal in his ordinary activities. But such behavior would not be practicable for the large proportion of laymen, however much they were intellectually convinced of the necessity for it. The other alternative was to make some kind of compromise with the necessities of lay life. But this compromise Buddhism was not prepared to make because it would mean sacrificing some of its principles.

The result was that the folk religion, or rather folk cults, had to fill in the gap left in the lay life, to make it possible for the common man to accept Buddhism as his religion while continuing with his secular activities. This result was different from those in the Mahayana countries, where Buddhism actually modified itself to suit the social milieux in which it had to establish itself. In Ceylon, it was the layman who adapted his own cults and practices to Buddhist ideology rather than the other way about. The gods and demons of the popular faith were placed under the supreme jurisdiction of the Buddha without whose final sanction they cannot operate. The powers of the Buddha, his greatness and goodness, were chanted for magical purposes, and legends grew up relating how the Buddha conquered the demons and relegated them to authority over certain spheres of human existence.

There thus came to be what can best be termed "the Buddhism of Ceylon" but which even today has not been elevated to that status. It is the religion of the Sinhalese villager, and it is a fairly satisfactory compromise between the individualistic-recluse ideal of pristine Buddhism and the needs of secular life. In a sense it does not violate the spirit of Buddhism, for the Sinhalese Buddhist is quite aware of the fact that his faith in the folk cults only relates to the sphere of his material existence. He does not pray to the gods for salvation from *saṃsāra;* he merely asks their succor in times of trial. He feels more than reverence toward them; he fears their power and knows that he needs their help, for which he is prepared to render service. He is aware that, where salvation is concerned, they are in a worse plight than mortals, for they must be born on earth and be cleansed of the roots of evil before they can ever hope to attain eternal beatitude. Toward the demons whom he propitiates, his attitude is even less reverent. He brings them under his power by the help of magical rites and demands, in the name of the Buddha, that they cease to harass and bring disease on human beings. He offers them things they like, he invites them to partake of certain foods, and he cajoles them or even deceives them into granting his wishes.

In regard to the life beyond and final emancipation from this vale of woe, the Sinhalese Buddhist accepts the basic teachings of the religion, and his values are, in the last resort, derived from Buddhism. He believes in the virtues of nonattachment, in the value of subduing one's passions, in the peace that comes from inward contemplation, and in the desirability of attaining the ultimate goal of Nirvana.

The religio-social life of the village is patterned on the basis of this ideology. The folk cults are organized by the priesthood and consist of elaborate ceremonies accompanied by all-night dancing, drumming, and chanting. For this purpose, images of deities and demons are made of clay, masks are carved of wood and painted, and altars are constructed by means of bamboo framework, tender leaves of coconut, the pith of the banana stem, and such material. The Buddhist monk, however, does not perform the function of a priest. He is a recluse concerning himself with the ultimate problems of human destiny and preaching to people on such matters.

The bulk of the village culture stems from these ritualistic ceremonies. But here we see a certain lack of integration, which is probably at the basis of some of the problems that must be faced today. The higher religion is Buddhism, and the higher culture is the one that arises from Buddhist belief and practice. Side by side with it is the folk culture, which, from the point of view of the common man, complements the higher culture. But the traditional elite, in strict adherence to the principles of Buddhism, has always looked down upon the folk cults and the arts that have developed out of their ceremonies, partly because they are of no use in and may even hinder the pursuit of higher ideals and partly perhaps because they are rustic and vulgar. There has thus arisen a kind of rift between the folk culture and the culture of the elite, not simply because actual fusions between them have not taken place, but also because the elite have regarded all such fusions as contaminations of the higher culture. The folk arts have not therefore received sufficient recognition to enable them to develop into national arts. For example, the art of the folk artist who created images of demons and deities, carved and painted ritual masks, and made ingenious decorations on altars is regarded almost with disdain compared with the arts of the temple painter and the maker of Buddha images. Dancing, drumming, and singing, which have no connection with Buddhist worship, are looked down upon as lower arts, and the ballads narrating the lives of the popular gods and demons, which form the bulk of the folk literature, are considered merely the amateur efforts of rustic versifiers and are not admitted to be literature.

But the higher culture of which we are talking can be described as a recluse culture, which inculcates an ideal of individual salvation by contemplation and the subjugation of passions and does not include the kind of faith and devotion that express themselves in artistic form. Even in the cases of painting and sculpture, which are the only two art forms springing directly from Buddhism, we find that they are not connected with the religion in the same ways as in the theistic religions. Theravada Buddhist painting inclines toward the narrative, descriptive, and didactic, with no attempt at a goal of emotive expression but with a quietistic, contemplative end. It is the same with sculpture. The Buddha image is not an individual artist's expression of his faith in the Buddha or his devotion to him. It represents rather a whole culture's symbol of its ideal of perfect joyousness and peace attained by realization of the truths of existence.

The arts of music, dance, and drama, which have in the past always sprung from religious ritual and congregational worship, could not arise from Buddhism in the nature of the case. Buddhism is antiritualistic and noncongregational and, from its intellectualist point of view, looks upon these arts as unwholesome activities that tend rather to rouse the passions than to calm them. The higher culture of the elite does not therefore provide the means for expression of some of the instinctive urges in man, for his impulse to translate his feelings into rhythm and melody, for his desire to gain satisfaction by the creation of beauty, and for his innate need to come together with fellow humans in common activities.

We see therefore that, in spite of attempts by the folk culture to integrate with the higher culture and thus to create an all-round, balanced pattern for secular living, this integration did not wholly take place. The traditional elite has always tended to look down upon the much more integrated pattern of living provided by the folk culture and has upheld and reiterated the recluse ideal. The result has been that the folk culture, in spite of its dynamism and its ability to provide a more satisfying pattern of organized living, has remained at the level of a folk culture and has not achieved the status of a national culture. The folk arts have remained static and undeveloped, there has been little impetus to creation, and in some cases folk arts have even been lost to posterity.

At the higher and more sophisticated levels of society, on the other hand, in the circles of the king and his nobles, for instance, the lacuna resulting from the failure of the higher culture to provide a satisfying pattern for secular living were filled by Indian culture. Royal institutions and ceremonials were almost completely based on those of Indian kings. The king and his ministers and those attached to the court formed a different class, living a different kind of cultural life. From the indirect evidence we can gather from literature and from quasi-historical records, we infer that the kings and nobles were patrons of

Indian music and dancing, as well as of Sanskrit learning, rather than of the indigenous arts. While Buddhist monks no doubt performed certain religious ceremonies, Brahmins officiated at functions like coronation and marriage, which, from the Buddhist point of view, would be regarded as secular ceremonials. The culture of the royal elite, therefore, appears to have consisted of a mixture of Buddhist practices and secularized Hindu ceremonials, and the members of the elite seem to have satisfied their emotional and intellectual needs by cultivating the classical arts and literature of India.

What I have described so far are the situations out of which have arisen the problems of today and tomorrow. These problems have become more complicated by such events of recent history as the colonization of Ceylon by Western powers and its recent emergence as an independent country. Present-day Ceylon is passing through a period of intellectual ferment in which, while there is a search for tradition on the one hand, there is questioning of the value of this tradition on the other. It is not surprising to hear that the question, What is the real tradition? is also raised. Younger writers are earnestly concerned with the quest for a set of values that will place human relations on more satisfying footings and thus establish a pattern of living more consonant with the wider awareness of human motives that modern knowledge has given to people.

The great question and one that people almost fear to face is How far are the values of a Theravada Buddhist civilization capable of survival today, or in what way can they be reoriented to contribute to our progress? On this question there is much conflict of views between the traditional elite and the Western-educated elite. But the point is that values are values, and one either accepts them or casts them away. One cannot say that a certain set of values is conducive or unconducive to progress, because "progress" is itself a value term, and everything depends on the meaning that we are prepared to give to this term. Any society can hold in esteem a set of values while being aware that they have no relation to material progress and may even be inimical to it. Only time can show whether a society is prepared to cast away its values or prefers to go down upholding them.

We have to leave the first question, therefore, as unanswerable at present. One thing, however, seems fairly certain, namely, that, whatever definition of progress we accept, a society cannot achieve such progress by completely casting away its traditional values. The reason is that values are beliefs about human ends, and they come to be accepted only after they have conditioned the thinking of people for centuries. Once discarded, they cannot be easily or quickly replaced, and it is better to have *some* set of values to guide the conduct of individuals or societies than to have none. The worth of a set of values has no relation to its validity because there is no way of testing that validity. It appears that, when traditions must adapt themselves to different circumstances, they must do so within the framework of the same set of values.

Perhaps I should illustrate by means of concrete examples. The practical Buddhism of the Sinhalese village, which I have described, seems to me to provide an instance of how, without damage to basic values, we can achieve a body of traditional behavior patterns leading to the inward harmony of the individual as well as to the outward harmony of the group. We may also take as an example the manner in which Zen Buddhism has adapted itself to secular living in Japan and has produced the aestheticism that has become almost a religious sentiment with the Japanese. Here, it seems to me, we have an instance of a society that has translated the highest ideals of Buddhism into a form of experience of which the layman can partake and through which he can prepare himself for the nobler life. In contrast, we find the Theravada Buddhist texts citing with approval the example of a monk who lived for more than thirty years in a rock cave but, because he was engaged in meditation, did not notice the paintings on the wall. This example represents an unnecessary narrowing of the path to realization and a confining of Buddhist ideals within small limits. There ought to be many paths for the many to trod, and Buddhist ideals should be spread over as wide an area of human experience as possible. According to Zen, the contemplation of beauty and harmony in nature, as well as the beauty and harmony created by man, leads to inward quietude, to a calming of passions, and to a stilling of the mind, which are necessary preparation for the realization of nirvana and which can serve in practical living as well. We thus arrive at a situation in which there is no antagonism between the highest ideals, the ultimate values, and practical day-to-day living.

Hindu society, too, has made an excellent adjustment between its ideals of renunciation and the needs of lay living in its doctrine of *Varnaśrama dharma* or the Four Stages of Man. In the first stage, a person lives the life of a celibate student, in which he learns the arts and sciences and passes his time in the company of his teacher and fellow students. In the next stage, he marries, brings up his children, and performs his domestic obligations and duties. When these stages are over, he retires to the forest, sometimes accompanied by his wife, and begins to contemplate seriously the problems of the afterlife and his own spiritual salvation. In the final stage, he becomes a true recluse intent on attaining the highest beatitude. This division of life into four stages makes possible the development of a man's whole personality. His instinctive urges find expression, and his character becomes purified through his relations with his wife and children and, through them, with the rest of the community.

Unless there is such total integration between ideals and realities, society is likely to produce schizophrenics or conscious hypocrites. Fiction writers have brought to light the existence of such character traits in the Sinhalese of today. Contemporary literature also portrays the more sensitive souls who, because they are keenly aware of this conflict of values and no more believe in the necessity for such a conflict, become almost psychopathic. This phenomenon is, of course, a modern one that results from the fact that people are aware of different and more harmoniously integrated patterns of living. The impact of modern knowledge in the fields of psychology and education has taught them the necessity to reorganize human relations on a saner footing, with a deeper and more sympathetic understanding of human motives. This change does not mean that they have thrown aside the higher values of the tradition, but it may mean that they are even prepared to do so if one aim cannot be realized without sacrificing the other.

A Buddhist society like that of Ceylon has to face today the challenge that comes both from the side of its cultural life and from the side of its moral life. On the side of culture, society must cure itself of an attitude of near-Philistinism that is the inevitable outcome of the recluse ideal's pervasion of the secular life. Along with painting and sculpture, the arts of music, dance, and drama, which Buddhism has not looked upon with favor, must develop, and society must unequivocally accept their intrinsic worth as well as their utility in character building, education, and the organization of community life. A different attitude toward the folk culture, such as has been taken by the Western-oriented elite and by the coming generation of educated village youth, may help to create the necessary mental disposition for this change. In the actual task of artistic creation, it is also necessary to have a less chauvinistic attitude and a readiness to admit the limitations of folk culture and its inability, in its primitive form, wholly to satisfy the sophisticated and, to some extent, internationalized taste of today. The folk arts obviously need the stimulus of outside contact in order to flower and be capable of attaining the status of national arts. And what seems most desirable, particularly in the arts of music and dance, is the inspiration that can be derived from a more developed allied tradition like that of India. In this respect, the tendency for Ceylon to isolate itself from the cultural context of Greater India, which began with British times and continues today, may act as a hindrance.

The traditional elite, which has emerged today as the lower

middle class, has unfortunately become the voice of chauvinism and near-Philistinism and exhibits beside a kind of prudery that cannot but be detrimental to the uninhibited growth of literature and the arts. Its view is that the West is immoral and that this immorality is expressed in Western literature and art. What its members advocate is a return to the recluse ideal; they are still expressing their traditional dislike of secularization. Needless to say, this expression of defeatism is not a realistic way of meeting the challenge of the modern world.

The problem does not arise merely as a result of one set of moral values confronted with another. It seems more a question of the proper definition of the term "morality" itself. I think it is necessary to distinguish between morality in the fundamental sense of the term and morality as a code of self-discipline that one imposes upon oneself as a prerequisite for the attainment of spiritual insight. Morality in the fundamental sense is imposed upon one as a necessity of community living. It arises from human relations, and we may say that the recluse has no need of it. A layman does not necessarily become moral by following, in his lay life, the self-discipline of a recluse. On the other hand, there may be instances in which he may have to neglect his duties as a layman if he attempts to follow the discipline of a recluse. It may also be that the discipline he imposes upon himself as a result of his desire to emulate the recluse may help him in his morality as a layman. But his moral nature must be judged always in the light of his relations with his fellow beings. There is a problem of morality, therefore, for the layman and not for the recluse.

There is much confusion in the sphere of moral judgments as a result of a failure to distinguish these two elements. The ordinary layman thinks that to be moral is necessarily to be ascetic. A "good" man is one who conforms as much as possible to this ideal, and a man is "bad" to the degree that he deviates from it. Practices that are neither moral nor immoral, like taking liquor, are thus used as criteria for judging man's moral nature.

Morality tends to be mistaken for mere external observance and conformity on one hand, and, on the other, all actions tend to be regarded as neither moral nor immoral if done in private. A result of this confusion is that today, when it is becoming more and more difficult for a layman in his everyday social life to follow an ascetic code, even the earlier one laid down for the Buddhist layman, many people resolve the problem by adopting a double code of morality, one public and the other private.

Perhaps it is necessary for us to probe even more deeply into moral questions, as writers in Ceylon are doing today, and to draw a distinction between conventional or institutionalized morality and morality in the fundamental sense. This distinction would be the only basis for re-establishing society on a sane footing and for curing prudery, moral schizophrenia, and hypocrisy. I do not believe that people should cast away the ultimate values of Buddhism or that these values cannot survive in the modern world. On the other hand, I do believe that something must be done to save them. We should become clear in our minds as to what these values really are and what their essence is, and we should reorient social living so that they can seep down into the day-to-day life and activities of people.

JOSEFA M. SANIEL

The Mobilization of Traditional Values in the Modernization of Japan

JAPAN'S RAPID METAMORPHOSIS within a generation from a "feudal" to a modern society has not yet been duplicated in any of the developing states of Asia—states all deeply rooted in traditional values. How the Japanese leaders of the Meiji period (1868–1912) mobilized traditional values in Japan's forced march to modernization is the main consideration of this paper. But first permit me to define two terms: "traditional values" and "modernization." By "traditional values," I mean sources of motivation within a premodern society; by "modernization," I mean the process of transforming a society's traditional political, economic, and social systems into modern systems ideally characterized by the highest possible degree of efficiency with the least expenditure of energy —in short, the rationalization of these traditional systems.

In the Japanese experience of modernization, the immediate goal was a modernized political system capable of controlling social action in such a manner as to produce strong social cohesiveness, which had not been attainable within the so-called "centralized feudal" system of the Tokugawa period (1600– 1867). Industrialization or the modernization of the economic system was thus only a means to achieve the first end. For modernization was Japan's response to the nineteenth-century challenge posed by the threatening military and economic aggression from abroad at a time when Tokugawa Japan was beset with continued unrest. And after the fall of the Tokugawa *bakufu*, it was a response to the challenge of continued infringement of Japan's sovereign rights by "extra-territoriality" and "uniform tariffs"—provisions of her "unequal treaties" with the Western powers—for as long as Japanese feudal institutions persisted.

We shall look at the Japanese experience in modernization from the perspective of almost a century later, when the consequences of actions taken can be clearly seen. From this historical perspective there is the danger of assuming that, because a measure had certain favorable consequences, these consequences were clearly foreseen and intended. We cannot, of course, say in every case how clearly the consequences were foreseen. The important point for us is the accomplishments of the Meiji reformers and not their prophetic abilities.

To modernize Japan, the leaders of the Meiji period—the Meiji oligarchs—sought within their society (which was not surprising at all because of Japan's comparative isolation from the rest of the world for more than two centuries) values meaningful to the Japanese that could serve both as mainsprings of motivation for the people to support modernization and as sanctions for necessary social changes entailing sacrifices and painful adjustments. The traditional values mobilized were the concepts of the emperor system and the family system. Both systems were powerful sources of motivation for conscious and purposeful action toward certain ends by means of the Confucian values of loyalty and filial piety.[1]

As simplified and reinterpreted by the Tokugawa scholars, who utilized Shinto beliefs and Confucian ethics, the emperor system includes the notion of a divine emperor, descended through unbroken lineage from divine ancestors, as the imperial sovereign. He is also coterminous with national polity (*kokutai*)[2] and the father of the nation, with the imperial house constituting the main house and the Japanese families its branches. The subject incurs duties toward the emperor as does a son to his parents; he owes loyalty to the emperor who is responsible for his well-being. In this context, the emperor system is the political expression of the family system, although the full notion of the "family state" only became explicit toward the end of the Meiji era.

Until the reforms of the Allied Occupation government were introduced, Japan's family system was the core of its social structure. A cohesive model for other basic social units, the family as a group was more important than the individuals composing it. Its lineage or its vertical ancestor-descendent relationship, traced to the male head of the house, made it essential for the house, composed of main and branch houses, to adopt a male heir in the absence of a son. Adoption was necessary because the head of the house undertook the worship of the house's ancestors who look after the continued prosperity of the house, a function that gave religious justification to the status of the house head within the family system. In return for the house head's interest in the house member's welfare, the latter had the duty of filial piety to the former, which took precedence over filial piety to his parents. On the other hand, filial piety to one's house was subordinated to loyalty to one's ruler. An individual who failed to behave accordingly suffered from "shame," "loss of face,"[3] or rejection by his social group. Conformity and hierarchy were the inevitable results; the individual was always aware of the group's judgment of his deeds. He was conditioned to recognize his "proper station" within the hierarchy,[4] to accept directions from above, and to submerge his interests in those of his group.

Under this scheme of social relations, the head of the house was central to the family system but constituted the lowest echelon within the emperor system. It is clear that even before Japan's modernization, the hierarchical superior-inferior relations manifested in the Japanese family system suggested tendencies away from personal to status loyalty, which can perhaps be viewed as "generalized particularism." That is, the family system was opened—in the sense of being made more universal—by such specific family mechanisms as adoption of a talented outsider into the family system, a step toward the universalistic relations in modern bureaucracies and industries. The Japanese family system also lacked the rigid familial boundaries of the Chinese family system, a precondition for modernization. Yet it manifested a strongly particularistic type of social control over nonconforming behavior. Patterns of dealing with nonconforming behavior were well defined: A son, for instance, had to abide by his mother's decision to break up his marriage even if he was happy with his wife.[5] His refusal to do so would have caused him "shame." The resulting conditioned behavior and unquestioning obedience to superior authority seem to have paved the way for the acceptance (with minimum opposition) of the revolutionary innovations the Meiji modernizers introduced into Japanese society.

These Meiji modernizers were among the group of *samurai* (military aristocrats of the Tokugawa period), aided by a few court nobles and wealthy merchants, who moved to restore full imperial power, which had been attenuated by the shogun's assumption of political powers during Japan's feudal period (the twelfth through the nineteenth centuries). Within the prevailing context of social action, this breaking through existing social forms was justified by the fact that these *samurai* were transferring their loyalty to the emperor, the restored legitimate head of the larger entity. And so disruption of the value of loyalty did not take place. The 1868 restoration of the emperor to the fullness of his sovereign powers ushered in Japan's modernization.

Meiji Political Reforms

It may not be out of place here to repeat that the modernization of the Tokugawa political system was the first task of Meiji Japan's leaders because of their desire to meet any foreign threat with confidence and because of their hopes for an early emancipation from the onerous "unequal treaties" with the Western powers. To rationalize the political system, the Meiji reformers mobilized both traditional values: the emperor system and the family system and the values of filial piety and loyalty embraced by these concepts.

We need not deal at length with the experiments in developing a central government to replace the complex system of the Tokugawas. What is important to note is that the first government established under a stipulation of the April, 1868, Imperial Charter—considered the basis of Meiji policy—was mainly inspired by the Chinese system, which held paramount the position of the emperor. Except for some modifications, the system functioned until the 1889 constitution provided for a permanent form of government. As the constitution was the emperor's gift to his people, his position as supreme head, by whom all rights were granted and to whom all duties were owed, was beyond the check of any organ of the political system.

Indeed, the Meiji social engineers manipulated the concept of the emperor system to effect a strong central government in Japan with powers symbolically concentrated in the emperor. The transfer of allegiance from the feudal lord to the nation-state, usually requiring time, was facilitated by substituting for the abstract idea of nation-state the concrete notion of the emperor as the father of the nation. Within a society undergoing revolutionary changes, as Japan was during the early Meiji period, the father image of a divine emperor also provided the people with an unchanging fixed source of authority, which aided the centralization of political control.

In the revival of the Shinto mythological concept of the emperor's divine origin and his position as head of the imperial system, religion strengthened the system by making it meaningful in an ultimate sense. That is, the individual's fulfillment of obligations to his superiors ensured for him continued blessings and ultimate protection from any difficulty or danger in this impermanent world. The family and nation partook of both secular and religious characteristics. And some kind of sacredness cloaked parents, house heads, and political superiors, who were intermediaries with, if not representatives of, the divine.[6] Such a view of the emperor system not only reinforced the central position of the emperor in the political system but also aided in achieving the rearrangement of centrifugal loyalties within the Tokugawa system into a direct vertical line of hierarchical ties from the emperor to the family, then the basic social unit of Japanese society, although not totally eliminating the possibility of factional cleavages between the several vertical structures subordinate to the emperor.

We need not go into the details of the establishment of provincial governments for purposes of unifying the nation under the throne. Suffice it to say that they included the feudal lords' return to the emperor of their registers of land and people and the subsequent organization of their feudal territories into prefectures directly under the emperor. The feudal lords and the *samurai* who lost their rice stipends were given pensions, which were commuted in 1876. Some of them invested their commuted pensions in business and in time became part of the rapidly increasing group of merchants, financiers, and industrialists of modern Japan. The abolition of feudal territories, the most crucial phase in the liquidation of the old order and the modernization of Japan's political system, was thus accomplished safely.

Two other laws fortified Japanese society's commitment to the centralized modern state with a divine emperor at the top. Because the efficiency and strength of the new political system depended largely upon a regular and adequate income to maintain the bureaucratic system and upon a national army to protect the state from internal and external threats, two essential laws were promulgated: the tax law and the conscription law. The first assured the government of a dependable income by providing that taxes be uniformly levied in cash instead of in kind, that taxes on land be based on assessed value, and that taxes be collected by agents of the central government. The second law ignored feudal class distinctions, which had already been legally abolished when the feudal lords surrendered their registers and fiefs to the emperor. In the conscript army, *Bushido*, a status ethic systematized during the Tokugawa period and emphasizing loyalty, was reoriented from a code of the *samurai* to that of the national army. Along with shinto beliefs, *Bushido* was a significant factor in the strength and cohesiveness of the modern Japanese army and an effective means of directing all loyalties toward a deified emperor. Commands of military officers were taken as dictates of the divine emperor and therefore had to be obeyed unquestioningly. The army became an instrument for carrying out the imperial will.

We have indicated that loyalty to the emperor, the social attitude of looking up to a superior, who was unquestioningly obeyed because he took charge of the individual's good and because he was divine, was duplicated in the family system. And so was the emperor's care for his subjects. It is needless to mention that the house head's obligation to take care of the members of his house, as well as the care of the father for his children, reduced the shock and pain of adjustment resulting from rapid and wrenching social changes. Because it was within the microcosmic replica of the larger entity that the process of internalizing traditional social norms that the reformers desired to preserve took place, the Japanese leaders sustained the family system in the civil code, one of the legal reforms of the Meiji period. Primogeniture, the basis for succession to the headship of the house, and the rights of the house head over the members of the house, both to represent them and to direct them in their activities, were legalized.[7]

The Meiji leaders, by the late 1880s, found it necessary, however, to reinforce the values of filial piety and loyalty (immanent in the emperor and family systems), which had undergone two decades of exposure to the dynamic influences of Western liberal ideas and rational thought. These forces inevitably aroused, however gradually and perhaps even silently, doubts about the vitality of the emperor and family systems. Nor could the development of modern industries and the concomitant growth of the market, to which the family gradually lost its economic functions, leave untouched the ideals of solidarity and the symbols of family authority. These developments, which threatened the modernizers' attempts to accommodate Western science within Eastern ethics were, in fact, the results of universal education instituted in 1872 and the process of industrialization. Until the 1880s, when the ethical basis of education was re-emphasized, education was utilitarian. It was a means of acquiring the tools of the West, its languages and its scientific and technical know-how, for the industrialization of the country—imperative for Japan's retention of political independence and her development into a "rich and strong country" comparable to the Western powers. In this undertaking, the Japanese leaders sent their own people abroad to learn all they could of Western science and technology and invited tutors from the West, from the United States, France, and Germany, for instance.

Between 1880 and 1890, as Western liberal ideas increasingly seeped into Japanese society, moral concepts were introduced into the educational system at all levels. Centralized control of education, including control of teachers, funds, curricula, and textbooks, made it possible for the leaders of Japanese modernization to manipulate the educational system for national ends. In 1890, because of the compelling need to preserve traditional values and to create greater ideological unity uncorrupted by Western ideas, the Imperial Rescript on Education was promulgated. It provided for the indoctrination of the Japanese in the traditional values of the divine emperor and the Confucian concept of loyalty and filial piety, as well as in such more modern precepts as respect for the constitution. Copies of the imperial decree were distributed to every school and were hung alongside the emperor's portrait, before which all made obeisance. The decree became almost the catechism (recited by all Japanese students) of a state cult. In an earlier move by the reformers to draw national loyalty to the emperor, an attempt to make Shinto the national religion was begun, but it had soon been subordinated to the principle of religious freedom, a principle subscribed to in the West. The function of building up a strong ideological unity was thus left to the educational system, which took charge of indoctrinating the students in the values of the emperor system and the family system, and to a cult of state Shinto, which was declared to be purely patriotic and "not a religion." The result was the intensification of conformity and unquestioning obedience to superior authority. Not that there was no one who behaved differently. But those who opposed or deviated were dealt with by the Meiji leaders also in the name of the emperor.

Loyalty to the emperor was the political strategy used by the government to hold the opposition at bay, but it was also a device utilized by some who opposed government policies.[8] The emperor system was especially potent when the emperor was considered coterminous with national polity (*kokutai*). This notion resulted from the identification of the emperor with the Shinto *kami*, interpreted as the pervading universal element. The equation implied that the will of the emperor was identical with the will of *kami*, which in turn became the source of motivation for the people to identify their wills with the emperor's, for they and the emperor were one in *kokutai*. We therefore find the reformers utilizing the Imperial Rescript—the emperor's statement of public policy or the expression of his desires and wishes (his will)—as an instrument to reconcile irreconcilable issues expected to arise during a period of social change.[9] Resolutions of conflicts of authority produced by rapid social innovations upsetting the old order were formally referred to the emperor for his decision or his will.[10] The emperor thus became the rallying point of all divergent groups. It did not matter very much to the Japanese if the supreme will of the emperor was preserved only in theory. For in fact it was the Meiji oligarchs who determined the emperor's "desires and wishes" and actually decided the policies of the modernizing state. Was it because loyalty to the emperor was status rather than personal loyalty?

The values of the emperor system and the family system were essential in smoothing the way toward modernizing Japan's political system. In the process of modernizing the system, therefore, two lines of development are observable: the centralization of the political system at one point, the emperor, who became the *sole* focus of national loyalty, a position never before enjoyed by him; the preservation of filial piety within the family system, a value similar to loyalty in its ability to motivate people to obey or to conform to the will of superior authority. Both developments, which motivated cohesive and disciplined response from the people, facilitated decision-making on policies regarding Japan's modernization and the speedy implementation of these policies. In such ways did the modernized political system acquire increasing power to channel disciplined social action toward national ends. One of them was the modernization of the economic system in the shortest time possible, while preserving the Japanese polity from foreign control.

Meiji Industrialization

Rapid industrialization of the economic system was of critical importance because Japan's traditional economy was being violently shaken under the disruptive impact of foreign trade and, if unmodified, could no longer endure as a base for political power. Industrialization was a means of building up the country's military strength—then the immediate national goal. A strong Japan could defend herself from any Western threat and could negotiate on the basis of equality the revision of the "unequal treaties." The dependence of the country's military defense upon its economy was aptly expressed in *Fukoku kyohei* (Rich country, strong army), an early Meiji slogan.

The major postrestoration economic problem was the speedy industrialization of Japan's feudal economy characterized by intense pressure on the land; meager resources; tradition-bound technology; a peasant population held in check only by widespread malnutrition, disease, and infanticide; isolation from the commercial and industrial revolutions of the West because of Japan's voluntary seclusion for about 250 years; and, finally, grinding poverty.[11]

It is obvious that under such economic circumstances, beside having to promulgate reform laws providing an environment favorable to economic development, laws like those leveling the feudal class barriers, providing freedom of occupational choice, decreeing uniform coinage, and establishing standard weights and measures, the Meiji leaders were faced with the specific problems of acquiring capital and an adequate labor force, as well as of planning the initial steps in the establishment of large-scale industries and the control of such industries to allow these reformers to manipulate them for the sake of national goals.

Once again, the Meiji social engineers fell back upon the traditional emperor and family systems, with their inherent values of filial piety and loyalty. Loyalty to the emperor required the people to help enhance by industrialization the greatness of the country over which their divine emperor ruled. Industrialization would keep the country abreast of the developments in the West responsible for the strength and power of the foreign countries then threatening Japan's territorial and sovereign integrity. Loyalty and filial piety to superior authority—father, house head, or lord—required high-level performance or strong achievement ethics and frugality. It was the duty of an individual to serve the head of his social group in the best way he could and to contribute as much as he could to the collective funds. All these duties were basic in channeling cohesive and highly motivated social action toward industrialization.

In Japan, the process of industrialization was hastened by certain pre-existing long-term economic developments favorable to the rationalization of the economic system. During the Tokugawa period, money was used as a means of exchange on a national scale. Although the different feudal territories did not use a uniform system of coinage and taxes as well as *samurai* stipends were generally paid in kind, the existence of the cash nexus implied that a universalistic means of exchange had emerged in Tokugawa society.[12] Universalism was also evident in the relations between employers and free labor, that is, laborers who did not own any of the means of production and who worked for wages either in agriculture or in premodern industries, even though wages were usually turned over to the laborer's family head and often saved in part to finance his marriage later on.[13] Tokugawa society witnessed the rise of rural capitalists who not only owned land but also engaged in money lending, trading, and the industries.[14] Experience in investing accumulated capital in productive enterprises was thus not wanting during the postrestoration period. Institutions that functioned like banks made possible flexible financing. Technology was mainly traditionalistic and usually ritualistic, but standardization of certain products[15] seems to have been widespread, a precondition for the introduction of the one-price system, a universalistic norm of a modern society.[16]

To industrialize Japan, the Meiji leaders' first problem was to decide the means of acquiring capital. Capital was needed to purchase industrial machines and to construct industrial plants; to employ foreign technical and organizational experts; to train Japanese managers, engineers, and industrial labor; and to build roads, bridges, railways, ships—all of which are essential to an industrial society. Furthermore, funds were required to liquidate feudal society[17] and to pay the Tokugawa government's indebtedness, not to mention the funds that had to be expended to underwrite the major innovations of the Meiji leaders' reform program like the new bureaucratic government, the educational system, and the conscript army.

To secure capital, the Meiji reformers refrained from large-scale foreign borrowings[18] lest Japan meet a fate like that of China.[19] Instead, they turned to their society for necessary capital. The process of solidifying "surplus" income available within the country into capital for financing government projects and liabilities could have caused a revolution or serious uprisings[20] in another society but not in Japan, where the values of loyalty and filial piety immanent in the emperor and family systems motivated the people—mainly peasants[21]—to part with their current income for the new government's reform program and justified the government means of siphoning "surplus" income by manipulating the evaluation of taxable land under the new tax law. Under the law, land tax was to be levied on the assessed value of the land. After the rate of taxation was determined, the weight of the tax burden was placed upon the peasants by arbitrarily assessing the value of the land (that is, not based on its market value) in such a manner as to guarantee sufficiently high total returns not less than the extremely high returns from land taxes in the last Tokugawa period.[22] When it is considered that the old method involved the payment in kind of a definite portion of the total harvest, it is easy to see that an unvarying cash tax from year to year inflicted privation, however acceptable, on the peasants. The value system that emphasized achievement was partly responsible for abiding peasant incentives to work hard in the face of decreasing individual gains from his labor on the land because of heavy taxation. It also cushioned the stress and strain of forced savings for distant and half-understood goals of the nation.

The traditional peasant's habit of taking his "proper station" within the hierarchy of his social unit and being loyal to the head of the larger unit encompassing it emphasized the importance of the family system, the microcosm of the imperial system, in conserving traditional habits of thought and attitudes. The Meiji reformers left local affairs under the control of the cohesive village organization, which survived as a center of co-operative action, communal or village resources, religious ceremonies, and other functions. The headman was the key figure in co-ordinating the cohesive action of the clusters of families constituting the village. As long as farming continued to be undertaken by the family organization using hand labor to work small units of land and as long as the extensive system of ditches, dams, ponds, tunnels, and water gates necessary for wet rice culture was collectively owned, the values of the family system would persist. Solidarity and obedience within a peasant family are matters of survival. Each member of the family is therefore taught the traditional values that unconsciously govern his behavior even outside the family.

Availability of a labor force sufficiently trained and mobile and psychologically oriented to the new ways of an industrial society is a precondition for industrialization of a country on a nation-wide scale. This prerequisite was not a major problem for the Meiji reformers because of certain economic developments during the Tokugawa period.

Among these developments was the experience of working for wages, mentioned earlier, which resulted from the rise in Japan of commercial farming, landlordism, and tenancy around the second half of the eighteenth century. The process of peasant expropriation moved faster than the development of capitalism both in agriculture and in urban industry, thus producing a vast body of "stagnant surplus population" either taken care of by the family or sent to the city by the family to keep its finances viable. Because of the inability of urban industries to absorb the swelling labor force, however, people were soon driven back to their families. The importance of the values of the family system in this instance cannot be overestimated. Because they aided the individual and the family as a social unit in adjusting to changing economic conditions of the early Meiji period, the values of the family system accounted for the comparative stability of the base of Japanese society while the Meiji leaders introduced revolutionary innovations from the top.

Beside the availability of a labor force that could respond to monetary incentives, making it relatively easy to draw peasants away from the village to the city, to separate them from their families, and to encourage them to work in factories, there was the added advantage in postrestoration Japan of an existing labor force half-trained in rural industries that had been spawned in the countryside during the Tokugawa period. This labor already possessed "quickness of hand and eye, a respect for tools and materials and adaptability to the cadences and confusion of moving parts."[23] Laborers were comparatively ready to train for work in modern industries. Between 1868 and 1881, the first period of modern Japan's industrialization, foreign teachers were employed by the Meiji government to teach this labor force modern industrial technology.[24] The organization of the industries that employed this labor force was, however, modeled after the family and motivated by the values of filial piety and loyalty.

The family pattern of organizing industries was a survival of premodern handicrafts industries, which persisted in both the small-scale and large-scale industries of modern Japan. The policy of the Meiji leaders toward industrialization intensified the Meiji industries' commitment to this type of organization. For these reformers desired an industrial system that could easily be controlled by the political system for national goals.

Because accumulated private capital was generally at a low level and capitalists were "too weak, too timid, and too inexperienced to undertake development,"[25] the government had no alternative but to act as entrepreneur, financier, and manager during the early stage of Japan's industrialization. Initiating industrialization in Japan and sustaining it could be done only by a government able to tax the people and to motivate them, by means of the values of the emperor and family systems, willingly to pay their taxes.

To invest the amalgamated "surplus" income in strategic industries, that is, in the heavy industries, including mining, ship building, and railways and telegraph, necessary for national defense, also called for an appeal to the values of the emperor and family systems because industrialization at that stage did not result in tangible benefits for the people.[26] The divine emperor desired the people to contribute all they could to the development of these industries in order to guard Japanese polity (*kokutai*) against the foreign powers. In the face of straitened financial circumstances early in the 1880s, however, the government was forced to sell at low prices the peripheral industries not directly contributing to the military needs of the state to favored families who had supported the leaders of the restoration turned Meiji reformers.

As a result of these relations between the government and the families who were to constitute the *Zaibatsu* or the "financial clique" of modern Japan, the country's industries continued to serve state goals. The ties with the government, further strengthened by various forms of paternalistic government subsidy to the *Zaibatsu* families, preserved the traditional awareness of hierarchy and the habit of looking up to superior authority for decision, aid, and guidance. *Zaibatsu* industrial concerns were thus closely related to the political system.

As previously pointed out, the *Zaibatsu* families' large-scale industries manifested their commitment to the hierarchic ties of the family system and the emperor system. To illustrate, let us briefly look into the Mitsui family industrial and business combine, which, like the other *Zaibatsu* combines, modeled its organization after that of the family. Hierarchic ties of loyalty between the Mitsui house head and the numerous family members and employees strongly integrated the complex and interlocking Mitsui combine. The Mitsui house council dominated by the head of the main family of the house of eleven families (before it was dissolved in 1946) regulated not only the business but also the personal lives of family members. Everything, from marriage, divorce, and adoption to handling corporate investment, savings, and profit distribution involving members of the eleven families, required the action of the house council. And even though the house council was not incorporated, its business decisions took precedence over those of the Mitsui *honsha* ("top holding company").[27] When the Mitsui house, because of an inadequate number of family members trained in management, was forced to fill executive positions of subsidiary companies with recruits from the cream of the university business faculty's graduates, who had to undergo periods of apprenticeship within any of the Mitsui enterprises, the relationship between these executives and the Mitsui house head became one of ritual kinship. It was not unusual for some of them to marry into the Mitsui house. As for the other employees, the strict house code of the Mitsui house called for absolute loyalty. Upon entering the service of any of the Mitsui companies, each employee was made to sign a written oath of loyalty to the house. Transfer from one *Zaibatsu* family combine to another, which hardly ever took place, was considered "shameful."[28]

It is needless to point out here that obedience, high-level performance, and frugality motivated by loyalty tended not only to assure the solidarity and efficiency of the *Zaibatsu* industrial and business combines but also to ease government manipulation of these combines for the service of the state: The *Zaibatsu* house head had influence over the individuals within the family combine. Government control over large-scale *Zaibatsu* combines extended down to the house heads of the small-scale plants or factories of five to fifty workers that crowded the cities and dotted the rural scene.

These traditional small industries, although less capitalistic and less modern, were very productive, were socially stabilizing in that they did not uproot the peasant population, and were able to absorb part of the increasing labor population. Depending largely on loans from local merchants and banks working within the *Zaibatsu* financial network, on small trading companies subsidized by the *Zaibatsu*, or on larger plants (also dependent on the financial and marketing aids of the *Zaibatsu*) that assembled parts of products (like bicycles) manufactured in these workshops, modern Japan's small-scale industries were indirectly subject to *Zaibatsu* and ultimately government control and manipulation. For instance, shifting the type of production and improving standards were dictated from above rather than by competitive market situations.

Unquestioning obedience to directions from superior au-

thority was possible because small-scale enterprises were organized on the basis of family organization. The entrepreneur
was usually the family head—a farmer or a townsman—and the
family members supplied the labor. Additional workers might be
recruited; they were assimilated within the family pattern
through long periods of apprenticeship under the house head,
who not only took care of their training but also of their personal needs, as a father would take care of his children. The
value of the family system released motivations for rigid discipline and long hours of work, which resulted in an unbelievably
low overhead for these small workships and certainly contributed
to the economic development of Japan.

These small-scale plants produced consumer goods for the
local market, which persisted in demanding local products because foreign ones were unfamiliar to the people as a result of
Japan's long isolation from the rest of the world. Consequently,
small-scale industries enabled the country to retain much-needed
capital for investment. Furthermore, these consumer goods, especially silk,[29] constituted Japan's main export during the early
period of modernization, which allowed Japan to pay for its
imported capital goods and know-how. Lockwood, an authority
on modern Japan's economic development, describes the decisive
contribution of Japan's small-scale industries to the country's
economic development: "The growth of Japan's agriculture and
other basic industries* built on ancient foundations . . . enabled
the island empire to support the growing population and expand-
ing political commitments . . ." during the early period of Japan's
modernization.[30] He continues, "Through a steady modernization
they produced the rising national income which supported large
State budgets for armament and colonial development. They provided the exports to pay for much of the heavy import of mu-
nitions, machinery, and other essentials for strategic industries.
Despite these charges upon the national dividend, they were the
means by which Japan carried herself through the first stages of

* most of them consumer goods industries.

economic development and emerged from her agrarian-feudal background to take on the aspects of modern industrial power."[31]

The rationalization of the economic system of Japanese society, which resulted in economic growth, was, however, the result of the system's subservience to the goals of the state. The speed of industrialization was not matched by a rapid rise of levels of living for the mass of the peasant population and urban workers.[32] Neither did the rationalization of the political and economic systems develop individual initiative and personal freedom. For the values of the emperor and family systems mobilized to hasten modernization froze the hierarchic ties within the society, and unquestioning obedience by the people to superior authority was manifested not only in the social system but also in the political and economic systems—all co-ordinated to serve the immediate goal of Japan: the freedom of the country from fear of foreign threat and violation of Japan's sovereign rights. Extending the good life to the people, who were called upon to make sacrifices for the sake of the country's modernization, was not an immediate end of Japan's modernization. Any improvement of the levels of living was incidental.[33]

Because of the values of the emperor and family systems, the Japanese leaders who worked behind the symbol of the emperor and decided for the nation what to change and what not to change were able to retain their strong control of the social, political, and economic systems of Japanese society.[34] Within these systems, the momentum of the process of rationalization or modernization, once started under such powerful leadership, continued with much force, pushing Japan into four major wars between the restoration and the end of the last Pacific war, for the sake of Japanese polity or *kokutai*. It seems ironic that the modernization or rationalization of Japanese society that was undertaken in the Meiji period for the purpose of warding off Japan's fall before the Western powers would, within a period of less than a century, lead to Japan's defeat by the Allied powers of the West.

Some Lessons for Asia

The values of the emperor and family systems were indeed successfully mobilized by the Meiji reformers in the process of rapidly modernizing Japan, the only Asian power strong enough to challenge a Western power until 1950. Can any of the developing countries of South and Southeast Asia repeat Japan's feat in modernizing a "feudal" society within a generation? Only time will tell. We must, however, not lose sight of the fact that the sociocultural and historical context of Japan's modernization precludes a one-to-one duplication of Japan's experience in the developing countries of South and Southeast Asia today. Yet, in addition to showing the possibility of mobilizing traditional values in the process of modernizing a country, the experience of Japan can yield these countries a few suggestions.

First, it demonstrates the need for strong and *responsible leadership*. I emphasize *responsible leadership* for a country that desires to modernize as fast as possible. Sacrifices have to be made not only by the bulk of the population but also by the leaders themselves. The early Meiji reformers—ambitious, restless, and imaginative as they were—did not aim for self-enrichment but devoted themselves to work for the nation, so that it could speedily transform itself into a modern state with the necessary power and prestige to face any foreign country. The early Meiji entrepreneurs likewise worked for the state. Achievement-oriented and frugal, they invested their capital in productive enterprises rather than in nonproductive investments like jewels, expensive clothes worn for single occasions, and other forms of conspicuous consumption.[35]

Second, Japanese experience shows the importance of determining the goal of modernization, as well as the time required in reaching this goal, and for keeping it always within the view of the leaders and the people. The Meiji leaders had one goal: the speedy release of Japan from fear of foreign attack and infringement upon her sovereign rights by the Western powers. This goal was presented in terms of traditional values understandable to the people. Tangible proofs of progress toward it effectively convinced the people that their sacrifices had not been in vain. They could look forward to a "rich and strong" Japan that would some day take its place among the powers of the world—as it eventually did. Not observable in the Japanese experience is the impatience or mass disillusionment with the rate of progress in economic development evident in most countries of South and Southeast Asia today. The usual response of these countries' governments to such public discontent has been *disproportional allocation* of their limited resources to "social" investments like consumer goods and housing rather than to "productive" improvements in agricultural technology, industry, and the like, thus retarding the rationalization of the economic system.

Third, there is the significance of strong national group consciousness and solidarity in Japan's modernization. A country with a common language and culture that escaped Western colonization, practically closed to the rest of the world for more than two centuries before her period of modernization, Japan, during the period of modernization, was not faced with vexing problems similar to those now facing South and Southeast Asian countries. I should like to cite a few of these problems here:

1. There is the need for trained people to fill positions of leadership in the political and economic spheres suddenly left vacant by the withdrawal of colonial control over these countries (Japan did not suffer from such dislocation; she trained men to fill positions as they were needed by the modernizing state).
2. There is also the existence of pluralistic societies manifested not only in unassimilated immigrants but often also in the diversity of the indigenous ethnic, linguistic, and religious groupings. Not that pluralism in a society is in itself a deterring factor in social change. There is some evidence to support the contrary assumption, that it could actually induce change, given certain conditions. What is suggested is that it is relatively easier to stimulate action toward common

goals within a homogeneous group that shares deeply rooted values than within a heterogeneous one.

3. Finally there is overurbanization developed by the "push" factors of low-levels of rural living and conditions of physical insecurity rather than by the "pull" factors represented by job opportunities and higher levels of living. This development is a recent manifestation of a historical fact: the emergence of the "great" or "primate" city in South and Southeast Asia, which serves as an entrepôt linking the imperial Western power and the local population in the colonial system. Among other things, overurbanization results in *disproportionate allocation* of limited resources to development in urban areas relative to rural areas, when agricultural development should have priority in the total plan of economic development.

Fourth, Japan's experience shows the urgency of establishing a political system stable and powerful enough to channel cohesive social action in the attainment of national ends. Meiji Japan's government, centralized around a divine emperor and strengthened by the values of the emperor and family systems, was able to magnetize centrifugal feudal loyalties and to solidify "surplus" income siphoned from the people for capital to finance Japan's modernization. There was a relative absence of what is referred to as the "atomism" or "individuation" evident in societies of South and Southeast Asia, which is the result of placing personal ambitions and familial loyalty above state goals. "Atomism" is especially manifest in the extreme competition and frequent conflicts for top positions and complete control among the relatively few officials, professional men, and technicians in these societies. The attention and energy of these trained men are thus concentrated on eliminating all competition in their struggles and maintaining power for personal or family ends rather than on attaining national goals. In the Japanese experience of modernization, the Meiji reformers saw that men needed for Japan's modernization were trained and then placed in positions where they could best utilize what they had learned and thus maximize their contribution to the modernizing state. Useless waste of training because qualified men are kept from positions that those in power continue to hold in addition to other important positions is not part of Japan's experience.

These suggestions are but a few that can be drawn from Japan's experience in modernization. Of course the example of Japan must be perused not only for its positive suggestions but also for its negative aspects, which may serve as warnings for all later modernizing nations. Before leaders of South and Southeast Asia can profit from the Japanese case, however, they must first look into their own societies, as the Meiji reformers did, to take stock of its problems, its human and material resources, and its sociocultural and historical heritage. Such knowledge is also necessary in considering which of a society's traditional values can be mobilized to speed up the process of modernization in each developing country.

What pre-eminent values in the society can be used as mainsprings of planning and action? What results, deliberate as well as incidental, may be anticipated? Which values may be safely countermanded by plans? Is it a case of either-or, that is to say, of a rejection of traditional values with an adoption of modernization schemes? Or the maintenance of such values at the cost of modernization? Or is there some intermediate possibility? These questions are some of those that need to be asked. Only a searching, disinterested scrutiny can reveal possible answers. In any case, the developing nations of South and Southeast Asia have to take action in order to achieve what seems a common desire: economic advancement. The question is Shall we of South and Southeast Asia act intelligently by weighing the facts and obtaining as certain knowledge as possible about our respective societies. Or shall we extemporize as each situation arises, preferring intuitive solutions? Or shall we depend on foreign assistance programs, which usually entail their own approaches to implementing social changes within a society, approaches that may not be based on the sociocultural context of the receiving nation? The choice is ours, but it is a critical choice, one that may well decide the future of our respective nations.

Notes

1. In Japan the ethical system of Confucius, involving filial piety and loyalty, was modified to fit the country's social system. See R. Benedict, *The Chrysanthemum and the Sword* (Boston: Houghton Mifflin Company, 1946), pp. 117–8.

2. For Aizawa Seishisai's concept of *kokutai*, one of the teachings of the influential Mito school of Tokugawa Japan, see R. Tsunoda, *et al.*, comps., *Sources of Japanese Tradition* (New York: Columbia University Press, 1958), pp. 597–600.

3. For more details on the concept of "shame" or "loss of face," see R. Benedict, *op. cit.*, pp. 222–7, 288–9.

4. See *ibid.*, Chapter III.

5. See *ibid.*, p. 121.

6. R. N. Bellah, *Tokugawa Religion, the Values of Pre-Industrial Japan* (New York: The Free Press, 1957), p. 194.

7. See K. Steiner, "The Revision of the Civil Code of Japan: Provisions Affecting the Family," The Far Eastern Quarterly, II, No. 2 (February, 1950), 177–82.

8. To illustrate, the Parliamentary Rescript of the emperor in 1881 was meant to check the opposition demand for the speedy establishment of the parliamentary system of Japan. Saigo Takamori, the leader of the 1877 Satsuma Rebellion—the first and last major threat to Japan's internal security—also justified his act of treason in terms of loyalty to the emperor.

9. For instance, the issue in the early 1880s regarding the advisability of borrowing ¥50 million from London to redeem government paper money as a measure to restore its value, which threatened to split the Meiji oligarchy, was referred to the emperor for his decision. See T. C. Smith, *Political Change and Industrial Development in Japan: Government Enterprise, 1868–1880* (Stanford: Stanford University Press, 1955), pp. 97–8.

10. Ike mentions a conflict of authority between two members of the oligarchy—Okuma and Ito—which was decided by the emperor. See N. Ike, *The Beginnings of Political Democracy in Japan* (Baltimore: The Johns Hopkins Press, 1950), pp. 94–6.

11. W. W. Lockwood, *The Economic Development of Japan. Growth and Structural Change, 1868–1938* (Princeton: Princeton University Press, 1954), p. 501.

12. Money had been used in Japan even before the Tokugawa period but not on a nation-wide scale. For details on the historical background of money economy in Japan, see D. M. Brown, *Money Economy in Medieval Japan. A Study in the Use of Coins* (New Haven: Institute of Far Eastern Languages, Yale University, 1951).

13. See T. C. Smith, *The Agrarian Origins of Modern Japan* (Stanford: Stanford University Press, 1954), p. 212.

14. On the accumulation of commercial and usury capital, see C. D. Sheldon, *The Rise of the Merchant Class in Tokugawa Japan, 1600–1868* (New York: J. J. Augustin Inc. Publisher, 1958), especially Chapters IV and VIII. See also Smith, *Agrarian Origins*, especially Chapters VI and VII.

15. Like the standardization of sizes of floor mats, clothing, and housing materials. See Bellah, *op. cit.*, p. 29.

16. *Ibid.*, pp. 27–30.

17. For instance, to pay *samurai* pensions and later to underwrite their commutations.

18. Foreign borrowings between December, 1867, and June, 1881, were limited to two small loans negotiated with London, which were self-liquidating. See Table XVI in Smith, *Political Change*, p. 75.

19. After 1842, when China signed the treaty ending the first Anglo-Chinese war, which was followed by similar treaties signed with the other Western powers, she ceased to exercise full control over her territory. Foreign encroachment upon China's territorial and sovereign integrity through such various means as money loans to pay her war indemnity, to build railways, to develop mines, and the like continued until it reached a peak in 1898. By then Japan was already one of the participants.

20. Agrarian uprisings did take place during the first decade of the Meiji period (1868–1878). In fact, there were 190 agrarian uprisings within this period as compared by Professor Kakusho Iwao (cited by E. H. Norman) to a total of fewer than 600 during 256 years of Tokugawa rule. Yet, no one of these uprisings developed into proportions serious enough to make it difficult for the government conscript army or the police force (which was a vital element in maintaining law and order during the critical transitional years) to suppress it. See Norman, *Japan's Emergence as a Modern State* (New York: Institute of Pacific Relations, 1940), pp. 72–3, 118.

21. According to T. C. Smith, in the 1870s no less than 70% of the population was engaged in agriculture as a primary occupation. See Smith, *Political Change*, p. 30.

22. *Ibid.*, p. 79. See also the chart "Sources of Japanese Government Revenue," showing what percentage of the total government revenue between 1875 and 1889 came from land taxes, Norman, *op. cit.*, p. 77.

23. Smith, *Agrarian Origins*, p. 212.

24. See Smith, *Political Change*, pp. 8–9, 48, 58–9.

25. *Ibid.*, p. 102.

26. Lockwood enumerates the factors that accounted for the lag between the improvement of living levels of the mass of peasants, as well as of urban workers, and rapid industrialization or economic development of Japan. Lockwood, *op. cit.*, pp. 140–3.

27. See T. A. Bisson, *Zaibatsu Dissolution in Japan* (Berkeley: University of California Press, 1954), pp. 9–10.

28. *Ibid.*, pp. 26–8, 32.

29. Regarding the growing foreign demand for Japanese silk that permitted the country to acquire a dominant position in the world market before World War I, see Lockwood, *op. cit.*, pp. 27–8.

30. *Ibid.*, p. 34.

31. *Ibid.*

32. Lockwood explains the reasons for the continued depressed living standards in Japan. *Ibid.*, pp. 140–3.

33. Lockwood describes the rise in consumption levels in Japan, especially in the early twentieth century. *Ibid.*, pp. 143–50.

34. It should be noted that the Meiji oligarchy essentially lost control in 1914. Since then Japan's leadership has alternated between more liberal and more authoritarian elements, but an examination of the later phases of Japan's modernization falls outside the scope of this paper.

35. The problems of South and Southeast Asia that are discussed in this part of the paper have been suggested by an article by Prof. P. M. Hauser, "Cultural and Personal Obstacles to Economic Development in the Less Developed Areas," *Human Organization*, XVIII, No. 2 (Summer, 1959), 78–84.

The Discussion

THE DISCUSSIONS in Manila lasted for six days, during which ten separate sessions were held. The transcript of the complete tape recording amounts to about 550 pages of typescript. The editor was thus faced with a formidable task of condensation if he was to present the results of the discussion within the compass of a single chapter. A running summary seemed the least satisfactory solution, and consequently it was decided to select a cross section of the discussion for complete presentation so that at least some of the ideas and points of view in all their concreteness and particularity could be suggested. The editor has chosen selections from the early sessions, which proved suggestive for later discussions and which had a certain degree of continuity and interrelationship among themselves. They are not necessarily the most interesting things said at the conference, but taken together they do represent the range of concerns expressed. The reader is reminded that, in the introduction, the editor has already commented at some length on the major conceptual axes along which the discussions developed. It is regrettable that space forbids a full documentation of the ways various ideas mentioned there were set forth.

The following remarks by Mr. Geertz were delivered as a

commentary on Soedjatmoko's keynote paper and opening statement at the first working session of the conference. Succeeding
comments were usually separated by other remarks not repro-
duced here.

Mr. Geertz: It seems to me that the first thing that both the design of the seminar and everything that Mr. Soedjatmoko said
this afternoon suggest is that we need, in our discussions, to keep
constantly in mind the distinction between what I would call
the cultural level and what I would call the social structural level,
that is, the level of notions, of ideas, of values, of orientations to
the divine and the sacred, on the one hand, and actual social
organizations, social structures, class systems, levels of economic
development, on the other. If we mix these two, or forget one or
the other, the discussion might become somewhat barren. A discussion only of the intellectual content of various religious
systems or various traditional value systems more or less independently of the kind of social conditions under which the new
states and nations are operating is likely to turn into a kind of
academicism that is not too profitable. On the other hand, a simple
decline into the details of economic development as it is usually
thought of, of savings, investment, and the organization of production, while useful, would of course defeat the entire purpose
of this seminar. Somehow or other we have to do what has been
for the sociology of religion characteristically its central task,
that is, to keep within the same framework—and I am not going
to offer a framework, because I am not sure how this can be done
—the conceptual intellectual belief aspects of religion and its
social institutionalization.

   To give an example, one that Mr. Soedjatmoko has been
talking about in his paper today, we can look at the identity
problem that was the main basis of his paper on somewhat these
lines, as a model of how one needs to think about these things.
Because it seems to me that there are at least two sources of
identity in the new states. One is a sense of identity that comes
essentially from the past, from what the people in the society

seem to take as the "givens" of their social existence—they are just there; they are Muslims because they were born into a Muslim society; they are Tamils because they were born to Tamil-speaking parents. This whole sense of identity that comes as an inheritance, as a heritage from the past, is the real essence of one's personality everywhere in the world. On the other hand, there is also the sense of identity that looks more to the future and that comes from the polity in which one is involved, the state in which one is engaged, the direction of one's whole country, the policies that it hopes to carry out, its aspirations, and so on.

So that the first kind of identity problem in the new nations (and I think Mr. Soedjatmoko is quite right that there is an extremely severe identity crisis in almost all of these countries) is, in Mazzini's famous phrase, the wish "to exist and to have a name," to know who one is, to be somebody, to decide what one is linguistically, culturally, and, in our case here particularly, religiously; to know what this means as an essential part of themselves.

On the other hand, there is a second kind of identity. There is what Mr. Shils calls "the will to be modern," the will to be part of the international world, to be respected as a member of a modern state that is like other modern states, that plays its role in a world of modern states. In a sense, this is the fatal ambiguity in English between the terms "nation" and "state," which seems to me terribly important in this connection. There is always a persistent problem in aligning them, because the boundaries of the polity very rarely, particularly in the new states, coincide with the boundaries of the given cultural traditions that define people. Japan is in a sense a limiting case for this situation; it is one place where the ethnic and to a certain extent the religious and cultural community coincide as highly as it perhaps has ever coincided, within the boundaries of the national state. But, if one thinks of India or Indonesia or the Philippines, certainly this is not the case. There is the problem of aligning these two sorts of identity and keeping them straight—one of which is I think an essentially conceptual one and the other essentially a social structural one. So what is identity on the cultural level is a problem of social integration and social organization on the sociological level.

And so, as I say, we need in thinking about a problem like this to have a kind of double image. And this sort of thinking has been extremely difficult to sustain in the first stages of the development of the new states since independence. Because of the fear of disintegration, the fear of dissolution, the weakness of the polities; because they were born out of almost no recent political tradition; because of colonial experience, there has been a tremendous fear of political disintegration that might go with any real facing of the facts of internal diversity, ethnic differentiation, religious differentiation, and so on. The response to this of course has been what Mr. Soedjatmoko calls a concentration on virtual images—a creation, in a sense almost by fear, of the nationality to go with these new states. This creation often involves an insistence whose very shrillness betrays the sense that lies below it of the fact that there are really two problems here: that a particular Indonesian is at one time both a Javanese in a cultural sense from the past and an Indonesian in the future sense of where he is going; that an Indian is both a Bengali, in terms of the great cultural tradition of Bengal and the religious tradition of Hinduism, and at the same time a part of an emerging India. In attempting to think about this problem clearly one must be able to face this double image, face the fact that one really has in a sense two identities, that one has—again to use another term that Mr. Shils has used—a primordial loyalty to one's group, that one can never really escape. On the other hand, one has what he calls a sentiment of civility toward the whole state, a loose attachment toward the general state, a commitment to it. One must be able to keep these things disentangled. But this is not to say that they are not related. In fact, the whole problem here is to show exactly how they are related. I just want to use this as an example of the initial necessity I talked about of discussing always at one and the same time both (in my terms) cultural and social structural issues.

The other thing, which I think follows from this, is that we must be very careful, in discussing these matters, not to fall into the logic of false dichotomies, which has been the characteristic trait of so much of sociology and anthropology from the days of the *Gemeinschaft* and *Gesellschaft* distinction forward. Here I am raising the question of whether the simple dichotomy of traditional versus modern is really a very useful way of thinking about things. In talking about these two kinds of identity I have been trying to emphasize not that they are opposed but that they are concurrent, that they will persist, that people will have these problems all the time, that they interact with each other in a systematic relationship, that it is not a simple matter of one versus the other. It is not a simple matter of tradition versus modernization, a simple matter of, the more of one, the less of the other. A distinction between the industrial process and the value process again must not be thought of in this kind of simple *yin-yang* opposition but as actually a variable in some sort of systematic process. This makes thinking a great deal more difficult because dichotomies are very easy ways to think about things, but they are, in my opinion, misleading.

The third general point that I would like to make concerns the kind of conceptual style we should adopt in attacking our problem. (Not the ideas that we should have, for I am not trying to put forth any propositions here, and any that I have put forth I will immediately withdraw my support from as soon as I am challenged.)

In that connection, the only emphasis we need to have is a very strong one not on how much we know but how little. We really don't know much about any of the things we are discussing here this afternoon, and we won't know much more about them by Saturday. It is really not possible for us to give reasoned answers to questions; I think what we need at this point are reasoned questions. We should spend a great deal of our time not trying to decide whether Hinduism or Islam or Buddhism or whatever is or is not modernizing, is or is not functional for the advancement of progress, and so on, but rather trying to think out what kinds of question we need to ask about these things, about these religions, and about these systems in order to think productively about them.

Just as a series of examples I'll list some things that I think we know virtually nothing about.

The first thing that we know obviously very little about, and it seems to me that it would be almost prerequisite to any kind of a definitive discussion of this sort—and of course we didn't come here to have a definitive discussion—would be the changes in the religions now going on. We know very little about really what is happening to Hinduism, to Buddhism, to Islam, or to Christianity in the Philippines, exactly what changes are occurring. In the informal "hallway" discussions at conferences such as these, one hears, all the time, fragmentary references to conflicts within religions, to different positions, to changes, but somehow they don't get into the formal presentations. The mere use of such terms as "Islam," "Buddhism," "Christianity," and so on, tends to make us think of a religion as a kind of block, an eternal object that is always the same—somehow outside of the historical process. But of course religion is not just a barrier to the changes that are going on in the modern world but is very much caught up in them, and these changes are going on now. And we know almost nothing about them; perhaps we will know more by the time we are finished here, but I still think that a great deal of very careful work has to be done. And we might think about the kinds of question that should be asked in this connection.

Another thing we don't know very much about, it seems to me, which is also central to our topic, is how the religious experience proper, which Mr. Soedjatmoko spoke about as the agony of private experience, the direct encounter with the divine in one form or another, how this reflects back on secular values, how men are changed once they have what they regard as contact with the divine or relationship with the divine, how this then changes their attitude toward secular matters. There are the great Weber studies in this area, but beyond that we have gone almost nowhere in thinking about the relationship between religious experience proper—the actual ritual experience, the actual worship experience that people have—and the kinds of mentality they have in the cold light of day when they are not being properly religious in the narrow sense of the term. That is, what effect does their religious experience have on their secular life?

Another thing we know almost nothing about is what the late Robert Redfield called the "social structure of tradition": how people learn traditional values, how they are transmitted, how they are distributed within the population, who holds which ones, what persons and what roles in society mediate them, how they mediate them, and so forth and so on.

There are lots of other questions that could be raised. I will give one more example. If I am right about the importance of a sense of identity from the past and how one views one's culture, then we need to know much more than we know about how religion affects this, because religion is only one of a number of things which affect it. We know that geography affects it, where you live affects it, what kinds of custom you follow affect it, and the role of religion in this situation, in defining one's identity, it seems to me, is not a constant but varies. If one thinks—this is quite offhand—of Chinese civilization compared with Indian civilization, the role of religious ideas and the divine in India seems much greater than it was in China. There are other contrasts one can make in the way in which religion enters into the consciousness of who one is. And even within a single society, as Mr. Soedjatmoko mentioned in passing, there is a tremendous variation in what people believe and how important it is to them. Some people seem to see almost every item of daily life under the aegis of their religious beliefs. They see everything, so to speak, under the aspect of the divine. Others much less so—they leave much wider areas of life to the merely secular. Not necessarily less religious, at least by general definition (they may be extremely pious). They are less concerned, for example, with extending their religious commitments to the details of business transactions. About all these matters we know almost nothing. And I think a proper humility will be useful to us here, rather than holding forth about matters which none of us here—and no one anywhere else—knows anything about.

In sum, I think we should try to ask questions instead of answering them—we just don't know enough. I am reminded, in conclusion, of an aphorism, overstated as aphorisms always are, by Jacques Berque, the French sociologist and anthropologist, that there are no underdeveloped countries, just under-analyzed ones.

Mr. Sayigh: I would like to throw some doubt as to the universality of the desire for development. How do we know that people really want development? We impute the desire for development to the masses, but there is the question whether people want development or not. The question Who are the modernizers? is not merely a rhetorical question. I think it is a very practical question for our purposes, because once we decide who the modernizers are, where the locus of the desire for development resides, we can tell to what extent there are cultural blocks or cultural hesitation in the way to development. Therefore, I think it will be essential for us, especially when we talk about specific countries, to locate the desire for development and to locate also the seat for decision-making in that specific society. Then it would be easier to speculate on the cultural motivation to development that exists in that society or, conversely, tends to block it.

I would like, in addition to this point, to suggest also that if we think of modernizers as a small group in society—and I personally have sympathy with that kind of view—then we should remember that almost by definition our modernizers are rebels. If so, then they are less bound by cultural ties and blocks than the mass of the people for whom development is being designed. And therefore it makes quite a difference in talking about the weight of the cultural factor, whether we are talking about the modernizers who are the initiators of development or the general population who are the beneficiaries of development.

One last comment in connection with something said with regard to economic growth as an inadequate definition of modernization or progress. I think it would be useful if in this seminar we thought of economic development as something broader than economic growth. Economists today—and I am an economist myself, so I am more sensitive to this confusion—equate the two, although Schumpeter about forty-five years ago made quite a neat distinction between the two, which we tend to forget. Economic growth is simply a rise in income per head, if you wish. Development must mean more than that. It must have a social content as well—some pattern of distribution of income must be borne in mind and the continuity in the rise of income—which cannot take place without some substantial change in social and political institutions, cultural attitudes, and so on and so forth. If so, then economic development can be more or less equated with progress because it spreads on a far wider front than economic growth purely and simply.

Mr. Soedjatmoko: You are wondering to what extent we might not be imputing a desire for development to the population of a country as a whole. This certainly is a legitimate question. On the other hand, I think there are situations in which economic development as such may be an objective requirement. That is to say, there are situations where, unless a higher level of economic life is reached, there is bound to be political disintegration. We are therefore not only facing the question as to the existence or nonexistence of the desire for development among the population at large—irrespective of this there may be an objective necessity for economic development. And it is this awareness that moves the modernizers. That is why it is important for us to think more about the locus of particular motivations and motivational forces within the social structure.

It certainly is true that the modernizers usually are rebels in their society. They have made a break with tradition. But if modernization is to proceed successfully, the problem is not in the first place how much desire for development there is in a society as a whole and in the traditional sectors of that society especially. The problem really is how effective these rebels are in communicating with the traditional sectors. So, while they may remain in such a rebellious stance vis-à-vis tradition, they must increase their understanding of what makes the traditional sector tick. Unless they do so, they run a great risk of failure. This is the reason why I have tried to build my opening remarks around this problem.

If in the course of our discussions we come to incline to the view that in most developing countries it is only a handful of people who think about development, who really desire it, and who give it its particular economic, social, and political content, then we should bring this out clearly, and we should not persist in hiding behind the cliché that it is the people who want this and the people who want that. The power elite in a developing country should certainly be able to differentiate between these two situations, for each calls for different economic and political strategies. In any case, there are situations where development is a must, because physical and social conditions are a disgrace, and that is why we are here perhaps. But this does of course not mean that this conscious and concrete desire for development is necessarily shared by the populations at large of all these countries.

Father Bulatao: I would like to address myself to this point of manipulation of values.

I think we have here very clearly two sets of values: You have the traditionalist values, and you have the modernist values, the modernizers' values. Now one of the big values of Christianity is the absolute inviolability and value of the individual person. And therefore a person, whether traditionalist or modernizer, has a right to hold his own values. It is not a question of manipulating values or of changing values from the outside.

I think I would rather use the analogy of psychoanalysis, where one does not go into an analytic situation and treat a person as an object, unlike what Father de la Costa says about analysis. The analyst approaches the situation in a very subjective, in a very respectful way. He tries to see things from the person's viewpoint; there is a real dialogue between him and the person; he treats the person as a person, not as an object. And in the course of this dialogue values are clarified; there is a change of values, but it is not a matter of manipulation. It is a matter of clarification of one's values, a communication of oneself, and therefore the ability to reorient oneself. There is a real interchange, a real communication between two sets of values. And between the two of them you may say a third generally emerges.

Now these values then are really the adaptation to a new existing reality. If a set of values has to be changed, it is because that set of values has up to now refused to enter into dialogue with existing situations. It has locked itself in. The purpose then of our modernization process is to open up a person's attitudes, a person's view on things, to the changed situation. Take for instance the whole problem of teaching farmers modern means of agriculture. One doesn't manipulate the farmer's values and force him to change his ways. As a matter of fact, you usually fail that way. It is a matter of allowing the person to experience for himself a new set of values and, in this experience, teaching these values. Therefore the point is a matter of opening oneself to the new situation and therefore a matter of, one might say, dialogue.

Someone mentioned something about people feeling that they have surrendered something when they adapt. I don't think it is so much a surrender; I think it is more a positive reorienting of oneself to changed conditions, so that it is not a loss; it is a positive forward step when even a religion changes to a certain extent. Because it is again an opening of oneself to new experiences.

The last point is this problem of changing attitudes or changing institutions. I agree that the two of them go together. It is only by experiencing new institutions that a person changes his attitudes. Again, the analogy of psychoanalysis—the analytic situation in the room is not enough. The person has to get out in the world and experience these things for himself, and then he clarifies his experience within the analytic situation. But the two of them go together. There has to be a change in institutions that changes attitudes, and the attitude itself changes too, is opened up to new experience. So the two of them go together. And that is the way I feel that a nation grows.

Mr. Sayigh: I have many doubts, actually, with regard to the relevance of the religious factor to people's motivations in our present day. It's mainly because I see so many exceptions. I take a look at Spain in Europe, and I find it way behind France or Italy economically and socially speaking. And I look at the Muslim world itself, and I see that it was very dynamic and a great force for progress in a certain period of time. But now it is lagging behind. So where does one go from there? I think that modernization today is carried by groups of people who do not attach a great deal of importance to the religious factor in their decision-making and the body of their ideas. Therefore, whether or not the religious factor is significant in the behavior of people must be looked at within two systems. First, a system where society is very stagnant in the Rostowian sense (I am thinking of his later book *The Stages of Economic Growth*, not *The Process of Economic Growth*), in which case breaking away from stagnation requires a dynamic leadership group. The power elite in this kind of society has usually a set of ideas of a universal type that cuts across religions. The modernizers of this category in Indonesia, in Egypt, in the Philippines, in Ghana, I think share the same body of ideas regardless of their religions. These people usually think of the dignity of man meaning more specifically equal opportunity for education and economic opportunity, a rise in income, educational facilities, health facilities; in a restricted sense the values they have in mind don't go as deep down as religious values.

On the other hand, you can think of a system where society

is slightly beyond that very elementary stage, places like Lebanon, Iraq, Syria, where, just to give a landmark, income per head is $150 or over a year. Now in these places the decision-making process is more diffuse. You can see more happening through the individual decisions taken by individual businessmen, hundreds and thousands of them. And you do not necessarily need a power elite to activate progress.

In this instance, the ideas that move these people, the motivation, is much more economic, much more material. And there again the religious factor is of less significance. In other words, what I am trying to do is to cast a great deal of doubt on the influence of religious ideas, religious values, today in the move toward progress in either of these two systems.

Mr. Dube: This constant reference to the elite or the political elite worries me. In what way do we expect its attitudes to change? What exactly do we mean by change? Does it imply that the elite would give up the traditional values altogether and adopt a new scheme of values and a new set of goals? Or do we assume that it will retain a base of its traditional values and will interpret these values in such a manner that some of the goals of modernization would be accommodated? Those of us who have been studying the emerging political culture of the countries in the region with which we are concerned perhaps feel that a complete change in the values of the elite is extremely difficult, if not impossible. Let us bear in mind the fact that in the new political culture religion may be used as an instrument. It is quite possible that a certain member of the elite may be an agnostic, if not an atheist, in his personal convictions and beliefs, but in order to get votes he may have to put up a show of being deeply religious. Examples of this are not difficult to find. For this reason I would suggest that when we discuss this business of change in the value system of the elite, we should keep in mind the larger framework of the political culture in which these principal characters organize their struggle for power and within which they have to maintain themselves in positions of power.

Mr. Soedjatmoko: I have the rather uneasy feeling that some of the real problems are still escaping us. I find, for instance, that a note of undue optimism has crept into the discussions. This is reflected in the remark one of us around this table made yesterday to the effect that maybe religion is not so important as an inhibiting factor. This optimism may be the result of the fact that we have been looking at things in a very microscopic way, as a result of which we may have been inclined to judge these inhibiting factors as not so great. But somehow, all this does not add up. For, if we look at the problem in the aggregate, in terms of the national unit, then with all due respect to Mr. Sayigh's optimism, looking, let's say, at the convulsions through which the Arab world is going at present, I really don't think that that optimism is justified.

Equally so, while one may derive some optimism from the attempts at modernization in the villages in India, at the same time when one is in India I don't think one can escape this sense of the terrible weight of tradition on this whole process of modernization and development.

Father Lynch: There are ways in which religious beliefs do block the acceptance of certain practices and attitudes helpful for community development. I can give two examples of this from the Philippines.

The first concerns the annual town *fiesta*. One problem, presently under direct attack by Senator Manglapus, is that of exorbitant spending to provide food for visitors, even to the extent of going into serious debt. Religious beliefs support this practice, in that they are often appealed to as a reason for the spending. Who spends more is more generous and virtuous; who spends more gives greater honor to the town's patron; who *could* spend more and *does* not is courting divine displeasure for his niggardliness. These folk religious beliefs encourage all-out fiesta spending.

The second example concerns an attitude that has not been closely examined to date, despite the fact that it influences a great amount of behavior. Many Filipinos refer to and recognize this attitude by the phrase *Bahala na* and will speak of it as being akin to Christian resignation and therefore a good thing. But what is *Bahala na* on analysis? Let me give you a typical case.

A boy is studying for an exam. His friends come by. They don't have an exam, or they don't think it worthwhile to study for it, and they say, "Come on, let's go to the movies." He says, "I want to study," but they insist, "Join us only." (Here they appeal to one of the most powerful values in Philippine society, group harmony—going along with the desires of the peer group.) What does the boy do? More often than not, he decides to go out with the other boys. When he starts to think of the possible consequences of his decision—a low grade or failure in the exam—he cuts off further thought with a *"Bahala na!"* (freely, "Let come what may!" or, in the American idiom, "Aw, what the hell!"). Put in these terms, or when seen as the dereliction of duty, which it often is, this kind of action is not easily confused with Christian resignation, at least by an outsider to the culture. But if you concentrate on another aspect, that of withdrawal from concern about something, and don't ask whose fault the something is, then even the outsider might see the likeness to Christian patience and resignation. What is important is that many actions that orthodox Catholicism could not approve receive the full approbation of folk Catholicism as acts of Christian virtue.

Unfortunately there is a conspiracy of ignorance even among the clergy, many of whom share the folk Catholic view of fiesta spending and of withdrawal from socially difficult situations. If these leaders were better theologians, with a more accurate knowledge of the content of orthodox Catholicism, and if they knew what was really in the minds of their people, they might be able to effect considerable change in these matters. At least they could remove an apparently official sanction placed on these ways of acting and erase the impression that many of the clergy approve a do-nothing or do-little attitude in community development.

In brief, religious beliefs can and do block needed innovations. I have yet to see this conflict occur at an official level,
the level of orthodox Catholicism, but folk religious attitudes
certainly have interfered, and continually do interfere, with the
type of change that is needed in community development.

Mr. Bellah: I just want to raise some doubts about this differentiation between orthodox and folk as a necessarily completely
satisfactory solution to our problems. It seems to me that we
have been concentrating far too much on hindrances and not
enough on the problem of positive mobilization of motivation
for modernization and the ways in which this can be brought
about.

Now we have heard from representatives of all the religions
with which we are concerned, Christianity, Islam, Hinduism, and
Buddhism, at the—to use the word that Father Lynch used—
orthodox level; none of them really is a hindrance to modernization. So that such hindrances as there are can't be blamed on
that level but are to be taken care of at the folk level, where
there can even be a doubt as to whether they are really religious
at all. (I wonder if that is entirely fair; what may not be ortho-
doxly religious still may be, using a broad sociological definition,
the actual operative religion of the people in question.)

But the question that I would like to raise is: Granted that
the hindrance comes mainly from the folk level, is the elimination of the folk level and the replacement of it by the orthodox
religion going to solve the problem? My question is, is there in
the orthodox statements of these religions, even if there isn't a
hindrance to modernization, is there a real basis for the mobilization of leadership to attain modernization? In other words, to
take the Philippine case, can you, out of orthodox Catholicism
as it has existed in the past, expect dynamic leadership toward
modernization to emerge? Maybe this is an unfair question.
Maybe the only thing that we need to do is neutralize the in-
hibitions that are placed by the folk religion, and then purely
secular leadership can be expected to emerge or, in Dr. Sayigh's
terms, maybe the pure economic factors can then take over. My

own way of thinking would lead me to doubt that. I would suspect that a new cultural or ideological or religious movement of some sort is necessary. Therefore I think the problem would not be solved, but rather that basic changes in the structure of the orthodox position of the several religions with which we are dealing are needed in order to cope imaginatively and dynamically with the problem of modernization. Now there is plenty of evidence that there is within the structure of the Catholic Church itself at the highest levels a serious realization that this is the case, that the existing social and ideological structures of the Catholic Church grew out of social situations like Dr. Coulson described for the Islamic law, which had an entirely different social base and are no longer appropriate in a modern highly educated society. Thus we may be seeing a fundamental reorganization within even so stable and ancient a structure as the Catholic Church. At least there are voices within the Church in various countries who are hoping that this will take place and working for it. Certainly this is also the case within the Islamic religion, where there are various attempts to construct a more open modern orientation of Islam. But at least we need to consider this as a problem and not say, as I think it is a little bit too comfortably easy for each of us to say, "Well, our own religions are perfectly adequate at the orthodox level, and all that we need to do is clear away some of this undergrowth of folk superstition and everything will then turn out all right."

Mr. Geertz: Well, I am very happy that at last the problem of the internal rethinking of religion has been brought up, as it seems to me the center of the whole problem.

I would like, however, to throw an apple of discord into the discussion in this connection—by suggesting that it may be true, if one really thinks about the core of religion (which we have done almost not at all here) and these economic and political developments, that they may not be capable of complete harmonization, that there may be an intrinsic tension between the spiritual needs of man and the material needs of man, which can never be completely done away with no matter how clever one is or how much one manipulates institutions or anything else. The real problem in any state or in any religious tradition is to decide first what is spiritually essential to it and what is not. And second, how to preserve on the one hand the spiritual values the religion is directed toward, and how, on the other, to get economic and political development—how to keep these two different things in balance. There is no way for example (to talk again about a society I know) that I can see to turn Javanese mysticism into an economically supportive force. But I don't think that it must necessarily be a hindrance to economic change either. It seems to me that the whole problem is how to secure for the Javanese what is their traditional religious experience so that they do not become spiritually impoverished, so that they should not become lost in a rapidly changing modern world without any bearings whatsoever, and at the same time keep a balance and a productive tension between this religion, which does not (and so far as I can see cannot) support directly economic activities, and economic, political, and social development. Being a fox rather than a hedgehog, I am always rather concerned with tensions between things, between radical incompatibilities that cannot be resolved. And I think there is a certain utopian quality in much of our discussion. We are going to use tradition for modernity and get away with it. We are going to have it both ways; we are going to have no conflict in society; we are going to have no tensions; the problems of the priest and the businessman are going to come right, they are going to see eye to eye. I rather doubt it. This hasn't happened anywhere else. I doubt if it is going to happen in the Philippines, Indonesia, Malaysia, or Ceylon.

I think we might reflect more about this intrinsic dynamic tension, which must exist in human life and which is not necessarily to be deplored.

ROBERT N. BELLAH

Epilogue: Religion and Progress in Modern Asia

IN THE INTRODUCTION and in the report on the discussion, the editor's role was mainly representative: to give as fair a picture as possible of the various points of view expressed at the conference. At this point, however, the editor, in the spirit of our seminar, resumes his essentially nonrepresentative stance and speaks solely in his own voice. The following discursive reflections, though stimulated by the conference, are not intended as its "conclusions" but only as examples of one way in which its central problems may be viewed.

Progress

The use of the word "progress" in scholarly discourse tends to make the present-day social scientist a bit squeamish. Is not "progress" a myth that has no place in scientific analysis? As Carl Becker said,

The modern idea of progress belongs in this category of answers to necessary but insoluble questions. Like the myths of primitive peoples and the religious and philosophical beliefs of more advanced societies, it springs from the nature of man as a conscious creature, who finds existence intolerable unless he can enlarge and enrich his otherwise futile activities by relating them to something more enduring and significant than himself.[1]

Nor has it been viewed as an entirely harmless myth. Indeed, Karl Popper has blamed many of the ills of the modern world on the doctrine of inevitable progress.[2]

Two of the chief criticisms of the idea of progress have been that it is subjective, depending entirely on the criteria chosen to judge it, and that there are no logical or empirical grounds for accepting its inevitability. With respect to the latter point, it seems that the participants at our conference were not vulnerable. We all had a lively sense of the grave problems in connection with any sort of progress in Asia, of the necessity for knowledge and action to do something about it, and of the serious possibility of failure, partial or total. On the subjectivity issue, there is more room for doubt. Certainly Soedjatmoko's definition of the idea of progress as "a present better than the past, and a future potentially[3] better than the present" gives rise to the question, "better from what point of view?" We cannot of course deny that the feeling that the present is bad and that the future must be better is a powerful one in much of Asia, is indeed a primary datum in understanding the process at work there. But even if we knew exactly what Asians mean by "progress"—better living standards are certainly part of it, but other, perhaps more varying, components can be discerned—we should have some valuable information but hardly a sharp analytical tool. Is there any way to extricate from the notion of progress, besides the important mythical or ideological aspects that it undoubtedly possesses, a theoretical concept that will be helpful in our analysis? It can at least be argued that there is.

Using a cybernetic model of society, we might define progress as an increase in the capacity of a social system to receive and process information from within and without the system and to respond appropriately to it. Progress thus involves not merely learning but also learning capacity, an increasing ability to "learn to learn." This kind of learning capacity includes the "capacity for deep rearrangements of inner structure, and thus for the development of radically new functions."[4] From the point of view of this definition, modernization can be conceptualized as an especially rapid increase in progress in recent times. According to Cyril Black, "Modernization may be defined as the totality of the influence of the unprecedented increase in man's knowledge of and control over his environment that has taken place in recent centuries."[5] If we include the inner environment of society and personality, as well as the natural environment, then this sentence may be accepted as a provisional definition of modernization.

Now it is at least an open question whether or not the "deep rearrangements of inner structure" and the "radically new functions" that seem to be necessary for any such rapid increase in learning capacity as that involved in modernization are exactly what most Asians who favor "progress" have in mind. There may, in fact, be a serious contradiction between the ideological notion of progress involving a "better" future and the analytic notion that begins to specify some of the conditions for continuous self-development. It may indeed occur to many that preservation or continuity of certain traditional cultural values and social structures may be "better" than "deep rearrangements" of them. From such a point of view, modernization can hardly be called "progress." It is exceptional, however, for the issue to be put in so sharp a form. The rhetoric of Asian revolution more usually promises social and economic improvement without loss of the "best" of the indigenous tradition. Nor is such a position, however uncritical it may turn out to be in particular instances, wholly without significance. This much can certainly be said: A society that gives itself up to continuous rearrangements without regard to its own inner continuity of structure may be in as serious trouble as a society incapable of any rearrangement at all. On this point, Karl Deutsch is very suggestive:

How is it possible for an autonomous organization to accept outside information in the making of its most crucial inner decisions without losing its own identity? To accept the impact of outside information in a sequence of decisions may lead to decisions incompatible with one another. To accept it in the rearrangement of inner structures may leave the system with a collection of partial inner structures among which little or no communication and coordination may be possible. In such cases the effect of indiscriminate receptivity may be the destruction of autonomy or even the destruction of the system. Even where the system as such survives and retains a measure of autonomy, its steering performance and its capacity for further growth may be substantially lowered.[6]

What this argument suggests is that progress requires some balance between structural continuity and structural change, between memory and receptivity, so that the society will become neither rigid nor disorganized. Naturally, the success or failure of a given society will depend very much on the nature of its inner structure, its deepest values and commitments. The degree to which the inner structures and values can provide identity, continuity, and coherence while actually encouraging profound structural changes is the degree to which they are conducive to progress. As religion in most societies provides or is closely bound up with core structures and values, it is worthwhile exploring the relationship between religion and progress.

Religion and Progress

We may consider religion as a set of symbols that may be institutionalized, considered as normative, in a society or internalized in a personality. What makes religious symbols different from other kinds of symbol is that they define in broadest terms the nature of reality. They state or suggest what reality ultimately is, what the source of order (and often of disorder) in the universe is, what sort of authority in the most general terms is acceptable to men, and what sorts of action by individuals make sense in such a world.[7] Of course, such symbol systems may exist in a society, in books, for example, or in paintings, oratorios, and so forth, without any groups' or individuals' being actually committed to them. Much of the religious symbolism of the ancient Greek and Roman world survives in this way. In a given society, there may be groups devoted to various sets of religious symbols. An individual may be committed to a set of religious symbols shared by no other in his society, or one individual may be partially committed to several different sets of religious symbols. Any particular set of religious symbols is itself a historical growth often composed of elements quite heterogeneous in origin.

In spite of the diversity and complexity that exist in these matters, a society is generally officially committed to a particular set of religious symbols shared usually by a majority of the groups and individuals in it, though not necessarily compulsory for all. Such official commitment may be at a very general level —as, for example, the American commitment to belief in God expressed in many ways and reaffirmed at the most solemn public occasions—and may leave quite a wide diversity of specific interpretations or even rejection as matters of purely private concern. Most societies historically have been committed to more specific and particular sets of religious symbols. It is possible for individuals to take little interest in what is conventionally considered religious, but most individuals do seem to have some generally orienting symbol system in terms of which the world makes sense to them, even if it is fragmentary and ill thought out. People raised in a particular religious tradition may find it difficult to discern in the positions of other groups or individuals anything that meets their own normal criteria of religion. For present working purposes we shall use only our broadest definition of "religion" as a set of symbols providing the most general level of orientation to reality, so that we may include such diverse positions as early Buddhism, Confucianism, and Communism, which might be disallowed in a more particular sort of definition.

Perhaps the central function of a religion is to act as a cultural gyroscope, to provide a stable set of definitions of the world and, correlatively, of the self, so that both the transience and the crises of life can be faced with some equanimity by the society or person in question. It is this stability, continuity, and coherence provided by commitment to a set of religious symbols (or perhaps better to what they symbolize) that give religion such a prominent place in defining the identity of a group or person. Identity is a statement of what a person or a group is essentially and, as it were, permanently. Identity does not change except under very severe pressure. Commitment to religious truth that holds "always and everywhere" operates to enhance the definiteness with which I know who I am or my group knows what it is. It has long been known that religious ritual tends to focus on moments of crisis or transition, when the sense of identity is threatened. At the moment of marriage, when one leaves father and mother to cleave to another, or of death, when one on whom he depends is taken away, there are religious ceremonies, weddings and funerals, that operate to reinforce or redefine threatened identity. Similarly, at a moment of great social crisis like famine or war or at a time of momentous political transition, solemn religious symbolism—for example the inauguration of an American president—by reference to what does not change helps to make change tolerable. On the other hand, the periodic, calendrical or seasonal, round of religious ritual operates to counteract the blurring of identity through sheer temporal attrition.

Another way of thinking about the identity function of religion is to view it as a cybernetic control mechanism, the highest cybernetic control mechanism in a society or personality. Through their general definition of the nature of reality and therefore of the self, the religious symbols project a set of "limit images,"[8] which indicate what sorts of action are possible and desirable. These limit images operate to bring social and personal actions within the framework of a "higher power" or "wider meaning," so that some sorts of action are encouraged and others avoided. By creating a sense of "humility" and "respect for the sacred," religion helps to give a regularity to human action and to place it within certain boundaries. In one sense, religion can be viewed as a collective heritage of reality testing on the most general level. By keeping action within certain limits, it may help a society or person to avoid disaster in uncontrolled deviation or extreme fluctuation. Of course, this limit function is itself relative and subject to disturbance. A limit based on reality testing at one phase of history may simply inhibit useful advance at another, as when the "superstitious dread" of sailors at crossing an open body of water, valid enough at one stage of marine technology, inhibits nautical discovery once a more adequate technology has gradually developed. On the other hand, the religious gyroscope may, in situations of great pressure, begin to wobble severely and generate extremely unrealistic fears and expectations, as is often the case in nativistic and millennial movements.

The identity function of religion seldom operates only at the level of the most general definition of reality. Usually it involves more specific conceptions of time and space as well. Eliade[9] has instructed us in the widespread notions of sacred time and sacred space in primitive societies. These notions operate to give positive meanings to time and space, so that one knows *where one is*. At the simplest level, knowing where one is in time and space may automatically indicate who one is, but at any level, it is usually closely relevant to the identity problem. The more advanced religions, because of their universalism, have often stressed conceptions of time more than of space. Because of the general nature of religious symbolism, these conceptions of time have usually been quite comprehensive. Some of the Indian religions have developed notions of time involving vast cosmic cycles on a scale approaching that of the modern astronomer. These notions have been directly related to the interpretation of human life in terms of endless series of rebirths. Jewish, Christian, and Islamic notions of time, on the other hand, have stressed the unilinearity of historical development from a single beginning to a single end in accordance with the divine plan. It is essential for the religious man in these traditions to bring himself into accord with the requirements of that plan at any given time. As Father de la Costa has pointed out, the modern idea of progress is a secular adaptation of the Christian conception of history, and, as we have quoted Becker, it has often played an orienting role for modern man analogous to that of myths and religions in the past.[10]

But spatial notions are also evident in the higher religions. One needs only to cite the notion of Zion or the general Islamic orientation toward Mecca. Even so unspatial a religion as Buddhism has developed on occasion a vivid spatial symbolism, as when Nichiren claimed that Japan is a Buddha land. Christianity has a varied set of spatial associations, focusing around the Holy Land, Rome, the Third Rome, and, particularly in the Protestant Reformation, becoming associated with the idea of nationalism. In America, this line of development has been very prominent, as H. Richard Niebuhr shows in *The Kingdom of God in America*.[11] But of course the idea of "one world" also has deep religious roots and, in secular form, continues to play a role in modern systems of orienting symbolism.

We see that religious symbol systems usually operate to give a sense of spatio-temporal identity, although conceptions have changed from primitive notions of sacred time and sacred space to modern ideas of progress and nationalism. It is evident then that, for all its stress on eternity, identity, and continuity, religion does change. Indeed its changes are central to the concerns of this book. Yet it is also true that religion shows remarkable stability over time. What political or economic system has survived as long as Buddhism or Christianity or Islam? What books survive in common use the way religious scriptures do? And, even when religions do innovate, their very sense of permanence and eternity makes them link themselves to the past as well as to the future.

Christ said, "I come not to destroy the law but to fulfill it." Muhammad claimed to be the seal of the prophets and accepted them all back to Adam. The Buddha was seen as only the most recent of a vast chain of Buddha incarnations. Even the Communist Manifesto is careful to place itself in the context of all time: "All previous history is the history of class struggle."

The real continuity and the insistence on continuity even in the midst of radical innovation remind us of the central function of religion—to provide stable points of reference for human action—but should not blind us to how radical change has been. On this earth, even that structure most oriented to changelessness (as Karl Popper has pointed out, even those who insist most on change thereby find a principle of constancy—change is "ever-present") inevitably changes and then not randomly but in accordance with the whole process of sociocultural evolution. A full development of the idea of religious evolution is not possible here,[12] but a brief sketch may be helpful in getting at our central problem of the relation of religion to change in today's world.

The central dimension of religious evolution is what may be called "the rationalization of religious symbolism." As Clifford Geertz has put it, what we might call primitive and archaic[13] religions

... consist of a multitude of very concretely defined and only loosely ordered sacred entities, an untidy collection of fussy ritual acts and vivid animistic images which are able to involve themselves in an independent, segmental and immediate manner with almost any sort of actual event. Such systems (for, despite their lack of formal regularity, they are systems) meet the perennial concerns of religion, what Weber called the "problems of meaning"—evil, suffering, frustration, bafflement, etc.—piecemeal. They attack them opportunistically as they arise in each particular instance—each death, each crop failure, each untoward natural or social occurrence—employing one or another weapon chosen, on grounds of symbolic appropriateness, from their cluttered arsenal of myth and magic.[14]

In what we might call the "historic religions" (what are often called "world religions"), on the other hand,

. . . the sense of sacredness was gathered up, like so many scattered rays of light brought to focus in a lens, from the countless tree spirits and garden spells through which it was vaguely diffused, and concentrated it in a nucleate (though not necessarily monotheistic) concept of the divine. The world was, in Weber's famous phrase, disenchanted: the locus of sacredness was removed from the rooftrees, graveyards and road-crossings of everyday life and put, in some sense, into another realm where dwelt Jahweh, Logos, Tao or Brahman.[15]

Important social and personal changes accompany this process of rationalization of the religious symbol system. In the primitive and archaic societies, religious roles, with few exceptions, are embedded in the whole societies. Every father, every clan chief or king is also a priest. In the historic religions, particular religious roles and structures tend to crystallize, so that there is at least partial differentiation of a church or religious institution. Such a religious institution may provide a point of view from which other social institutions may be criticized or altered, may outlive any particular society, or may exist in several societies at once, possibilities that are available in only the most limited way at earlier stages. For the individual, the historic religions provide the possibility of personal thought and action independent of the traditional social nexus to a quite unprecedented extent. A new consciousness of the self defined in relation to the divine takes shape at this stage. The modern period seems to represent still another main stage of religious evolution—but that is the subject of the last part of this chapter.

Having given a general sketch of the place of religion in human action, let us now turn to the problem of relating religion to progress as we defined it in the analytic sense. How does religion relate to the increase in learning capacity, which we have seen as the heart of an analytical definition of progress? Clearly a religion with its general definitions of the cosmos, society, and self, its particular symbolism of time and space, and perhaps especially its consequent set of limit images will have very considerable implications for the learning capacity of the society in which it is institutionalized or of the individual who

has internalized it. It may imply fixed commitment to a detailed
pattern of traditional action with little room for structural change
or increase in learning capacity. It may, on the other hand,
exercise a steady pressure toward continuous expansion of learning capacity. Or it may simply remain indifferent to the possibility of learning or change in a wide variety of areas. Any
particular religion is apt to contain all these implications in varying degrees and to shift its emphases over time. On the whole, the
more rationalized religious symbol systems of which Geertz was
writing seem to have more favorable implications for progress
than do the less rationalized systems, although this generalization
is certainly not true of every case. As general laws in this connection are still far from clear, it is perhaps better to turn to some
concrete cases—first the traditional religious systems of several
parts of Asia and then some of the changes that have occurred in
recent times.

Religion in Traditional Societies

The historic religions that we find institutionalized in the
great traditional societies up to the eve of modernization differed
from primitive and archaic religions in a number of ways. We
have already noted that the historic religions had more differentiated conceptions of the transcendental realm, conceptualizing
it more distinctly over against the world. Socially, certain dif-
ferentiations incipient at the archaic level became much more
marked. The sharper distinction between elite and nonelite
groups in the society and the differentiation of the elite into
political and cultural-religious elites and of the nonelite into
rural and urban nonelites to mention only the major distinctions,
had profound consequences for the place of religion in society.
Although religion did provide stabilizing central value systems
and social integration in such societies, the very degrees to which
they were differentiated meant that religion took on distinct
forms in the different groups, with increased potential for con-

flict and innovation within the societies. Indeed, as inequality and lack of communication among subgroups in the society were perhaps more characteristic of these great traditional societies than of either primitive or modern societies,[16] differences in religious orientations of the subgroups were also perhaps more marked at that stage.

From the point of view of the religious elite, the great aim of life was to come into a right relation with the realm of the transcendent. The whole purpose of society was, in fact, to guarantee to individuals the opportunity to attain eternal salvation. Christianity, Islam, Hinduism, and Buddhism are the classic salvation religions, but even Confucianism, at least from Sung times, with its great stress on personal purity and enlightenment, can be considered in this same category. In most of the traditional societies, certain subgroups of the religious elites withdrew more or less completely from involvement in secular life in order to pursue lives of meditation and purification. Buddhist and Christian monastic groups are obvious examples, but the Hindu *sannyāsin* and the Confucian retired scholar were functionally similar. In all cases, these withdrawn groups, at least from the point of view of the religious elites, which was more or less widely shared by other groups in the society, had the highest prestige and were considered in a sense the "best" elements in the society. The great emphasis on otherworldliness (Islam seems to be an exception, but the importance of the Sufi ideal at least from the twelfth century on makes it only a very partial exception), which directs the attention away from mundane matters, seems to have made the historic religions singularly fruitless from the point of view of a general increase in social learning capacity. This description is not the whole story, as we shall see, but even within the sphere of otherworldly religion itself these historic religions might be viewed as generating certain capacities that, under favorable conditions, could become available for general social advance.

There was, for example, within the sphere of religious thought itself, a very considerable development of the capacity for rational systematic thought. It is true that basic religious positions were taken as fixed and final, whether through revelation or by some other means, in all the historic religions, but the job of exegesis, systematization, and application remained a major one. The achievements of Thomas and other medieval Christian theologians or of al-Ghazzali or Shankara or Chu Hsi were major cultural advances, and, even when barren of immediate practical consequences, they provided a more complex and articulated cultural resource for the understanding of reality. Of course, it is also true that, in every case, the great systematizers and commentators themselves came to be accepted as final and unchallengeable authorities, and in this way inhibited further cultural rationalization. And indeed some of them may be viewed as sanctified cultural dead ends. But, unless we are to buy the specious argument that Aristotle, for example, simply because he was often blindly followed, did not himself make any important contribution to the development of cultural capacity in the West, then the significance of the great religious thinkers should not be minimized.

The other area in which the historic religions even or perhaps especially in their otherworldly aspects contributed potentially to the increase of general learning capacity was that of motivation. Monasticism and the high evaluation of purification and meditation generally contributed to the development of more self-disciplined personalities capable of tolerating considerable frustration and controlling impulses. This type of personality control easily became pathological and was, in any case, usually confined to quite restricted groups in the society. Nevertheless, a disciplined personality capable of subordinating all personal interests to "higher" obligations, as Weber so often pointed out, seems to be a prerequisite for the capacity to rationalize social existence.[17] Whether or not motivation "mobilized" through religious discipline was channeled into the mundane sphere, rather than remaining exclusively otherworldly in aim, varied greatly from case to case among and within the historic religions.

Viewing human life as a great salvation drama, as most of the historic religions did, gave meaning to the cosmos and provided a comprehensive orientation for individual existence. The predominating atmosphere of world rejection shared to some degree by all (even Confucianism, the most optimistic, developed a settled mood of pessimism toward historical actuality in later centuries) seems to have given little positive basis for a sense of social as against purely personal identity. Nevertheless, in every case, they were able to provide dominating ideals and values for the societies in which they were institutionalized. To some extent, this influence involved a purely passive tendency to validate the existing social status quo in religious terms. This tendency might take the positive form of including the particular patterns of social existence in immutable religious truth, as did Confucianism, Hinduism, and, to some extent, Islam. The adoption of the "natural law" idea in Christianity had partially this same effect. Or the validation might be negative—the world would be accepted as it was because it lacked inherent meaning or would soon pass away, as the early Buddhists and primitive Christians believed. But, just as Christianity drew on classical traditions in working out a more positive orientation toward the world, so Buddhism drew on Brahmanism in South Asia and Confucianism in East Asia to effect an accommodation with existing social institutions when it became the dominant religion.

The purely passive validation of existing social realities, however, would alone hardly qualify the historic religions for a major role in the long-term shaping of social institutions or in any increase in social learning capacity, both of which they achieved in some degree. In spite of their world-rejecting tendencies, all of them developed active ideals of the good or just society implicitly or explicitly critical of existing social structures. As Troeltsch pointed out, Christianity developed an active conception of the Christian society for the first time in the Middle Ages,[18] a conception that had a long history of development with important implications for modern Western history. The conception of the realm of Islam as a realm of justice stood as a permanent norm against which the kaleidoscopic series of dynasties and sultanates could be judged. Although the *dharma* ideal in Hinduism usually meant, for practical purposes, the detailed prescriptions of the various castes, nonetheless the conception of a society in which *dharma* was embodied implied a just society as opposed to tyranny. And Confucianism never failed to hold up a model of just and harmonious society as it had existed at the time of the ancient kings, in contradistinction to the sad decay of later days. In every case, it was the specifically religious concern that dictated the model of the good society in which religious values could be most readily realized. Insistence on these religiously determined social ideals for centuries and millennia by religious institutions established in the various historic societies gradually shaped social institutions in the direction of greater value implementation, even though compromises with social realities were frequent and complete penetration of society was never attained.

It was religious pressure that gradually gave the great historic societies their characteristic forms and justifies our use of religious labels in characterizing them. Of course, the ability of religious values to exert long-term pressure on a society is dependent on some degree of structural differentiation of the religious institutions from other social institutions, especially the political institutions. The degree and mode of the tension between religious and political institutions had an important bearing on the capacity of the society for progress, as we shall see a bit more fully later.

All of the historic religions provided, together with definitions of ultimate reality, of the nature of the human condition, and of the good society, some general time and space definitions as well. The time conceptions of most of the historic religions were pessimistic about the future, at least the immediate future. The cyclical theories, like that of Buddhism, implied that earthly conditions would deteriorate continuously until the inauguration of a new cycle, not to be expected very soon. Christianity and

Islam, though each looked forward to an eschaton, viewed historical existence in the meantime as, on the whole, a decline.
Indeed, a condition of extreme social breakdown was viewed as
almost a precondition for the end of time, which was certainly
not regarded as a culmination of earthly human endeavors. Confucianism too saw history as a decline from the age of the ancient
kings and hardly expected a just ruler in latter days.

Beside these macroscopic conceptions of time, indicating
a downward slant in the historical process, there was also a more
microscopic tendency to glorify the past. When religious groups
did press for some social reform or improvement, they almost
always took as their models earlier phases of historical development. This impulse to change might be expressed as a desire to
return to the conditions of the primitive church, the community
of the prophet at Medina, or the rule of Yao and Shun, or it
might involve simply holding up the conditions at the beginning
of the dynasty or at the time of "good king so-and-so" as worthy
of imitation. Quite often the model of a simpler stage of social
organization, when the society had been more completely agricultural or pastoral, was romanticized and taken as a goal for
social reform, as can be seen not only in Christendom and Islam
but in China and Japan as well. The conception of the future
as open to really new social developments is scarcely to be found
in any of the historic religions outside the realm of millennial
expectations.

Although the conscious idea of progress even in ideological
form, not to mention the analytical concept, was not present in
the historic religions, their time conceptions nonetheless held
some positive implications for social advance. For one thing,
models for the future, ostensibly based on the past, were seldom
accurate representations of a past largely forgotten or misun-
derstood in contemporary thought. Consequently, under the
guise of "returning to" this or that phase of previous development, it was sometimes possible for quite new social conceptions
to be put forward. Furthermore, the idea that history did have a

meaning, even if largely a depressing one, gave impetus to historical thought in all the great traditions except possibly Hinduism, and this historical thought in turn did lead on occasion to some practical thought about social change, as in the case of Ibn Khaldun or a Chinese thinker like Huang Tsung-hsi. Millennialism, found in Buddhism, as well as in Christianity and Islam, and indeed an endemic possibility for religious orientation even in primitive and archaic religions, could contribute only under very special conditions to social innovation, for it was usually a symptom of severe social pathology. Its consequences were often destructive, or the energies it released were quickly rechanneled into traditional forms, as in the millennial movements accompanying the emergence of some of the Chinese dynasties.

Each of the historic religions offered space as well as time definitions. The Islamic notion of a *Dar al-Islam*, the realm of Islam, defined a civilizational entity transcending political divisions, within which a common religion and a common law were supposed to obtain. Christendom until the Reformation was a directly comparable idea and indeed, in secular form, lies behind the modern notion of an international community of nations, originating as a Western club in which Western members are now greatly outnumbered. The Chinese notion of a "Middle Country" (*Chung Kuo*) radiating its influence to "all under heaven" (*T'ien Hsia*) was the Confucian version of spatial symbolism. These various conceptions served to divide the world into at least potentially opposed spheres (explicitly in the case of Islam, with its designation of the non-Islamic world as *Dar al-Harb*, realm of war), although in fact conflicts and wars within spheres were probably much more common than between them. The converse of the divisive function of this spatial symbolism, however, was its insistence on inclusion of all those within the delimited sphere, at least all those within who accepted the dominant religious orientation. Most of the historic religions did show some capacity to tolerate alien religious groups within their gates, but at best the aliens were marginal members of society, having a "special status" (as the *dhimmis* in Islam), and at worst they were mercilessly persecuted. Yet the insistence on inclusion of (usually) the majority of the members of a society in the dominant religious group was in itself a matter of great social consequence.

It should be remembered that in most of the historic societies there was no well-developed conception of citizenship. Although some idea of rights or limits to political authority usually existed, frequently couched in religious terms, there were usually no expectations of participation in the political process on the part of the great majority of the people. Membership in the religious community did, however, provide a basis for active inclusion in society, even when political inclusion was not emphasized. It is true that most of the religious communities were themselves stratified, and the lower strata were not fully "religiously enfranchised," as it were. This stratification can be seen in the distinction between educated and uneducated in Confucianism, between the degrees of religious perfection in medieval Christianity, and between Brahman and non-Brahman in Hinduism. Under special circumstances, a rather full degree of religious inclusion combined with a fusion of religious and political functions to render, for premodern societies, a rather high degree of general social participation. The clearest examples are the ancient Mediterranean, especially Greek, city-states and ancient Israel. Early Islam momentarily showed a similar pattern. Similar tendencies have developed sporadically elsewhere, as in the Shin sect of Pure Land Buddhism in Japan. These socioreligious communities did not include the religiously alien. The *gerim* or "strangers" in ancient Israel were precursors of the *dhimmis* or "protected [non-Muslim] peoples" in Islam. Worship of the city gods was always a prerequisite for Greek citizenship, and even in Hellenistic times the Greeks were organized as *politeumata* in cities of mixed residence—only the Greeks having full citizenship, others being organized in their own *politeumata* with usually more limited rights and duties. Tendencies toward political absolutism rendered citizenship in Hellenistic Greece and imperial Rome and membership in the religious community in Maccabean Israel or Ummayyad Islam politically meaningless. But the conceptions of full social inclusion never died out and in modern times form part of the background of emergent nationalism. Even where the notion of inclusion in the religious community had little or no political significance, as was usually the case in Buddhism, for example, the conception of society as a single all-embracing religious collectivity did provide a basis for social integration and, on occasion, amelioration. Certainly the religious structure often played an important role in communication between the political elite and the mass of the population. In medieval Islam, the *ulama* operated almost as a general facilitating medium in the society.[19] The Confucian educated literati-gentry in China performed similar functions, as did the Christian church in medieval Europe.

So far we have stressed the aspect of stable integration of religion in societies of historic type. But conflict was endemic in such societies and nowhere more than in the realm of religion. We shall discuss briefly the conflict-generating tensions in three major areas: the relations between religious and political institutions, the relations between religious and secular cultural elites, and the relations between established religions and heterodoxy.

As we have already noted, religious and political institutions were relatively well differentiated in historic societies, compared to primitive and archaic societies. On the other hand, although the degree of differentiation was variable, it never approached the "separation of church and state" found in some modern societies. The political structure, especially at the highest levels, had an important religious dimension, and religious organization was closely supervised by the government and was of a public or official nature. Truly private religious groups were marginal and viewed with suspicion if they were allowed to exist at all. The close integration of religious and political institutions in such societies placed important restraints on both of them, restraints that religious or political groups tried from time to time to throw off or reduce, thus generating serious strains between them. Particularly in times of marked political expansion or innovation, vigorous political elites might seek to maximize political power at the expense of the traditional restraints placed upon it, and they would inevitably have to attack or undermine the religious sanctions supporting those restraints. Frankly antireligious or cynically manipulative attitudes toward religion were expressed by such groups of political thinkers as the Legalists in ancient China, the *artha* writers of ancient India, the Greek Sophists, the writers of "Mirrors for Princes" in the Islamic Middle Ages (especially Nizam al-Mulk), and the Renaissance political theorists of whom the extreme example is Machiavelli. There is no doubt that political regimes in areas where such thinkers were active did utilize the techniques they preached to greater or lesser degrees. The theories and actions of such political secularists were often highly favorable for the growth of social learning capacity and the ability to undertake innovations in the political sphere, at least in the short run. Nevertheless, purely secular political rationalization in historic societies gave rise to serious social disruptions when the limit images of religion were too sharply abrogated. The typical case is the Ch'in dynasty of China, which, under legalist domination, violated the interests and values of virtually every major group in Chinese society. The dynasty rapidly came to an abrupt and disastrous conclusion, and it was no accident that it was during the following Han Dynasty that Confucianism attained the position of state cult and official ideology. The political innovations of the Ch'in were by no means abandoned. The great Chinese bureaucratic system was in major respects a heritage of Ch'in. But the stable incorporation of the new political system depended on establishing it in the context of a newly elaborated version of the traditional religious-philosophical system, with limit images sufficiently institutionalized to withstand the severe dislocations to which the Ch'in system was prone. Of course, the balance attained was only relatively successful, and tension between dynasty and literati, between Legalism and Confucianism, was endemic throughout imperial Chinese history.

Some rulers (Constantine, Ashoka, Han Wu-ti, Shotoku Taishi) have aided the growth and establishment of various religions and others have persecuted them. Religions have supported state structures and opposed them. Particularly interesting are the cases in which rulers have attempted new religious rationalizations on their own (examples are Ikhnaton, Alexander, and Akbar, none of them particularly successful) and the cases in which religions have given rise to new state forms (Islam is the great example). As Eisenstadt has pointed out, the possibility of structural innovation in either the religious or political field and of the contribution of each to the development of the other is partly at least a function of the degree to which they are differentiated.[20] Too close a fusion tends to inhibit progress in either, a rule of thumb that will be of importance to us when we survey the modernizing potential of the several world religions. On the other hand, in periods of very rapid structural change, a partial dedifferentiation may be an important phase in the development toward a new level of differentiation.

The next important area of tension that we must discuss is the relationship between religious and secular cultural elites. The religious-secular distinction is a difficult one to make in societies of historic type, where the religious and the secular were not separated in quite the same way as they are in modern societies. Each historic society presents its own particular problems when we try to apply this distinction. Yet we can use it in two fairly general senses. We can differentiate between intellectuals who were part of the official religious structure and those who were not, even though, as in the case of the Greek and Chinese philosophers, those not in the official religious structure were often concerned with theological problems; and we can differentiate between those concerned with religious problems and those concerned with all other intellectual problems, regardless of their official structural positions. Normally, in historic societies, intellectuals not in the religious structure were part of the political structure, the religious and political groups being the two dominant ones. Nevertheless, the cases in which the intellectual was an independent farmer or merchant or, even more significantly, a professional, though relatively rare, are of great importance, for they imply the existence of an independent or private intellectual class. On the whole, it should be said that the existence of such private intellectual groups in historic societies was precarious. Patronage from members of the political or religious elites was usually important, and vulnerability to pressure from such elite groups was great.

Private intellectuals concerned with religion and intellectuals in whatever structural positions concerned with nonreligious issues both contributed to religious development in important ways. The vitality of religious thought in ancient China, India, Israel, and Greece would have been gravely weakened had it been confined to official priestly groups. Creative religious thought in the world religions came more often from within the religious structures but depended in no little degree on capacity to convert or attract talented secular intellectuals to the religious life. The contributions of intellectuals concerned with nonreligious problems, particularly science and ethics, to religious thought, through stimulating new answers to new problems, is well known in the West from the sixteenth and seventeenth centuries forward but is actually a very old process, particularly discernible in the Hellenistic period. Of course, on occasion, the contributions of the secular intellectuals were purely destructive, undermining the traditional religions but putting nothing in their places. The temptation of the isolated intellectual to gnostic speculation, in which all limit images are broken, gave rise to the Faust symbol and the profound suspicion with which medieval Christianity, Islam, and Judaism, for example, viewed the philosopher.

Even though the danger to social order from groups of

secular intellectuals may have been real at times, it seems that on balance the contribution such groups had to make to the increase in social learning capacity was very great. The establishment of some *modus vivendi* or, even better, encouragement from religious institutions for such groups therefore seems to have been a positive element in the progress or potential progress of historic societies. Particularly strategic in this connection was the educational system. Although it was often dominated by religious and political forces, room was occasionally made for the relatively free operation of secular intellectuals and the pursuit of secular subjects, above all in the medieval Western university. The development of the Islamic *madrasa*, with its narrowly restricted religious curriculum, illustrates the opposite tendency. Confucian education, on the other hand, though in no narrow sense religiously limited, was so preoccupied with ethical-political concerns and so dominated by the prestige of literary texts that its cultural creativity on any broad front was quite limited. The vulnerability of secular intellectuals in societies of historic type is illustrated by the fitfulness of scientific advance. Periods of marked advance, like the Hellenistic age or medieval Islam, were followed by long periods of sterility when religious and political forces undermined the positions of the secular intellectual groups that had been scientifically creative. In modern societies, although science is by no means absolutely secure, its institutionalization goes far deeper than in any historic society.

The final area of tension with which we must deal is that involving the relationship between established religion and heterodoxy. This problem I believe is essentially a problem of religious communication between different groups in a society. The degree to which religious communication between groups can be kept open is the degree to which a religious system can respond to new needs and creatively adjust, as well as contribute, to social development. Blockage of communication can occur through what might be called "overtolerance" as well as through intolerance. An overtolerant religion is one that fails to communicate its message to important groups in the society and passively assents in their adherence to heterogeneous and often less developed orientations. Perhaps the extreme case is Hinduism, which left the mass of Indian people hermetically sealed in caste-bound religious systems only rarely and usually ineffectively challenged through movements based on Hindu religious universalism.[21] Buddhism, through passive acceptance of pre-existing religious orientations, frequently found itself overwhelmed by them in time. The extreme case, perhaps, is Japan, where Buddhist universalism and individualism were almost entirely swallowed in a recrudescence of magical, collectivistic religious orientations of archaic type and semi-archaic Confucianism. Christianity, on the other hand, has often seen the break in communication develop through intolerance and minority groups driven to extremes by hostility and persecution. Of course religious persecution has often occurred in the Orient, and overtolerance has on occasion been characteristic of Christian countries.

Overtolerance, which is endemic to all historic religions to some degree, probably because of the tenuous communication systems characteristic of historic societies, is responsible for the distinction between folk and orthodox religion, which received frequent comment in our conference. Where this distinction is clear cut, large elements in the population, the peasantry and lower urban groups, are left in relatively archaic stages of social development. They are not therefore mobilizable, in terms either of motivation or of loyalty to larger groups and universalistic values, to the extent that those members of society who have been thoroughly penetrated by the historic religion are. They are therefore less able to contribute to or even to accept increases in social learning capacity. Furthermore, the existence of a large reservoir of archaic religion, what Max Weber called "a garden of magic," in a society means that there is a permanent possibility of regressive religious movements overwhelming the more advanced historic religious tradition. The rise of magic in the late Hellenistic world, the spread of Sufism in Islam after the eleventh century, the parallel spread of Kabbalism in medieval Judaism, as well as the Buddhist cases already mentioned, are examples of this process.

Intolerance, on the other hand, may lead to the long-term alienation of potentially creative groups in the society. Shi'ism, especially Isma'ili Shi'ism, in medieval Islam is perhaps the best example, for it had attracted artisan and intellectual groups whose catholic philosophical and scientific interests might have contributed to a widening of the Islam cultural world. The great countermovements of antiquity, of which gnosticism was typical, the Christian heresies in the Middle Ages, and Taoism in some stages of its development are comparable cases. Of course, the cultural creativity of each of these examples is debatable, and each did pose a deadly threat to the dominant religious orientation. But the incapacity of the dominant system to respond to the needs and conditions that gave rise to these heterodox movements was a sign of its own failure to contribute to social development.

Where religious communication has broken down severely either through overtolerance or intolerance or a combination of the two, the established religion is very likely to be replaced by another dominant religion, perhaps one of its own heterodoxies, and certainly not inevitably one of a more advanced type. A situation of prolonged stagnation, in which religious communication between groups is small but in which no vigorous religious groups are rising, seems the one in which religion could make the least contribution to social development.

In concluding this section on religion in traditional societies, it might be well to summarize the respects in which religion in such societies was or was not favorable to progress. First, it should be emphasized again that no religion before modern times ever consciously preached that it had a major obligation to further progress in the sense of endless self-improvement through increase in learning capacity. Rather, religions conceived their functions as we have defined them—to provide a sense of meaning and identity, to show men what is ultimately true and good.

Two conditions seem especially unfavorable for the religious encouragement of progress: too close a fusion between religious symbolism and the actual world and too great a disjunction between them.

Where religion simply sanctifies a given social-cultural situation, it provides little leverage to change it. If the religion lacks a complex theoretical structure and accepts most of its categories from traditional cultural concepts and if the ideal of religious action is simply conformity to social expectations, with little stress on any transcendent goal, then the capacity of the religion to contribute to progress is even smaller. Actually, fusion of this sort is characteristic of primitive and archaic religions. Religions of historic type have, by definition, broken through such fusions. Yet the tendency to fall back into such fusions is endemic in all historic religions. Perhaps Confucianism, the most archaic of the historic religions, best illustrates this tendency, especially in its central cult of the family.

On the other hand, where religion stresses the utter disjunction between what is religiously valuable and the actualities of this world, the ability to contribute to progress may be equally weak. Religious action consists of avoiding any participation in the normal routine of social existence. It stresses the attainment of states of emptiness or ecstasy, which are least like normal life. Even if elaborate theoretical structures and complex techniques of self-discipline are developed, they can have little impact on social change in such a context. Of course, there are many ways of building bridges from the beyond to social realities, and religious motivation may be rechanneled in new ways. But where empirical existence is felt to be totally evil (gnosticism) or totally meaningless (early Buddhism), it is hard to see how such religions can exert much leverage on the world, unless, as has often happened, heterogeneous social ideals are grafted onto them.

The situation in which progress is most likely to be advanced seems to be that in which transcendent ideals, in tension with empirical reality, have a central place in the religious symbol system, while empirical reality itself is taken very seriously as at least potentially meaningful, valuable, and a valid sphere for religious action.

Most religions have all three tendencies—fusion, disjunction, and creative tension between religious ideals and the world—in some sort of combination. "Hinduism," indeed, is a term covering a wide variety of tendencies illustrating both extremes, as well as the middle ground. Even in religions like Christianity and Islam, which seem to represent the third position, there may arise many situations that effectively block contributions to progress. Some of these conditions have been mentioned already in this section. Although all the historic religions contributed to progress in aiding the development and consolidation of historic societies, as distinct from archaic societies, only a few religious movements have made major contributions to progress beyond historic society in the direction of modern society. Of these few, Max Weber singled out for particular attention Protestant Christianity,[22] which was undoubtedly the first religious movement to make a significant contribution to modernization. Following Weber, indeed, it can be maintained that Protestantism was a necessary, though not sufficient, condition for the emergence of modern society in the first place.

Religion and Modernization in Asia

Before turning to our primary concern, the examination of the Asian situation, it is necessary to say a few words about modernity itself and about its first emergence in the West. One way of thinking about modernity is to note that, though progress in the sense we have defined it has been, with many reversals and variations, fairly constant through human history and particularly in the great historic societies, it nonetheless emerged as a conscious principle and rational aim only in the modern period. Historic cultures viewed society and personality within the framework of established patterns, given once and for all in revelation or tradition. The chief conscious problem was how to embody in actuality the fixed and given patterns. Endless development and continual innovation were not believed possible and would have been rejected with horror had they been suggested. The artificer or explorer beyond fixed bounds was a negative image, as in the medieval conception of Odysseus. It is only in the modern period that development and innovation have come to be viewed as good in themselves.

It is a serious weakness of some discussions of modernity that they define it too narrowly in terms of technology. It is true that technological development shows in admirably simple form the nature of endless development and innovation. But it is not technology that grounds modern culture—it is modern culture that gives scope to technology. For beside the rationalization of means, of which the insistence on technical efficiency is the typical case, modern culture is characterized by increasing insistence on the rationalization of ends. The modernization of societies and personalities is not concerned solely, as some of the critics of modernity have asserted, with maximization of technical efficiency. Such modernization has increased the possibility of rational conscious choice of ends. It is this point, indeed, that our definition of "progress," in terms of communication theory, as an increase in learning capacity primarily implies. Modernization involves the increased capacity for rational goal-setting because it gives the system—society, organization, personality—a more comprehensive communications network through which it is possible to assess the needs and potentialities of all parts of the system. Where modernization means only an increased effectiveness in goal attainment, with no increase in the rationalization of the goal-setting process, very serious pathologies can result.[23] Empirically, such pathologies of modernization have occurred, but they are the product of partial or disturbed modernization, not the inevitable result of modernization itself.

If we define modernization in this way, it must be evident that modernity cannot be merely an external problem for religion. It is not something to which religion can merely adjust or not. For modernity involves a changed sense of identity and a new way of posing limit images. It is an internal problem for religion, in that it involves the heart of religious concerns. It is not surprising therefore that modernity in the West arose not only in the sphere of science and technology but also in the core of the religious tradition itself. It is in this context that the significance of the Protestant Reformation is to be understood.

Of course, the Protestant Reformation should not be seen as an isolated event. Protestantism was the crystallization and culmination of tendencies and possibilities inherent in previous Christian development and shared in varying degrees with all branches of Christianity.[24] Movements and tendencies within Catholicism, itself far from monolithic in either thought or organization, anticipated and paralleled Protestantism in the past as well as in the present. Yet it is true that Protestantism, particularly in its Calvinist and sectarian forms (for it should be remembered that Protestantism too is a heterogeneous movement with many varieties and conflicts), first worked out in detail a Christian pattern of life that led directly to the emergence of major features of modern society.

Despite the lingering medievalism of doctrinal statement, several developments crucial to modernization are already visible in Calvin's Geneva. The attack on the medieval sacramental system led to a new emphasis on conscience and responsibility in individual action. The attack on the monarchical principle in the Church led to the emergence of the voluntaristic principle of social organization within the Church and a re-emphasis on voluntarism as a principle of civil society (even though at first the scope of voluntarism was gravely restricted by commitment to fixed doctrinal positions). The attack on the monastic life and on the idea of levels of Christian perfection gave new religious significance to action in worldly occupations. This world, "the theater of God's glory," became the only valid context for religious action—the fulfillment of a tendency long implicit in Christianity.

By the seventeenth century, the implications already present in the early Reformation were becoming fully evident. The Protestant emphasis on this world had channeled ascetic religious motivation into economic and political roles (all the world was a monastery), with remarkable consequences in the emergence of capitalistic and democratic institutions. Protestant intellectuals, believing that God's glory could be praised through science and philosophy as well as through theology, were making major contributions to natural science and to political thought. In the English Revolution, the implications of Protestant social voluntarism came to fruition with momentous consequences for the modern world. In the words of Hans Kohn,

The religious enthusiasm of the Puritan Revolution blazed the trail for a new liberty. The feeling of a great task to be achieved was not restricted to the upper classes; it lifted the people to a new dignity. They were no longer the common people, the object of history, but the nation, the subject of history, chosen to do great things in which every one, equally and individually, was called to participate. Here we find the first example of modern nationalism, religious, political, and social at the same time, although it was not yet the secularized nationalism which arose at the end of the eighteenth century. But it was infinitely more than the statism and patriotism of the Renaissance and of the age of absolute monarchies: a people aroused and stirred in its innermost depths, feeling upon its shoulders the mission of history and finding a new meaning and a new luster in the word "liberty."[25]

As the Puritan Revolution first gave expression to modern nationalism, though not yet in fully secular form, so did it give rise to the modern notion of progress, although not yet fully divested of religious apocalyptic.[26] It was in the seventeenth century that Protestantism accepted the idea that religious obligation has primarily to do with human welfare—in Milton's words, "The great and almost only commandment of the Gospel is, to command nothing against the good of man, and much more no civil command against the civil good"—and that this obligation implies never-ending effort—again Milton speaks of "the reforming of Reformation itself." For individuals, it means, as Milton said, to be "governed by reason" and to oppose the "double tyranny, of Custom from without, and blind affection within."[27] The ideal type of the modern man, not at the mercy of tradition or impulse but able to act in the full light of the requirements and possibilities of his situation, had already emerged.

It would be useless to deny that the modern world, whose birth Protestantism did so much to bring about, has created profound problems for Protestantism in particular and Christianity in general. Doctrinal positions that could be taken for granted in the seventeenth or even the eighteenth century became deeply problematic as a result of the advances in science and historical research in the nineteenth and twentieth centuries. The ways in which Christianity, both Protestant and Catholic, has responded, often with great vitality, to the more recent situations is of interest but lies outside the direct concern of this paper. For it is early modern religion in the West, above all Protestantism, that provides the most interesting analogies and contrasts to the religious situation in Asia in recent times. Modernity in Asia is not four or five centuries old but often only one century old or even less. Today's Asia shares with the age of the Protestant Reformation the problems of the first emergence of historic society and historic religion into the modern world. More recent developments in Western secular culture are indeed significant in modern Asia, and one further word about them is required at this point.

It was in England and perhaps even to a greater extent in America that the social and cultural implications of Protestantism were most fully worked out. Partly in accordance with the logic of Protestantism itself, the main themes of seventeenth-century

Protestantism as we have discussed them developed into an
independent secular cultural and political ideology in the Anglo-
Saxon world, for which we can use the term "liberalism." Liberalism contained the same basic commitment to individual responsibility and social voluntarism that emerged from the Puritan
Revolution. It preached a moderate nationalism, justifying the
nation in terms of higher universal values (which sometimes undoubtedly became a hypocritical cloak for imperialism) and
refrained from making the nation itself an ultimate. It also
preached faith in social and cultural progress without claiming
any final blueprint of the forms such progress could take.

Anglo-Saxon liberalism seldom cut all ties to religion, meaning mainly Protestant Christianity. In late eighteenth-century
France, however, a militantly secular liberalism emerged as the
ideology of the French Revolution. Under the economic impact
of the Industrial Revolution spearheaded by England and of the
political revolution spearheaded by France, the whole European
continent was, by the early nineteenth century, feeling intense
pressures toward modernization. In response to these pressures
and in reaction to the early modernizing ideologies of England
and France, there arose the great Continental ideologies of the
nineteenth century—romantic nationalism and scientific socialism.[28] Romantic nationalism turned the moderate nationalism
of Anglo-French liberalism into what might be called a "secular
religion," in which the nation—usually defined in terms of primordial loyalties to blood, soil, language, or religion rather than
to the civil solidarities of Anglo-French political thought[29]—was
taken as the ultimate value. Marxian socialism, which can also be
viewed as a secular religion, turned a particular theory of social
progress into an absolute, providing a complete blueprint for
world revolution. As both romantic nationalism and scientific
socialism were responses, partly pathological, to pressures to
modernize, it is not surprising that both proved highly resonant
in the non-Western world when it too came under heavy pressure to modernize.

It has been necessary to go into this much detail about Western history, not only in order to define some of the features of modernity that first emerged in the West, but also to be able to differentiate some of the disparate components involved in the Western "impact" on Asia. We shall argue that the chief ideological influences from the West on modern Asia have been Christianity (especially Protestantism), liberalism, nationalism, and socialism. And the latter two, nationalism and socialism, have been influential in both liberal and absolutist forms.

The superior social effectiveness of modern organization and the tendency to continuous development and expansion that it contains mean that, once modern forms of organization had come into existence, they began to exert pressure on premodern organizations and societies in their environment. We have already noted this phenomenon in Europe itself. During the course of the nineteenth century (in a few instances beginning even earlier), the whole world began to feel the political, economic, military, and ideological pressures generated by the early modernizing societies. It is common to speak of the Western "impact" on the non-Western world. Such a metaphor if anything underestimates the profound shock that the premodern societies suffered as a result of the expansion of modern organization. All previous forms of military, political, economic, and ideological organization were called into question. In some cases, premodern forms were quickly destroyed by occupying Western powers. In other cases, they survived in battered form in some kind of uneasy symbiosis with impinging structures. And in some cases, traditional forms were able to adapt modern organization to their own ends or to new syncretic ends. But whatever the particular outcome, traditional assumptions and traditional values could no longer be taken for granted. Each society, as the relentless pressure mounted, found its own identity becoming problematic.

It was, of course, the intellectuals who felt earliest and most severely the cultural trauma of the modern pressure. They were forced into a re-examination of their own cultural identity symbols, which meant, in most traditional societies, as we have already noted, religious symbols. The pressure on traditional religious symbols was often acute, even in the early stages, because Christian missionaries were among the shock troops of the modernization process, quick to point out the barbarous and unprogressive consequences of traditional religious beliefs and practices. Here we may briefly outline the major responses of traditional cultural elite groups, reserving a more detailed treatment for later.

A few traditional intellectuals were won over to Christianity, rejecting more or less vigorously their cultural past under the impact of the missionary critique. More common was a tendency to reject totally the whole of Western culture, to insist, even in the face of disastrous defeats, on the superiority and complete self-sufficiency of traditional forms. These were the "proud, stiff-necked men of the 'old school' who 'nail their colors to the mast' and kill and die."[30] But much more frequent, especially after the early stages of contact, was the attempt to maintain some continuity with traditional culture while coming to terms somehow with the modern situation. There seemed to be two main alternatives. One was to construct a "modernist" or "reformist" version of the traditional religion, in order to show that it is compatible with modernity and in fact that its "essence," when divested of historic perversions, is to further social and cultural modernization. The other, which we might call "neo-traditionalism," was to use modern ideas and methods to defend traditional cultural values, which are held to be superior to those of any other tradition. The difference between the two seems to lie in whether modern culture and society are accepted as good in themselves or elements from them are used simply as means for the defense of other values. Although movements of these two types often appear highly similar in many respects, it is usually possible to distinguish them in particular situations. Finally, there appeared, in most of the non-Western societies, as in the West itself, groups of intellectuals who more or less consciously reject religion in favor of some secular ideology—liberalism, nationalism, socialism. The appearance of secular intellectuals usually must await the emergence of a modern cultural elite alongside the traditional one, an elite composed of graduates from modern educational systems either in the West or in their own countries.

All of these cultural positions are characterized by some balance between the need to defend and the need to adapt, between memory and receptivity. Where defensiveness becomes absolute, the capacity to deal with the treacherous conditions of the modern world fails. Where adaptation leads to the total rejection of the traditional culture, the intellectual finds himself isolated and irrelevant. Let us consider, on the basis of what we have said about traditional religion and about the religious contribution to modernization in the West, what a religion of historic type must do if it is to contribute maximally to modernization. It must be able to rephrase its religious symbol system to give meaning to cultural creativity in worldly pursuits. It must be able to channel motivation disciplined through religious obligation into worldly occupations. It must contribute to the development of a solidary and integrated national community, which it seeks neither to dominate nor to divide, although this necessity certainly does not imply sanctioning the nation as a religious ultimate. It must give positive meaning to the long-term process of social development and be able to value it highly as a social goal, again without necessarily taking social progress itself as a religious absolute. It must contribute to the ideal of a responsible and disciplined personality. As part of the new balance between religious and secular in modern society, it must be able to accept its own role as a private voluntary association and recognize that this role is not incompatible with its role as bearer of the society's ultimate values. This list of requisites is of course an ideal typical construction. Certainly no religion of historic type has completely transformed itself in such a way, and probably no religion of historic type could do so completely. Some, by the very nature of their own religious symbol systems, would rather be destroyed than change in these ways. But if modernization is to be successfully accomplished, either traditional religion must be able to make this transition, at least in large part, or it must be able to withdraw from major spheres of life and allow secular ideologies to complete the transition. Let us turn then to the chief sorts of cultural response to modernization that have occurred in Asian societies, in order to examine the kinds of effect they have had. We have stated some of the conditions that seem to be necessary if modernization is to be successful. But, of course, modernizing societies frequently fail to meet these conditions, and disturbance, stagnation, breakdown, and regression are as frequent as success.

CHRISTIANITY. Christianity, through missionaries and local converts, has had an influence on cultural modernization in Asia out of all proportion to the small number of people involved. Research on this topic[31] is in its infancy, but enough is now known to indicate that, although there is great variability from country to country, Christianity and Christian institutions, especially schools, have been important catalysts for change.

In only one Asian country, the Philippines, was a majority of the population converted to Christianity. But this conversion took place in the sixteenth century and was essentially the triumph of a historic religion over religions of primitive and archaic type.[32] The problem of modernization did not arise until the nineteenth and twentieth centuries, long after Catholic Christianity was well entrenched in the islands. The confrontation with nationalism and secularism, the threat of separation, and the problem of inner reform were some of the issues facing religion in the Philippines in the last hundred years or so—issues not appreciably different from those facing other Christian societies. Christianity itself did not, therefore, play a major role in introducing pressures to modernize, as it did in many Asian countries, although in recent decades certain elements within the Catholic Church, notably the Jesuits, have provided leadership in that direction.

In a number of countries, early converts became ardent advocates of social and political reform, notably in late nineteenth-century Korea[33] and Japan. Even where converts were few, the Christian schools and colleges that began to appear everywhere in Asia transmitted modern ideas and expectations to the newly emerging Western-educated elites. In Japan, for example, converts or those influenced by Christian education made important contributions to the movements for constitutionalism, women's rights, prison reform, labor unions, and socialism. In colonial countries, Christian radicalism was tempered by the knowledge of the privileged position of the churches under the colonial regimes. Because of this close association with the imperialist powers, Christianity throughout Asia, especially in the colonial countries, was increasingly isolated by the rising tide of nationalism in the twentieth century. But, though the indigenous churches were small and often defensively closed, Christian ideas continued to circulate in the intellectual marketplace.

One of the most important effects of Christianity in Asia was to stimulate movements of reform and reorganization in the local religions. One of the best-known examples is the Hindu reform movement known as the Brāhmo Samāj founded by Rāmmohun Roy in the early nineteenth century. Rāmmohun sought to show that the essence of Hinduism is a humanitarian ethical monotheism and attacked such customs as suttee and child marriage (prime targets of the missionaries) as corruptions of pure Hinduism. The receptiveness to Christian ideas shown by Rāmmohun Roy, who believed that Christianity and Hinduism could ultimately be reconciled, was not shared by all subsequent Indian thinkers, though Gandhi was notably open to Christian thinking. But in India, as in many other Asian countries, even those most vehement in expressing anti-Christian sentiments often unconsciously responded to the Christian stimulus. In the Islamic world, on the whole the most barren ground for Christian proselytization, missionary criticism of polygamy, casual divorce, and the low status of women has helped to arouse consciousness of and movements to change these conditions. Although the missionaries were often critical of what they found, they also produced more than their share of Orientalists, who by their translations and scholarly studies not only helped to make the great traditions of Asia known to the West but also encouraged young Asians to become conscious and proud of their own pasts.

However much Christianity may have contributed to the emergence of modernity in the West and its propagation in Asia, it is clear that some forms of Christianity are in tension with many modern ideas and attitudes. As Western education spread, it became common for Asian intellectuals to use Western secular thought to attack Christianity. For example, in the anti-Christian movement that swept Chinese universities and student groups in the 1920s, Western philosophy and science were taken as conclusive refutations of Christianity. The fact that missionaries and convert groups were often fundamentalist in theology made them especially vulnerable to this kind of attack. On the other hand, some Western Christian denunciations of modern society as materialistic, atheistic, and inhuman have been picked up by Asians to show the superiority of their own "spiritual" traditions to that of the modern West. This context is only one within which the inner conflicts and tensions of modernization in the West have affected Asian thinkers.

TRADITIONALISM. Turning from those influenced by Christianity who, especially if they became converts, found themselves profoundly at odds with their traditional society, let us consider those who found change to be neither necessary nor desirable. From the Turkish Janissaries who murdered Selim III for his foreign innovations in the opening years of the nineteenth century to the Chinese Boxers who murdered foreign missionaries and diplomats in its last years, there were many throughout Asia whose simple formula for dealing with the challenge of modernization brought by the West was to destroy the foreigners, their local associates, and all their works and to return to the *status quo ante*. In its more violent forms, this response was necessarily brief and unsuccessful. But in its more passive form, not destroying but ignoring the modernizers, foreign and domestic, and their works, this response has been and continues to be widespread.

Many forms of erosion, some of which we shall touch upon, have weakened the pure traditionalists, but paradoxically enough, modern conditions have actually strengthened traditional religion in many areas and among many groups. While traditional ideas have been declining among elite groups, it is precisely among nonelite groups, at least in many cases, that religious ideas and attitudes characteristic of the traditional cultural elite have been spreading. Better public order and increased communications have provided the conditions for the spread of great traditions to lower-prestige groups and remote peoples. This process can be discerned throughout the Islamic world, where folk magic is in retreat in the face of orthodoxy and where pagan peoples in remote and border areas are being converted. The Christian Church in the Philippines has carried missions to some pagan hill peoples for the first time only in the twentieth century. M.N. Srinivas has noted the process of what he calls "Sanskritization," which involves the adherence of intermediate and lower-caste groups to the values and practices of the Brahmans. He notes that, although it is a long-term tendency, it has greatly accelerated in recent times.[34] Although this tendency for the great traditions to spread to formerly "culturally deprived" groups does not have anything directly to do with modernization, it may yet play a role in that process. For what is involved is the attrition of primitive and archaic traditions as they are replaced by what we have called "historic traditions." By breaking down local particularism, the spread of the historic religions contributes to the establishment of broader loyalties and universalistic principles. In premodern times, the spread of Islam, for example, among the primitive or archaic peoples of Africa and Malaysia has provided the possibility for larger and more effective political structures and more extensive trade relationships. Although it might be argued that a sort of quantum evolution from primitive to ultramodern, without assuming the many liabilities associated with the great religions, would be an effective course of development, the very grave difficulties of survival in any form that primitive peoples seem to face in the modern world make this possibility dubious. It seems more likely that upgrading to the level of historic culture will provide a more effective platform from which to modernize. On the other hand, to the extent that it succeeds in ignoring modernity, a strong and growing traditionalism must be a definite barrier to modernization.

Of course, no group existing in the modern world can wholly ignore modernity or fail to be affected by it. To speak of "pure" traditionalism in the modern world can only be misleading. The traditionalists shade imperceptibly into the neo-traditionalists—the former often do unconsciously what the latter do consciously, that is, utilize modern ideas and organizational forms for the sake of traditional value commitments. But before considering neotraditionalism it is useful to analyze briefly the frankly "modernist" or "reformist" movements.

REFORMISM. We have defined religious reformism as a movement that reinterprets a particular religious tradition to show not only that it is compatible with modernization but also that, when truly understood, the tradition vigorously demands at least important aspects of modernity. This position is one of the most fruitful and one of the most unstable of the several types of response to modernity. It is fruitful in that it provides the potential impetus to modernization, while also providing a continuity with traditional identity symbols, thus furthering change with a minimum of traumatic disturbance. It is unstable in that it not only requires a quite sophisticated understanding of both modernity and tradition but also must reconcile some very deep tensions between them. The problem has been acute enough in the West, where modernity has been an indigenous development to which the religious tradition has clearly made major contributions. In Asia, where modernity has come largely from without, wrapped in the symbols of an alien culture, the problems have been doubly difficult. As a result of the difficulties involved in maintaining the reformist position, such movements have often broken down either in the direction of wholesale acceptance of modern liberal culture under a veneer of religious phraseology or in the direction of neotraditionalism, in which the modern components are maintained only as instruments for furthering nonmodern or antimodern values and ends. Tendencies in these two directions have been very evident in Protestant Christianity, which has produced liberal "culture Christianity" on the one hand and neo-orthodoxy on the other, although attempts to maintain a genuine reformist position, associated with such various theological positions as those of Niebuhr and Tillich in America and Bultmann and Bonhoeffer in Europe, continue. In Asia, reformist movements are vigorous in only a few areas and have attained major success perhaps only in India.

The relative success of reformism in India seems to arise from a number of factors. The British-sponsored educational system gave the Indian cultural elite an understanding of modern Western culture almost unique in Asia in its sophistication. At the same time, the cumulative growth of scholarly study of the Indian past contributed to a deepening awareness of its varied resources. Another advantage was the factor of time—serious reformism dates from Rāmmohum Roy in the early nineteenth century. The receptiveness of Hinduism to syncretic reformulation was also an advantage relative to some other Asian religions, although one that could cut two ways, in that it also generated vagueness, diffusion, and what we have called "overtolerance."

The culmination of Indian reformism was certainly the person and work of Gandhi. It was he who showed the relevance of Hindu spirituality to contemporary worldly problems, political, social, and economic. Even though some of his particular solutions may have been chimerical, he opened the channels of communication between the spiritual and secular spheres. Perhaps his major contribution to the emergence of a modern India was

his insistence on the differentiation between religion and caste.
A tireless champion of Indian spirituality and a tireless enemy of
caste, he showed that the two could be separated. In fact, he
argued that the divisive and exploitive aspects of caste were in
direct contradiction to the highest teachings of Indian religion.
He thus contributed immeasurably to the emergence of a new
Indian nation united in religious commitments transcending
caste.[35] On the basis of Gandhi's achievement, it has even been
possible to give a new interpretation to the caste ethic as an ethic
of occupational contribution to the general welfare entirely
divorced from its traditional hereditary and totalistic implications.[36] Of course, many problems remain, and Indian reformism
has much to do if it is to provide an adequate ideological basis
for the Indian modernization that is still largely a matter for the
future. Vigorous rivals in the forms of purely secular ideologies
and conservative neotraditionalism exist. Yet it seems that the
success of Hindu reformism has played an important part in the
relatively smooth and largely voluntaristic nature of Indian development, which on the basis of socioeconomic indices alone
was hardly to be expected.

Although reformist movements in the rest of Asia have been
on the whole less successful than in India, they are also on the
whole more recent, exist in countries less culturally sophisticated
than India, and therefore may yet play an important role as
conditions change. Certainly the potentialities for contributing
to progress in all the historic religions discussed in the preceding
section on religion in traditional society have been fully exploited
by few modernist movements. Much more can certainly be done
to bring out the genuinely progressive potential in many of the
great traditions. On the other hand, a number of the traditional
barriers to progress mentioned in the last section are still far from
overcome.

Particular factors that have hindered the development of a
reformist movement may be briefly surveyed. Japan, with the
highest literacy rate and the most developed educational system

in Asia, might be expected to have produced vigorous reformist movements. Although individual reformists have appeared, on the whole few movements of any significance have developed, apparently because the regime in the first decades after the opening of the country in 1868 largely succeeded in appropriating the major symbols of traditional culture for an orthodox neo-traditionalism. Opposition to the establishment therefore tended to take the form of one of several secular ideologies or of Christianity, rather than of reformulation of past tradition. Even today, when there is little government interference in the cultural sphere, proponents of a reformist position are few.

China had one extraordinary outburst of creative reformism in the thought of K'ang Yu-wei, T'an Ssu-t'ung, and their associates in the 1890s. Here we can see many of the familiar devices of reformism: a return to the early teachers and text, a rejection of most of the intervening tradition, an interpretation of the pristine teaching, in this case Confucianism, as advocating social reform and national regeneration. The thought, particularly that of T'an, was original and occasionally profound, but the movement was destroyed by the palace coup of the Empress Dowager, which led to the death or exile of the leaders. Thenceforth the tradition was increasingly identified with the *status quo*, which, unlike the case in Japan, seemed incapable of even a minimal response to the modern world. After the revolution of 1911, political issues dominated the thought of the cultural elite, although a few individual reformists like Liang Shu-ming appeared. When, under Chiang Kai-shek, the Nationalist movement embraced a neotraditionalist form of Confucianism, reformism practically died as a significant movement, lost in the great struggle between the neotraditionalist Nationalists and the secularist Communists.

Except in Turkey, where the existence of the sultan-caliph as the virtual embodiment of neotraditionalist Islam tended to force the modernizing opposition in the direction of secularist rather than reformist ideologies, the situation in the Islamic world has been quite different from those in China and Japan, and reformism has had different problems to face. Where colonial governments existed, as they did in most of the Islamic world until quite recently, even the neotraditionalists could not be wholly in favor of the *status quo*, and the religious tradition was therefore not linked so definitely to an antimodernizing position.[37] Indeed, a promising Islamic modernist movement did get underway in Egypt in the late nineteenth century under the leadership of Muhammad Abduh. Abduh taught that the original Islam of the prophet and the Qur'an was essentially in accord with modern science and democracy. He attacked Sufi mysticism and magic as perversions of the true Islamic spirit. He began to reinterpret the bases of Islamic law, the heart of Islamic religion and the chief problem for any modern interpretation, so as to provide for the flexibility and innovation that modernity implies. But aside from insisting, for the first time in centuries, that modern Muslims have the right to go back to the original texts, rather than accepting the position of generations of commentators and subcommentators, he provided few general principles on which such a reinterpretation might develop. Indeed, his individual interpretations often seem to rest on rather arbitrary readings of texts. Subsequent generations have on the whole not advanced beyond Abduh in developing a coherent reformist position. In fact, his followers have tended to divide into liberal lawyers and politicians, for whom religious commitment signifies little more than ethical probity, on the one hand and those who have drifted further and further in the direction of neotraditionalism on the other. Of the latter, Rashid Rida and later the Muslim Brethren are the chief examples.[38] Abduh's influence spread throughout the Islamic world, including areas beyond the Middle East. But, as in the Middle East, his disciples have not moved beyond him, even in Indonesia where they were especially influential. The somewhat parallel development in British India, associated with the teaching of Muhammad Iqbāl, had a similar outcome. Iqbāl analyzed the history of culture to show that it was the Qur'an that had laid the foundation for the empiricism and realism of modern science as against the purely speculative tendencies of classical philosophy. He preached a dynamic, activistic Islam opposed to fatalism and quietism. But even less than Abduh did he come to grips with the central problems of adapting Islamic law to the problems of modern life. He undoubtedly gave impetus to the emergence of Pakistan as an Islamic state for the Muslims of the Indian subcontinent, but after the emergence of that state reformism was overshadowed by neotraditional and secular tendencies.[39]

There is no room here to attempt a complete account of the weakness of reformism in the Islamic world. Two factors seem to be salient. One is the resistance of Islam as a relatively sharply defined religious system to any easy syncretic reformulation and the concomitant vulnerability to charges of heresy of those who attempt such reformulations. The other is the concern with national independence and with political and economic viability once independence has been attained. These concerns seem to have turned the attention of the cultural elite away from religious reformism. What has often emerged is an elite motivated mainly by secular ideologies and appealing for mass support in terms of neotraditionalist phraseology because it strikes a deeper and more ready response than does reformism.[40]

What has been said about Islam outside Turkey is also, to a considerable extent, true of the Theravada Buddhist countries. Reformist movements have made modest beginnings there, especially perhaps in Ceylon,[41] but secular ideologies, with their strong appeals to the elites, and neotraditionalism, with its strong appeal to the masses, have proved to be formidable rivals.

NEOTRADITIONALISM. Neotraditionalism was a natural and early response to modernizing pressures in most Asian nations. The Chinese phrase "Eastern morality and Western technique" had parallels in most other places. The idea was simply that one could maintain the traditional orientations as basic but utilize modern technology as auxiliary. It was the easiest position to fall back on once an intransigent traditionalism had proven disastrous. But long after the intellectual inadequacies of neotraditionalism have become evident to many in the cultural elite, neotraditionalism has continued to be a force, not only because neotraditionalism often taps emotional depths in the masses through its direct use of traditional symbolism, but also because the intense assertion of the superiority of the indigenous tradition to any other and particularly to Western culture has aroused responses in almost all social groups during independence struggles or periods of intense nationalism, which most Asian countries have been experiencing. Reformism has suffered from the inability of a relatively complex and intellectual restatement of the tradition to appeal to the masses and from the inhospitable atmosphere that extreme nationalism provides for the intense self-criticism of tradition that reformism always implies. The relation of neotraditionalism to nationalism bears further discussion.

Neotraditionalism has been often adopted by traditional elite groups in noncolonial Asian societies as an ideology designed to keep change to a minimum and defend the *status quo* as far as possible. Neotraditionalism has, however, in at least one striking case, Japan, been used by the elite of a noncolonial nation to provide the ideological basis for sweeping social innovation. The Japanese example, because of its dynamism, is a limiting case of neotraditionalism, yet it clearly falls within that rubric. The ideology of the emperor system, with its heavy doses of Confucianism and Shinto symbolism crystallizing in the 1890s, was based neither on a serious assessment of modern culture nor on a searching re-examination of the tradition. It was simply a statement of the values to which the ruling elite was committed, decked out in the symbolism most readily understood by the Japanese masses. In the name of this ideology, sweeping technological change and social reorganization could be carried out, but these changes amounted only to a rationalization of means. Serious consideration of changes in goals was ruled out by the sacrosanct character of ideological orthodoxy. Some flexibility remained for the elite groups in the early period. As they had in large part created the emperor system, they were to some extent "esoterically" able to see beyond it. But with succeeding decades the elite became the prisoner of its own creation, subject to intense pressure from less sophisticated second-level groups like the army officers for any sign of deviation. There was indeed an attempt to interpret the emperor system in democratic terms by liberal constitutionalists and politicians in the period of the First World War and the early 1920s, but this attempt failed to generate widespread popular support and was itself repudiated in the neotraditionalist reaction of the 1930s. The only serious challenges to the emperor system came from Christianity in the 1890s and Marxism in the 1920s and 1930s.[42] Here indeed there was radical criticism of neotraditionalism but from entirely nontraditional positions, rather than from a reformist point of view. The consequences of Japan's course of development were spectacular success in the rationalization of means and serious pathology in the rationalization of ends. Neotraditionalism not only thwarted effective parliamentary democracy, but it also hindered the emergence of a modern secular nationalism. The conceptions of popular sovereignty and the citizen state could not emerge in the atmosphere of the emperor system.[43] Yet the successes of the neotraditional road to modernization in Japan, limited though they were, were striking in contrast to the slowness of any kind of development in many other Asian nations. The neotraditional way, where it can generate intense energy and where that energy can be effectively channeled, may be a tempting alternative for other modernizing nations. But the Japanese case may serve as a warning of the serious hazards involved in this course. The Japanese case, however, may be unique, in that Japanese tradition provides a natural support for certain kinds of rationalization that is very rare in most other traditions.[44] Certainly in other instances where neotraditionalism has come to the fore—Spain, Portugal, certain Latin-American nations, Nationalist China, and certain

Muslim and Buddhist nations, for example—the result has more often been stagnation than one-sided modernization. In some of these cases, the elite has utilized neotraditional symbols, though itself more oriented to secular ideologies, simply to mobilize the support to remain in power. Like that in Japan, these elites can become the victims of their own manipulations, although the result may simply be stagnation and corruption rather than imperialism and militarism.

The four types of religious response to modernization that we have discussed so far—conversion to Christianity, traditionalism, reformism, and neotraditionalism—are all mutually exclusive alternatives, although they may shade into one another. When we come to the three secular ideological responses, however, there is no assumption of mutual exclusiveness. Each may be combined with the other or with any variety of religious response, except perhaps pure traditionalism. It is true that each of the three secular positions—liberalism, nationalism, and socialism—has been on occasion a self-sufficient and absolute commitment: a secular religion. We shall be interested in them both as ultimate forms and in their capacity for combination with other religious and ideological components.

LIBERALISM. Of the several secular ideologies, liberalism has been least successful as a secular religion, although it certainly played that role in the French Revolution. Liberalism has been most successful in Protestant countries, where it is grounded, often unconsciously, in the religious tradition. In the Catholic nations of southern Europe and Latin America, where liberalism has frequently been anticlerical and grounded on enlightenment or positivist philosophies accessible only to the educated elite, it has been far less stably institutionalized. Whether or not the historic changes in Catholic orientation signaled in the current Vatican Council will provide a new lease on life for liberalism in the Catholic world remains to be seen, but it is a possibility to be closely watched.

In Asia, it is extraordinarily difficult to gauge the strength of liberalism. Until the end of the First World War, liberalism, because it was the ideology of the dominant colonial powers, seemed to be a powerful key to success in many Asian countries. But the rise of an authoritarian Germany in the late nineteenth century and especially the emergence of leftist and rightist totalitarianisms in the 1920s have made liberalism seem far less muscular to Asian minds. The wish for the decline of imperialism and its partial fulfillment have given rise to the widespread idea that liberalism is dead. Certainly there are few places in Asia where an avowedly liberal movement is a powerful force. Yet, wherever Western education has spread, and there are few countries where it has not, there are liberal ideas. Insistence on individualism, civil liberties, and social voluntarism may be combined with nationalism, socialism, or a religious orientation, but it is by no means wholly lacking. The Communist Chinese hysteria about liberalism is an indication of how deep the penetration has been not only among the intellectuals at large but also within the party. Even Mao Tse-tung was deeply influenced by T. H. Green in his early years.[45]

Although it is possible for individual intellectuals to base their liberalism on particular philosophies, as Kawai Eijiro did with Kantian idealism, liberalism as a social force requires a more popular symbolic grounding. Religious reformism, as we have discussed it, appears to be a natural basis, as the relative strength of liberalism in India perhaps confirms. In Indonesia too, it has been the reformist Islamic Masjumi Party that has been most inclined to liberalism. In Japan, where liberalism seems to be the dominant ideology at the moment, it is hard to detect its symbolic grounding, a fact that gives some concern to both Japanese and foreign observers. A deep commitment to liberal values seems often to be associated more with a moderate socialist orientation than with support of the ruling Liberal Democratic Party. Although serious efforts to ground liberalism in Japanese tradition are being made, it remains to be seen how successful they will be.

It seems to be no accident that the countries with the most developed modern educational systems, like Turkey, Lebanon, Israel, India, the Philippines, and Japan, are also the strongest centers of liberalism in Asia. Where the educational system is only beginning to develop and the modern-educated group is small, liberalism may be quite weak, although, as in Malaysia and some African countries, it may be able to maintain a balance-of-power position. Egypt, with its relatively well-developed educational system and its authoritarian regime, may seem an exception to this generalization, but the markedly liberal aspect of Nasserism—its disinclination to use totalitarian methods of coercion—is perhaps partly attributable to the large sector of the population with modern education. But even where the modern educational system has succeeded in disseminating liberal values, as was the case in Japan in the 1920s, this factor alone will not guarantee their effectiveness unless they are grounded in the common value system and institutionalized in the social structure.

NATIONALISM. Nationalism is generally agreed to be a powerful factor in modern Asia. Yet the term is used loosely, and varieties of nationalism are often overlooked. The broadest definition of "nationalism" is perhaps the consciousness of belonging to a nation, but the grounds and consequences of such belongingness can be phrased quite variously. The nation may be taken as the ultimate standard of value or viewed instrumentally. Nationalism may be linked to liberalism, socialism, or religion or may be opposed to one or more of them. It is important to keep these variations in mind in assessing the significance of nationalism for modernization.

Purely secular nationalism, without major admixtures of reformist or neotraditionalist religion, has been relatively rare in Asia. In Japan, though secular nationalism was characteristic of such Meiji thinkers as Fukuzawa Yukichi, it was gradually absorbed by the neotraditionalist emperor ideology. Secular nationalism in China tended to be crowded out by resurgent neotraditionalism among the Nationalists or combined with a dominant commitment to socialism among the Communists. Secular nationalism and anticlericalism appeared in the Philippines during the struggle for independence from Spain but became progressively muted due to the absorption of liberal values through the period of American occupation and the growing sense of identification with Catholicism as against largely Protestant America or non-Christian Asia. Nationalism in Indonesia has drawn on a medley of traditional religious symbols. Nationalism in the Theravada Buddhist countries has quite generally had a strong overlay of religious identification, and we have already commented on the importance of religious reformism in Indian nationalism. Pakistan is understandable only in terms of intense religious self-consciousness and would never have become a nation without it.[46] In most other Muslim nations, strong Islamic elements have been present. It is true that Arab nationalism was originally secular in orientation and included some Christians among its early activists. The Baathists represent a type of Arab nationalism that is largely secular and committed to socialism. The Nasser movement is also to some extent secular and has recently emphasized socialism. Yet, in spite of these secular tendencies in Arab nationalism, there seems to have been from the beginning and increasingly up to the present a strong Islamic note, perhaps exacerbated by the conflict with Israel.

The one great example of a relatively pure secular nationalism, which in this case amounted virtually to a political religion, is that of Turkey. Definitely anticlerical although not avowedly atheistic, it relegated religion to the sphere of private conscience and to some degree competed with it as a world view. Nationalist historians emphasized the glorious pre-Islamic history and achievements of the Turkish people and took pride in ancient inhabitants of Anatolia like the Hittites. In these respects, Turkish nationalism was parallel to that of Mexico, for example, rather than to those of most other Asian nations. Nevertheless, the Muslim identification remained strong. The small Christian and Jewish minorities, for instance, were never regarded as "Turks,"

a term reserved for Muslims, although they were of course Turkish citizens. In the period after the Second World War and the
return to parliamentary democracy, the Democratic Party began
to use demagogic neotraditional religious appeals. Yet the army
coup that ousted them was in part justified as thwarting a return
to religious "fanaticism," as the followers of Ataturk had dubbed
traditional Islam. The success of secular nationalism as a modernizing ideology in Turkey is still somewhat in doubt. Its appeal
has been largely to the educated elite. The quick response of the
masses to religious slogans in the postwar period indicates how
little they had really been touched by secular nationalism. And
it is indeed the "stickiness" of the masses, especially the rural
masses, that poses the major problems for Turkish development.

Nationalism, in the sense of the integration of most of the
population into a national community through what Karl
Deutsch calls "social mobilization,"[47] seems to be one of the
requisites of modernization. The widespread use of religious
symbols in nationalist rhetoric in Asia is clearly a consequence
of the fact that religious identification is virtually the only trans-
local identity of the masses. Where there is religious homo-
geneity within the national community or where religious
diversity is functional rather than by social group,[48] the appeal
to religious identity may reinforce national consciousness, although, as we have seen in the case of Japan, it may restrict some
of the consequences of that national consciousness. But where
the national community is composed of heterogeneous religious
groups, the appeal to religious identity may prove severely disruptive to nationalism or may lead to the development of region-
alist or separatist subnationalisms. Where religious diversity exists
on a substructure of shared religious and cultural orientations as
in Indonesia, Hindu India, and Islamic countries with mixed
Sunni and Shi'i populations, nationalism can appeal on the basis
of the common elements in the religious tradition and play down
the diversities. Where the religious division is too deep, as between Muslim Malays and Buddhist-Confucian Chinese in Malay-

sia, Buddhists and Catholics in South Vietnam, Hindus and Muslims in British India, Christians and Muslims in the Middle Eastern countries, Christian Greeks and Muslim Turks in Cyprus, the alternatives seem to be three. Either a basis of unity in secular nationalism is found, or there is partition, or one of the groups becomes a (disgruntled) minority with some degree of social, if not civil, disability. Successful integration on a secular basis seems to require a degree of differentiation between religious and other social commitments that is not common in Asia outside the most modernized groups or else a balance of power, like those in Lebanon and perhaps Malaysia, in which each group for the sake of its own interests seeks to maintain the *status quo*. On the whole, religious reformism seems to be more congenial to the development of a religiously pluralistic nationalism than does neotraditionalism. Gandhi, for example, was assassinated by a fanatical Hindu communalist who felt that the great leader was being soft on Muslims during partition.

SOCIALISM. Socialist ideology is almost as widespread as nationalism in Asia, but it equally requires an examination in terms of its various forms and the varieties of its alliances with other religious and ideological trends. Socialism is the form in which the general idea of progress seems to have most appeal to Asians. Many of them have accepted the idea that progress under the aegis of "capitalism" means advantage only for the few and exploitation of the many. For them, the idea of socialism combines the commitment to progress with the commitment to social welfare, often with strong eschatological overtones. It is socialism, with its promise of general social improvement, that makes modernization attractive and its hardships and sacrifices bearable. It is therefore an important motivational component in the modernizing ideologies of Asia.

Perhaps the most common form of socialist ideology is the official commitment to socialism in general terms combined with nationalistic and religious symbolism. Such official socialism can be found in Israel, Egypt, Syria, Iraq, India, Ceylon, Burma, and Indonesia. In many of these countries, opposition movements more exclusively committed to socialism or communism urge more exclusive attention to or more rapid progress toward socialism. It does seem that socialism as part of the official ideology of these countries is often more of symbolic than of practical significance. Yet the general commitments of all of these countries to economic planning and social welfare, however well or badly they may be carried out, does indicate that the socialist conception is not entirely nominal. In a few countries, socialism exists primarily as an opposition movement, particularly in Japan, where the Socialist and Communist Parties resemble those in some European countries with large socialist oppositions. In Iran, socialism is an important ingredient in the nationalist ideology of the opponents of the regime, which relies mainly on neotraditionalism for its ideological support. In a few countries like Turkey or the Philippines, external or internal tension with Communism has tended to eliminate socialism both from official symbolism and from the legal opposition, although socialist ideas are by no means without influence.

In only one major country, however, has a pure commitment to socialism become the dominant ideology. In China, socialism, as the ideology of the Communist Party, has become, in alliance with nationalism, a secular religion, in opposition to all forms of tradition. China shares with Turkey, the only other Asian nation to experience an important period of secular religion, the experience of domination by a neotraditional elite opposed to fundamental change. An extreme antitraditionalism seemed to be a major requisite for social progress in both countries. The critique of tradition was far more radical in China than in Turkey, especially from the period of the May Fourth movement of 1919. A host of writers, of whom perhaps Lu Hsün was the most influential, castigated the Chinese tradition root and branch, demanding an entirely new start. Although Communism in China has probably not succeeded in eradicating all traditional ideas from the minds of the people and indeed has itself undoubtedly been influenced consciously or unconsciously by many aspects of that tradition, it has still promoted ideological and social change at every level of the social structure in a way approached by no other Asian nation. Progress, though considerable, has been uneven and the price paid high, sufficiently so that socialism *à la chinoise* is not overwhelmingly attractive to other Asians. Whether or not it continues to be viewed dubiously will depend on the relative successes of the Chinese and those committed to alternative courses in the years to come. The central question posed by the Chinese experiment seems to be whether the frontal assault on tradition is highly favorable to rapid development or is in itself so disruptive as to impede development.

Conclusion

We have tried to suggest that progress, in the sense of increased learning capacity, is essential if Asian societies are to cope successfully with the modern world. We have also pointed out that progress can be self-defeating if it so disrupts a society's identity pattern as to cause a breakdown in its functioning. Let us consider now how the various religious and ideological tendencies relate to the two problems of progress and identity.

There is little doubt that, of all the alternatives, traditionalism and neotraditionalism are oriented most strongly to the defense of identity—traditionalism at any cost, neotraditionalism at the least possible cost. Nationalism, especially the variety that includes a heavy dose of neotraditionalism, sometimes also places primacy on the defense of identity. The problem with these positions is not only that they often relegate progress and development to the level of secondary considerations, compared to the continued reiteration of identity symbols, and thus handicap actual advance. The problem is also that, when these defensive positions begin to break down under the strain of sustained social failure, there are no prepared positions on which to fall back, and their adherents become vulnerable to a variety of extremist and pathological social movements.

Christianity and reformism are both also concerned with the

identity problem, as much and perhaps more than they are concerned with progress. Both make critiques of past identities and seek to mold new cultural identities, identities by and large more relevant to the modern world than are traditional identity patterns, although by no means without their own tensions with modernity. By stressing worldly activism and individualistic responsibility (as most but not all Asian Christian and reformist movements do), they contribute to the increase of learning capacity in individual personalities. To the degree that they influence official ideologies (except for the Philippines, this point applies more to reformism than to Christianity), they may effect changes in institutionalized value systems and their transmission through the educational system and other public communications channels. Christianity, because of its close association with Western culture, usually implies a sharper break with past identities than does reformism, although indigenous churches are trying hard to divest themselves of the taint of "foreignness." For this reason, reformism is usually a more attractive and viable alternative than Christianity, although it may be in its own way very revolutionary and bring down on its adherents the violent hostility of traditionalists.

The secular ideologies are all ostensibly more oriented to progress than to identity, with the exception of the more conservative forms of nationalism. But all the secular ideologies too, unless they are held very superficially, have implications for the pattern of identity. Liberalism is usually incompatible with deep adherence to traditional religion and requires either the abandonment of traditional religion, severe compartmentalization of religion and ideology, or commitment to a reformist version of religion that corresponds with liberal values. Both nationalism and socialism can become all-embracing ideologies implying new identity patterns. More commonly, they combine with various components of traditional religion and culture and serve to point in the direction of new goals of national community and social progress. Extreme forms of nationalism and socialism can involve as sharp breaks with traditional identity as can Christianity and reformism. It is clearly impossible to maximize defense of traditional identity and progressive change at the same time. The various responses seek to emphasize one or the other or to maintain an often uneasy balance between the two.

Related to the dichotomy between ideologies stressing defense of identity and those stressing progress is the distinction between movements that have elite appeal and those with mass appeal. On the whole, the movements stressing identity defense have had more mass appeal, and those stressing progress have had more elite appeal, although this distinction is not universal. Reformism, which has usually been an elite movement, struck a popular response in India through the charismatic figure of Gandhi in the context of the national struggle for independence, and Nehru continued to symbolize the reformist position. In Turkey and China we have noted the mass appeal of nationalism and socialism, respectively, to peoples disaffected with neotraditionalism, although how deeply the masses were affected in the long run has come into question in Turkey and may be doubted in China.[49] Usually nationalist and socialist appeals have been most effective when used as slogans for more syncretic ideologies with strong traditional overtones. But, as the general level of education rises and other indices of development begin to climb, these secular ideologies may be expected to have more appeal in their own right, as they have in the West.

To the liberal Westerner or Asian, there is little doubt that a syncretic ideology, stressing continuity with the best of the past and progress toward a better future, preferably underpinned by a reformist religious position and a commitment to liberal values, seems the best solution for Asians to follow. The question is Can such a harmonious combination break the myriad clinging tendrils of tradition that keep society from making any real advance? Radical, indeed fanatical, solutions often seem more able to break loose from tradition and stimulate rapid social change. Yet there is the evident danger that such sharp breaks in identity may produce severe pathology leading to social breakdown. The limit images of tradition may block any advance, but a collapse of all limit images can lead to a system out of control, madly oscillating to destruction, which in this nuclear age may mean destruction for us all.[50]

We have stressed the variety of patterns and outcomes in the Asian cultural response to modernization. This variety we may express in a few concrete images by calling to mind the memorials to the heroes of modernization in three Asian countries. The memorial to the Meiji Emperor, the Meiji Shrine in Tokyo, is a Shinto shrine in perfect taste and perfectly traditional. The tomb of Ataturk in Ankara, immense as a Hittite palace on its high hill, is totally un-Islamic in architecture and atmosphere, especially with its great relief sculptures. It is a severe monument to modern nationalism. The Rajghat (Gandhi memorial) and the Nehru memorial in Delhi, without at all suggesting traditional religious architecture, still avoid the severe secularity of the Ataturk Mausoleum. The atmosphere is one of spiritual and moral commitment, with Nehru's interest in the Buddha represented by a deer park associated with his memorial and Gandhi's by the recesses in the walls of Rajghat, which are reminiscent of Ajanta. These expressions of neotraditionalism, nationalism, and reformism in three countries indicate only what has been the dominant note in each of them. All the various currents can be found in each Asian society. We have only been able to hint in this essay at explanations of the varying outcomes. Much research remains to be done before we can speak with any confidence of the causes of the variation.

Modernization is in a sense never "completed." At least no limit to increased learning capacity is presently evident. But in most of Asia, except for Japan, which has its own problems, modernization has not even reached the self-propelling stage. In many countries, stagnation is as evident as progress—in others, although progress continues, collapse into stagnation is a real and present danger. This essay and indeed this book are based on the assumption that religion and ideology are important elements in Asia's success or failure in further progress.

Notes

1. "Progress," *Encyclopedia of the Social Sciences*, XII (New York: The Macmillan Company, 1934), 495.

2. Karl R. Popper, *The Poverty of Historicism* (London: Routledge & Kegan Paul, Ltd, 1957); and Popper, *The Open Society and its Enemies* (London: Routledge & Kegan Paul, Ltd., 1945). See also Reinhold Niebuhr, *Faith and History* (New York: Charles Scribner's Sons, 1949).

3. *N.B.:* not "inevitably."

4. Karl Deutsch, *The Nerves of Government* (New York: The Free Press, 1963), p. 253. My definition as a whole leans heavily on Deutsch, *ibid.*, pp. 248–54. It is quite similar to the conception of evolutionary progress in biology put forward by Julian Huxley in *Evolution in Action* (New York: Harper & Row, Publishers, 1953), Chapters 1 and 5.

5. "Political Modernization in Historical Perspective," mimeographed, 1959, p. 1. Professor Black's extremely suggestive comparative work on political modernization is soon to appear in book form.

6. Deutsch, *op. cit.*, p. 240.

7. See Talcott Parsons, Introduction to Part IV of Parsons, *et al.*, eds., *Theories of Society*, (New York: The Free Press, 1961).

8. Deutsch, *op. cit.*, p. 212.

9. Mircea Eliade, *Patterns in Comparative Religion* (New York: Sheed & Ward, 1958), Chapters X and XI; and elsewhere in his numerous writings.

10. Father de la Costa's discussion can be found on page 18. Becker's position is spelled out at length in *The Heavenly City of the Eighteenth-Century Philosophers* (New Haven: Yale University Press, 1932). See also Ernest Lee Tuveson, *Millennium and Utopia* (Berkeley: University of California Press, 1949). Tuveson stresses the specifically Protestant character of the early modern idea of progress.

11. Niebuhr, *The Kingdom of God in America* (New York: Harper & Row, Publishers, 1957).

12. For a preliminary statement of this theme, see Robert N. Bellah, "Religious Evolution," *American Sociological Review*, 29 (June, 1964), 358–74.

13. By "archaic religions" I mean the Bronze Age religions of Egypt, Mesopotamia, China, and so forth, and more recent religions of similar type.

14. "'Internal Conversion' in Contemporary Bali," mimeographed, 1961, p. 3.

15. *Ibid.*, p. 5.

16. Lloyd Fallers, "Equality and Inequality in Human Societies,"

in Sol Tax, ed., *Horizons of Anthropology* (Chicago: Aldine Publishing Co., 1964).

17. Max Weber, *The Sociology of Religion* (Boston: Beacon Press, 1963).

18. Ernst Troeltsch, *The Social Teaching of the Christian Churches*, I (London: George Allen & Unwin, Ltd, 1931), Chapter II.

19. This point has been made with special clarity in an as yet unpublished work by Ira Lepidus on the Mamluks. See also H. A. R. Gibb and Harold Bowen, *Islamic Society and the West, I: Islamic Society in the Eighteenth Century* (Oxford: Part I, 1950; Part II, 1957), on the Ottoman Period.

20. S. N. Eisenstadt, "Religious Organizations and Political Process in Centralized Empires," *Journal of Asian Studies*, 21 (May, 1963), 271–94.

21. M. N. Srinivas has pointed out the long-term percolation of Brahman values and orientations into the middle and lower castes, although it was a very slow process in premodern times and did not materially affect religious diversity, especially of lower-status groups. See Srinivas, "A Note on Sanskritization and Westernization," *The Far Eastern Quarterly*, 15 (August, 1956), 481–96.

22. Max Weber, *The Protestant Ethic and the Spirit of Capitalism*, (London: George Allen & Unwin, Ltd, 1930).

23. The importance of the rationalization of ends for any adequate conception of modernization was brought home to me by Ishida Takeshi.

24. On pre-Reformation aspects of Christian development in the West that were especially favorable for the emergence of modernity, see Talcott Parsons, *Societies: Evolutionary and Comparative Perspectives* (Englewood Cliffs: Prentice-Hall, 1965), Chapter 4. Almost all this short book is relevant to the problems of this epilogue.

25. Hans Kohn, *The Idea of Nationalism* (New York: The Macmillan Company, 1944), pp. 166–7.

26. Tuveson, *op. cit.*, pp. 71–92.

27. Kohn, *op. cit.*, pp. 169–71.

28. I have explored the problem of the "ideologies of disturbance" a bit more fully in "Values and Social Change in Modern Japan," *Asian Cultural Studies 3*, (Tokyo: International Christian University, 1962).

29. On primordial and civil solidarities, see Edward Shils, "Primordial, Personal, Sacred and Civil Ties," *British Journal of Sociology* (June, 1957); and Clifford Geertz, "The Integrative Revolution," in Geertz, ed., *Old Societies and New States* (New York: The Free Press, 1963).

30. Deutsch, *op. cit.*, p. 132.

31. Research on this topic has been plagued by the narrowness of both church and secular historians. Church historians seem too preoccupied with purely internal church matters to discern the larger impact of Christianity on Asian culture. Secular historians have tended to view the influence of Christianity too simply in socio-economic or political terms. A new and much more adequate approach to the problem of the impact of Christianity in several Asian nations has been begun by the Committee on Asian Cultural Studies at International Christian University in Tokyo, under the leadership of Kiyoko Takeda Cho. Mrs. Cho has herself already made an important contribution to the subject with respect to Japan in her *Ningenkan no Sokoku—Kindai Nihon no Shisō to Kirisuto-kyō* (*Conflict of Views of Man—Modern Japanese Thought and Christianity*) (Tokyo: Kōbundō, 1959).

32. See J. L. Phelan, *The Hispanization of the Philippines* (Madison: University of Wisconsin Press, 1959).

33. See especially Chung Chai-sik, *Protestantism and the Formation of Modern Korea, 1884–1894*, unpublished doctoral dissertation, Boston University, 1964.

34. Srinivas, *op. cit.*

35. Joseph Elder, in a paper read at the March, 1964, meeting of the Association of Asian Studies, presented evidence based on an all-India survey that religious beliefs do not vary directly with attitude toward caste and that religious commitments usually continue among those who consciously reject caste.

36. See Joseph Elder, *Industrialism in Hindu Society*, unpublished doctoral dissertation, Harvard University, 1959.

37. Nikki R. Keddie, in her article "Western Rule Versus Western Values," *Diogenes* (1959), surveyed the major Asian cases, concluding that on the whole traditional religion has been the ally of the modernizers in the colonial nations, their enemy in the noncolonial ones.

38. On the development of modernism in Egypt, see especially Nadav Safran, *Egypt in Search of Political Community* (Cambridge, Mass.: Harvard University Press, 1961).

39. On Islamic reformism in general and Iqbal in particular, see Muhsin Mahdi, "Modernity and Islam," in Joseph M. Kitagawa, ed., *Modern Trends in World Religions* (La Salle, Ill.: Open Court Publishing Co., 1959); and Marshall G. S. Hodgson, "Modernity and the Islamic Heritage," *Islamic Studies* (Karachi), 1 (June, 1962).

40. Soedjatmoko's discussion of the relationship between modern elites and tradition in his paper in this book is especially illuminating on this point.

41. See Michael Ames, "Ideological and Social Change in Ceylon," *Human Organization*, 22 (Spring, 1963), 45–53.

42. It should be noted that only a few Christians or Marxists remained in opposition during the 30s and early 40s. Most compromised with the prevailing tendencies of thought when pressures to conform became extreme.

43. My understanding of Japanese modernization has been strongly influenced by the work of Maruyama Masao and Ishida Takeshi and by conversations with them. Among many works of theirs that might be cited are Maruyama's *Nihon no Shisō (Japanese Thought)* (Tokyo: Iwanami Shinsho, 1961); and Ishida's *Gendai Soshiki Ron (An Essay on Modern Organization)* (Tokyo: Iwanami, 1961).

44. See Bellah, *Tokugawa Religion* (New York: The Free Press, 1957).

45. Stuart R. Schram, *The Political Thought of Mao Tse-tung* (New York: Frederick A. Praeger, Inc., 1963), p. 12. Mao also read Adam Smith, Darwin, Spencer, Mill, Rousseau, and Montesquieu in his youth. *Ibid.*, p. 9.

46. Israel is another case of a nation resulting from religious self-consciousness. Even though Zionism can be considered a secular ideology of the Jewish people, it is hard to deny that religion has been the primary force in the formation of that people.

47. Karl W. Deutsch, "Social Mobilization and Political Development," *American Political Science Review*, 55 (September, 1961), 493–514; and Deutsch, *Nationalism and Social Communication* (Cambridge, Mass.: M.I.T. Press, 1953).

48. Religious diversity is functional in a country like Japan where, with some exceptions, Buddhism, Shinto, and Confucianism are not three distinct religious groups but three aspects of the religious life of most Japanese. The average Japanese, for example, is married in a Shinto shrine, carries on a Confucian family cult at home, and is buried in a Buddhist temple.

49. In dealing with the classical personal religious problems like death, guilt, and suffering, specifically religious positions seem to have an advantage over the secular religions. The latter do have relevance to these personal problems but lack the specialized symbolic and ritual means to handle them that the religious traditions have developed over the centuries. The salience of these personal problems to the ordinary citizen and his relative lack of involvement in society-wide political issues may help to explain the hold of the explicitly religious positions relative to the secular religious ones. Some reflections relevant to these issues are contained in David E. Apter's essay "Political Religion in the New Nations," in Clifford Geertz, ed., *Old Societies and New States* (New York: The Free Press, 1963).

50. This paragraph and indeed much of the epilogue can be seen as developments of themes initially put forward by Soedjatmoko.

Bibliography

I. Religion and Society

Bellah, Robert N. "Religious Evolution," *American Sociological Review*, 29, 1964.

Eliade, Mircea. *Cosmos and History*. Harper Torchbooks, 1959.

———. *Patterns in Comparative Religion*. Sheed & Ward, 1958.

Nakamura Hajime. *The Ways of Thinking of Eastern Peoples*. UNESCO (Tokyo), 1959.

Parsons, Talcott. "Religious Perspectives in College Teaching: Sociology and Social Psychology," in H. N. Fairchild, ed., *Religious Perspectives in College Teaching*. The Ronald Press Company, 1952.

———. *Societies: Evolutionary and Comparative Perspectives*. Prentice-Hall, Inc., forthcoming.

Smelser, Neil J. *Theory of Collective Behavior*. The Free Press, 1963.

Talmon, Yonina. "Pursuit of the Millennium: The Relation Between Religion and Social Change," *European Journal of Sociology*, 3, 1962.

Thrupp, Sylvia L., ed. *Millennial Dreams in Action*. Mouton & Co., N.V., 1962. (Supplement II to *Comparative Studies in Society and History*.)

Troeltsch, Ernst. *The Social Teaching of the Christian Churches*. George Allen & Unwin, Ltd, 1931.

Weber, Max. *The Sociology of Religion*. Beacon Press, 1963.

II. Religious and Ideological Aspects of Modernization

Bellah, Robert N. "Reflections on the Protestant Ethic Analogy in Asia," *The Journal of Social Issues*, 19, 1963.

———. "Religious Aspects of Modernization in Turkey and Japan," *American Journal of Sociology*, 64, 1958.

Binder, Leonard. *The Ideological Revolution in the Middle East.* John Wiley & Sons, Inc., 1964.

Bury, J. B. *The Idea of Progress.* The Macmillan Company, 1932.

Deutsch, Karl W. *Nationalism and Social Communication.* M.I.T. Press, 1953.

———. *The Nerves of Government.* The Free Press, 1963.

Geertz, Clifford, ed. *Old Societies and New States.* The Free Press, 1963.

Hauser, P. M. "Cultural and Personal Obstacles to Economic Development in the Less Developed Areas," *Human Organization,* 18, 1959.

Kautsky, John H., ed. *Political Change in Underdeveloped Countries.* John Wiley & Sons, Inc., 1962.

Keddie, Nikki R. "Western Rule Versus Western Values," *Diogenes,* 1959.

Kitagawa, Joseph M., ed. *Modern Trends in World Religions.* Open Court Publishing Co., 1959.

Kohn, Hans. *The Idea of Nationalism.* The Macmillan Company, 1944.

Matossian, Mary. "Ideologies of Delayed Industrialization: Some Tensions and Ambiguities," *Economic Development and Cultural Change,* 6, 1958 (also reprinted in Kautsky, *Political Change*).

Mehden, Fred von der. *Religion and Nationalism in Southeast Asia.* University of Wisconsin Press, 1963.

Parsons, Talcott. "Christianity and Modern Industrial Society," in Edward A. Tiryakian, ed., *Sociological Theory, Values, and Sociocultural Change: Essays in Honor of Pitirim A. Sorokin.* The Free Press, 1963.

———. *Structure and Process in Modern Societies.* The Free Press, 1960.

Pye, Lucian W., ed. *Communication and Political Development.* Princeton University Press, 1963.

Shils, Edward. "The Concentration and Dispersion of Charisma: Their Bearing on Economic Policy in Underdeveloped Countries," *World Politics,* 11, 1958.

———. *Political Development in the New States.* Mouton & Co., N.V., 1962.

———. "Primordial, Personal, Sacred and Civil Ties," *British Journal of Sociology,* 1957.

Sigmund, Paul E., Jr., ed. *The Ideologies of the Developing Nations.* Frederick A. Praeger, Inc., 1963.

Thayer, P., ed. *Nationalism and Progress in Free Asia.* The Johns Hopkins Press, 1956.

Troeltsch, Ernst. *Protestantism and Progress.* Beacon Press, 1958.

Tuveson, Ernest Lee. *Millennium and Utopia, A Study in the Back-*

ground of the Idea of Progress. University of California Press, 1949.

Weber, Max. *The Protestant Ethic and the Spirit of Capitalism.* George Allen & Unwin, Ltd, 1930.

Wertheim, W. F. "Religious Reform Movements in South and Southeast Asia," *Archives de Sociologie des Religions,* No. 12, 1961.

III. Studies of Particular Areas

THE ISLAMIC WORLD

Anderson, J. N. D. *Islamic Law in the Modern World.* New York University Press, 1959.

Coulson, Noel J. *A History of Islamic Law.* University of Edinburgh Press, 1964.

Gibb, H. A. R. *Modern Trends in Islam.* The University of Chicago Press, 1947.

Grunebaum, Gustav von. *Modern Islam.* University of California Press, 1962.

Smith, Wilfred Cantwell. *Islam in Modern History.* Princeton University Press, 1957.

TURKEY

Gokalp, Ziya. *Turkish Nationalism and Western Civilization,* tr. by Niyazi Berkes. Columbia University Press, 1959.

Lewis, Bernard. *The Emergence of Modern Turkey.* Oxford University Press, Inc., 1961.

Mardin, Sherif. *The Genesis of Young Ottoman Thought.* Princeton University Press, 1962.

ISRAEL

Halpern, Ben. *The Idea of the Jewish State.* Harvard University Press, 1961.

THE ARABS

Adams, Charles C. *Islam and Modernism in Egypt.* Oxford University Press, Inc., 1933.

Berger, Morroe. *The Arab World Today.* Doubleday & Company, Inc., 1962.

Haim, Sylvia, ed. *Arab Nationalism: An Anthology.* University of California Press, 1962.

Hourani, Albert H. *Arab Thought in the Liberal Age.* Oxford University Press, Inc., 1962.

Husain, Taha. *The Future of Culture in Egypt,* tr. by Sidney Glazer. American Council of Learned Societies, 1954.
Safran, Nadav. *Egypt in Search of Political Community.* Harvard University Press, 1961.

IRAN

Banani, Amin. *The Modernization of Iran 1921–1941,* Stanford University Press, 1958.
Binder, Leonard. *Iran: Political Development in a Changing Society.* University of California Press, 1962.

PAKISTAN

Binder, Leonard. *Religion and Politics in Pakistan.* University of California Press, 1961.
Schimmel, A. *Gabriel's Wing. A Study of the Religious Ideas of Sir Muhammad Iqbal.* Supplement to *Numen,* 6, 1963.
Smith, Wilfred Cantwell. *Modern Islam in India.* Victor Gollancz, Ltd, 1946.

INDIA

Farquhar, J. N. *Modern Religious Movements in India.* The Macmillan Company, 1931.
Nehru, Jawaharlal. *The Discovery of India.* The John Day Company, Inc., 1946.
Sarma, D. S. *The Renaissance of Hinduism.* Benares Hindu University Press, 1944.
Shils, Edward. *The Intellectual Between Tradition and Modernity: The Indian Situation.* Mouton & Co., N.V., 1961.
Singer, Milton. "Cultural Values in India's Economic Development," *The Annals,* May, 1956.
———. *Traditional India: Structure and Change.* Publications of the American Folklore Society, Vol. X, 1959.
Smith, Donald Eugene. *India as a Secular State.* Princeton University Press, 1963.
Srinivas, M. N. "A Note on Sanskritization and Westernization," *Far Eastern Quarterly,* 15, 1956.

CEYLON

Ames, Michael. "Ideology and Social Change in Ceylon," *Human Organization,* 22, 1963.
Wriggens, W. Howard. *Ceylon: Dilemmas of a New Nation.* Princeton University Press, 1960.

BURMA

Pye, Lucian W. *Politics, Personality and Nation Building.* Yale University Press, 1962.

234   BIBLIOGRAPHY

Slater, Robert Lawson. *Paradox and Nirvana*. The University of Chicago Press, 1951.

INDONESIA

Geertz, Clifford. *Peddlers and Princes*. The University of Chicago Press, 1963.
———. *The Religion of Java*. The Free Press, 1960.
Sjahrir, S. *Out of Exile*. The John Day Company, Inc., 1949.
Skinner, G. W., ed. *Local, Ethnic and National Loyalties in Village Indonesia*. Yale, Southeast Asia Studies, Cultural Report Series, No. 8, 1959.
Wertheim, W. F. *Indonesian Society in Transition*. N. V. Uitgeverij W. Van Hoeve, 1956.

PHILIPPINES

Achutegui, Pedro S. de, S.J., and Miguel A. Bernard, S.J. *Religious Revolution in the Philippines*, I. Ateneo de Manila Press, 1960.
Bulatao, Jaime, S.J. "Philippine Values: The Manileño's Mainsprings," *Philippines Studies*, 10, 1962.
Coquia, Jorge R. *Legal Status of the Church in the Philippines*. The Catholic University of America Press, 1950.
Lynch, Frank, S.J. "Organized Religion," in Fred Eggan, *et al.*, *Area Handbook on the Philippines*. HRAF Press—Human Relations Area Files, 1956.
McHale, Thomas Riley. "Religion, Religious Change and Economic Development in the Philippines," *The Philippine Economic Journal*, 1, 1962.
Phelan, J. L. *The Hispanization of the Philippines*. University of Wisconsin Press, 1959.

CHINA

Chan Wing-tsit. *Religious Trends in Modern China*. Columbia University Press, 1953.
Chow Tse-tsung. *The May Fourth Movement: Intellectual Revolution in Modern China*. Harvard University Press, 1960.
Levenson, Joseph R. *Confucian China and its Modern Fate*. University of California Press, Vol. I, 1958; Vol. II, 1964.
———. *Liang Ch'i-ch'ao and the Mind of Modern China*. Harvard University Press, 1953.
Schram, Stuart R. *The Political Thought of Mao Tse-tung*. Frederick A. Praeger, Inc., 1963.
Schwartz, Benjamin. *Chinese Communism and the Rise of Mao*. Harvard University Press, 1951.
———. *In Search of Wealth and Power: Yen Fu and the West*. Harvard University Press, 1954.

Teng Ssu-yu and John K. Fairbank, eds. *China's Response to the West*. Harvard University Press, 1954.

Wright, Mary C. *The Last Stand of Chinese Conservatism*. Stanford University Press, 1957.

JAPAN

Bellah, Robert N. *Tokugawa Religion*. The Free Press, 1957.

———. "Values and Social Change in Modern Japan," *Asian Cultural Studies*, 3, International Christian University, Tokyo, 1962.

Blacker, Carmen. *The Japanese Enlightenment, A Study of the Writings of Fukuzawa Yukichi*. Cambridge University Press, 1964.

Brown, Delmer M. *Nationalism in Japan*. University of California Press, 1955.

Holtom, D. C. *Modern Japan and Shinto Nationalism*. The University of Chicago Press, 1943.

Jansen, Marius, ed. *Changing Japanese Attitudes Toward Modernization*. Princeton University Press, 1965.

Kosaka Masaaki. *Japanese Thought in the Meiji Era*. Pan-Pacific, 1958.

Maruyama Masao. *Thought and Behavior in Modern Japanese Politics*. Oxford University Press, Inc., 1963.

Smith, W. W. *Confucianism in Modern Japan*. Hokuseido, 1959.

Participants in the Conference

ANWAR, ROSIHAN
   Indonesia
BELLAH, ROBERT N.
   Harvard University, United States
BULATAO, JAIME, S.J.
   Ateneo de Manila University, Philippines
CASTRO, AMADO A.
   Development Bank of the Philippines, Philippines
CORPUZ, ONOFRE D.
   University of the Philippines, Philippines
DE LA COSTA, HORACIO, S.J.*
   Ateneo de Manila University, Philippines
COULSON, NOEL JAMES
   School of Oriental and African Studies, University of London, England
CUYUGAN, RUBEN SANTOS
   University of the Philippines, Philippines
DOHERTY, JOHN, S.J.
   Ateneo de Manila University, Philippines
DUBE, S. C.
   National Institute of Community Development, India
FERNANDEZ, CARLOS
   Philippine Columbian Association, Philippines
FONACIER, TOMAS
   University of the Philippines, Philippines

   * Father de la Costa was unable to attend the conference though
he did contribute a paper.

GEERTZ, CLIFFORD
  University of Chicago, United States
KOENTJARANINGRAT
  Indonesia
LYNCH, FRANK, S.J.
  Ateneo de Manila University, Philippines
MAJUL, CESAR
  University of the Philippines, Philippines
MANGLAPUS, RAUL S.
  Senator, Philippines
MORALES, ALFREDO T.
  University of the Philippines, Philippines
ORTIZ, PACIFICO, S.J.
  Ateneo de Manila University, Philippines
PASCUAL, RICARDO R.
  University of the Philippines, Philippines
QURESHY, ISHTIAQ H.
  University of Karachi, Pakistan
SANIEL, JOSEFA M.
  University of the Philippines, Philippines
SARACHANDRA, EDIRIWEERA R.
  Ceylon
SAYIGH, YUSIF A.
  American University of Beirut, Lebanon
SOEDJATMOKO
  Indonesia
SOLIVEN, MAXIMO V.
  Philippines
TANCO, ARTURO R., JR.
  Philippine Investment-Management Consultants, Inc.,
  Philippines
VENKATAPPIAH, B.
  State Bank of India, India
WANG GUNGWU
  University of Malaya, Malaysia

Index